SHAKESPEARE'S VIOLATED BODIES

This timely study looks at the violation of bodies in Shakespeare's tragedies, especially as revealed (or concealed) in performance on stage and screen. Pascale Aebischer discusses stage and screen performances of *Titus Andronicus, Hamlet, Othello* and *King Lear* with a view to showing how bodies which are virtually absent from both playtexts and critical discourse (due to silence, disability, marginalisation, racial Otherness or death) can be prominent in performance, where their representation reflects the cultural and political climate of the production. Aebischer focuses on post-1980 Royal Shakespeare Company and Royal National Theatre productions but also covers film adaptations and landmark productions from the nineteenth century onwards. Her book will interest scholars and students of Shakespeare, gender, performance and cultural studies.

PASCALE AEBISCHER is Lecturer in Shakespeare and Renaissance Literature in the Department of English, University of Leicester. She has contributed to a number of books and has published in journals including *Restoration and Eighteenth-Century Theatre Research, Journal of Dramatic Theory and Criticism, Etudes Anglaises* and *Studies in the Novel*. She is also the principal editor of *Remaking Shakespeare: Performance across Media, Genres and Cultures*.

SHAKESPEARE'S
VIOLATED BODIES

Stage and Screen Performance

PASCALE AEBISCHER

CAMBRIDGE
UNIVERSITY PRESS

PUBLISHED BY THE PRESS SYNDICATE OF THE UNIVERSITY OF CAMBRIDGE
The Pitt Building, Trumpington Street, Cambridge, United Kingdom

CAMBRIDGE UNIVERSITY PRESS
The Edinburgh Building, Cambridge, CB2 2RU, UK
40 West 20th Street, New York, NY 10011–4211, USA
477 Williamstown Road, Port Melbourne, VIC 3207, Australia
Ruiz de Alarcón 13, 28014 Madrid, Spain
Dock House, The Waterfront, Cape Town 8001, South Africa

http://www.cambridge.org

First published 2004

Printed in the United Kingdom at the University Press, Cambridge

Typeface Adobe Garamond 11/12.5 pt.   *System* LATEX 2ε   [TB]

A catalogue record for this book is available from the British Library

Library of Congress Cataloguing in Publication data
Aebischer, Pascale, 1970–
Shakespeare's violated bodies : stage and screen performance / Pascale Aebischer.
p.   cm.
Includes bibliographical references (p. 203) and index.
ISBN 0 521 82935 6
1. Shakespeare, William, 1564–1616 – Knowledge – Anatomy.   2. Shakespeare, William, 1564–1616 –
Stage history.   3. Shakespeare, William, 1564–1616 – Film and video adaptations.   4. Body, Human,
in motion pictures.   5. Body, Human, in literature.   6. Death in motion pictures.   7. Death in
literature.   8. Dead in literature.   I. Title.
PR3069.B58A68   2003
822.3′3 – dc22   2003055765

ISBN 0 521 82935 6 hardback

Contents

Illustrations

Acknowledgements

The beginning is an ending: my last English class in summer 1989. My teacher, Thomas Rüetschi, had repeatedly insinuated that my entire form, myself included, were too dim to understand Shakespeare. Now, as a 'farewell present' to us all, he asked me to read Katherina's final speech in *The Taming of the Shrew* aloud – I had never read it before, didn't know the play, and as I worked my way through 'Why are our bodies soft and weak and smooth, / Unapt to toil and trouble in the world . . .' I was increasingly outraged by its import. What better motivation could one possibly have to launch into a resisting reading of Shakespeare? My deep thanks to Thomas for stinging my pride and teaching me to love Shakespeare.

Since then, many teachers, friends and colleagues have nurtured that love and helped me during the gestation period of this book. Warm thanks are due to my supervisors in Oxford, Emrys Jones and Ann Pasternak Slater, who gently guided me through the process of thesis-writing and allowed me the freedom I so desperately needed. Meanwhile at home, John E. Jackson, Werner Senn and Margaret Bridges offered continuing support. I am also grateful to the 'ghosts' who haunt this book in its margins: my drama teachers at the London Academy of Performing Arts, where I learnt how much thought goes into the performance of violence, and my twenty-five fellow graduate students at Lincoln College, Oxford (you know who you are), who helped me stage the production of Q1 *Romeo and Juliet* which, though nearly entirely absent from this book, informs so much of my thinking about performance and how to read early modern playtexts. In this context, I must acknowledge the strong influence exercised both by Tiffany Stern and Paige Newmark, who have regularly challenged my assumptions and made me think of the present in terms of the past, and by Regina Schneider, who acted as a sounding-board for my ideas in the early stages of this book.

Many more people have responded to drafts, helped answer specific queries or discussed questions that have eventually had an impact on this book. I would like to single out Lukas Erne, Emma Smith, Blair Worden, Paromita Chakravarti, Simone von Büren, Kathy Henderson, Bill Worthen (an inspiring examiner), Deborah Cartmell, Kathy Wheeler, Peter Holland, Carol Rutter, John Kerrigan, Karen Junod and Ginger Vaughan, whose generous, sensitive and perceptive feedback on different chapters has provided much food for thought and greatly assisted me in formulating my ideas. More than anything else, these readers have combined an encouraging belief in my work with responses that have not shied away from occasionally pointing to its immaturity. I hope that now they will agree that the book is 'ripe'. Andrew Gurr, Dominic Oliver, Patricia Lennox, Marjolijn Vlug, Robert Shaughnessy, Mary Luckhurst, Jonathan Burch, Peter Donaldson and Claire Preston have responded to some sometimes odd queries with wonderful aplomb, while Richard Schoch, Drew Milne, Helen Cooper, David Hillman and Harry Berger Jr have pushed me in the right direction at crucial moments. Special thanks are due to my 'South African informants', as I like to think of them: Andrew Vandervlies, Natasha Distiller and Ndumiso Luthuli have helped more than they are probably aware, while Azmeh Dawood and Anshuman Mondal have assisted me in the tightrope-walking exercise of talking about race. Bernard Rappaz taught me a few things about journalistic cheek, while Cécile Crettol, with Lucien and Anaïs, asked all the right questions. José Ramón Díaz Fernández, meanwhile, made sure that I was up-to-date with my reading by providing me with his extraordinary bibliographies.

As I write these acknowledgements and the list of names grows longer and longer, I cannot help feeling deeply moved by the generosity of all the individuals who have supported me over the years. This is particularly true of the next group of names, those of inspiring artists and back-stage miracle-workers who have taken the time to answer questions, sometimes at great length, and who have given me thrilling insights into their work and world. It has been a privilege to talk and correspond with Janet Suzman, Julie Taymor, Nicholas Hytner, Lee Beagley, Jane Hartley, Xavier Leret, Jo Carr, Jenny Tiramani, Jonathan Holloway, Kate Ward, William R. Lockwood, Roger Howells and Claire van Kampen. Thanks also to Louise Teal and Gerald Murray for their generosity.

Generosity is the keyword for the next acknowledgement, too: every little girl should have a fairy godmother, and I have certainly had more than my fair share of one. Barbara Hodgdon is 'the star to every wand'ring barque, / Whose worth's unknown although his height be taken'. If one day some younger scholar is only half as grateful to me as I am to her for her friendship, unstinting support and guidance, it will make me very proud indeed.

My research was greatly facilitated by the assistance and initiative of the staff at the Shakespeare Centre Library in Stratford-upon-Avon, in particular Jo Lockhart, Sylvia Morris and, more recently, Karin Brown. Thanks also to Vera Ryhajlo at the Bodleian Library in Oxford and Camille Seerattan and Georgiana Ziegler at the Folger Shakespeare Library in Washington DC. I have received practical – and meticulous – help with bibliographies and copy-editing from Erica Longfellow and Angie Kendall, to whom I am deeply indebted, as I am to Caroline Howlett, the fabulous copy-editor at Cambridge University Press. In recent months, Elaine Treharne has been instrumental in making me realise what is important – many thanks to her and to the Department of English at the University of Leicester for moral and financial support. The University of Leicester (especially Carl Vivian at AVS, who spent hours creating 'video grabs' with me) is only one of several institutions that have assisted me with this project: thanks are due to the Folger Shakespeare Library for a short-term Research Fellowship; Darwin College, Cambridge, where I was elected to a Research Fellowship in 1999; and the Swiss National Science Foundation which supported my research for several years. I am equally indebted to Lincoln College, Oxford, where I spent the three very happy years of my tenure of the Berrow Scholarship (many particular thanks to the late Marquis de Amodio) and where I also held a Senior Scholarship.

On a very personal note, I am grateful to my late grandmother, Elisabeth Aebischer, for the computer which has travelled to so many libraries with me; to my other late grandmother, Lucie Crettol, for teaching me what it means to be strong, good and humble; and to my fabulous, inspiring, supportive parents whose love has seen me through several rough moments and who have coped so well with the rather odd course my life has been taking. Finally, David Jones is responsible for the absence of many a comma, the readability of many a sentence and the presence of my sanity (?) and good humour (!). Saying 'thank you' just doesn't come near to meaning enough.

Some parts of this book have appeared in print before. I would like to gratefully acknowledge Paula Burnett of *EnterText*, Jean-Marie Maguin and Patricia Dorval of the Société Française Shakespeare, Kathrin Heyng of Gunter Narr Verlag, John E. Jackson and Olivier Pot, François Laroque on behalf of *Etudes Anglaises* and Gilly Duff of Pluto Press for permission to re-use material from the following articles: 'Yorick's Skull: *Hamlet*'s Improper Property', *EnterText* 1:2 (2001), 206–25; '"Yet I'll Speak": Silencing the Female Voice in *Titus Andronicus* and *Othello*', in Patricia Dorval (ed.), *Shakespeare et la voix* (Paris: Société Française Shakespeare, 1999) pp. 27–46; 'Looking for Shakespeare: The Textuality of Performance', *SPELL* 13 (2000), 157–73; '*Hamlet*, mémoire, langue, action, et passion', in Olivier Pot (ed.), *Emergences et formes de la subjectivité littéraire aux XVIe et XVIIe siècles* (Geneva: Droz, forthcoming); 'Women Filming Rape in Shakespeare's *Titus Andronicus*: Jane Howell and Julie Taymor', *Etudes Anglaises* 55:2 (2002), 136–47; and 'Black Rams Tupping White Ewes: Race and Gender in the Final Scene of Six *Othellos*', in Deborah Cartmell, I. Q. Hunter and Imelda Whelehan (eds.), *Retrovisions: Reinventing the Past in Film and Fiction* (London: Pluto, 2001), pp. 59–73.

Note on texts used

The desire to have a clear and reader-friendly referencing system has led me to select for each play the most recent comprehensive and accessible scholarly edition. Thus references to *Titus Andronicus* are to the 1995 Arden 3 edition by Jonathan Bate (London: Routledge, 1995), an edition which includes the Folio-only 'fly' scene (allowing me to base my discussion of the play on the Folio text). In its sensitivity to the theatre, the edition lends itself particularly well to the type of readings I propose in this book. The same is true for E. A. J. Honigmann's 1997 Arden 3 edition of *Othello* (London: Thomas Nelson, 1997). Though at times sadly biased against the character of Desdemona, as when, on page 291, he reattributes her lines about Lodovico in act 4 scene 3 to Emilia because 'For Desdemona to praise Lodovico at this point seems out of character', the edition shares the Arden 3 series' concern with textual and theatrical issues and is much more comprehensive and up-to-date than its rivals. For *Hamlet*, a play which I treat here as consisting of all the different playtexts and performances that make up its corpus, I use Harold Jenkins's conflated Arden 2 edition for references (London: Methuen, 1982). The lines I quote in the chapter are present (with minor variants) in both the Second Quarto and the Folio texts. For the First Quarto text, the edition I work with is Paul Bertram and Bernice Kliman's 1991 *The Three-Text Hamlet: Parallel Texts of the First and Second Quartos and First Folio* (New York: AMS Press, 1991). It is only for the chapter on *King Lear*, where the textual differences between Quarto and Folio have a direct bearing on my argument, that I quote from the two texts separately, using René Weis's *King Lear: A Parallel Text Edition* (Harlow: Longman, 1993). I generally quote from the Folio text, using the Quarto text only for the Quarto-only lines, marking both types of quotation with F and Q respectively.

Prologue: the gravedigger's daughter – a story of loss

Art which stays new, in Ezra Pound's phrase, is art in which the question 'what does it mean?' has no correct answer. Every narrative has, at least, a capacity to suggest a metanarrative, and art that 'works' is highly suggestive in this sense, as though the story were really a metaphor for an idea that has to be almost tricked out of hiding into the audience's consciousness.

– Tom Stoppard[1]

The gravedigger and his daughter will need protective rainwear? . . .
The gravediggers daughter during block 11 will bring on 'a stoup of liquor' . . . and possibly a picnic for herself and her father . . .
After the funeral . . . the gravedigger and daughter will tip the skull and bones back into the grave and nail the trap lid onto the trap.

– Royal Shakespeare Company Rehearsal Note[2]

The gravedigger's daughter is surely one of the most elusive 'Shakespearean' characters. Absent from all early modern playtexts of *Hamlet*, she left this tantalising tiny trace in the cartload of production materials for the 1989 Royal Shakespeare Company *Hamlet* that one of the Shakespeare Centre librarians wheeled into the reading room for me one day – and then was heard no more. As much as I searched for other pieces of evidence documenting the existence of the gravedigger's daughter, no other rehearsal note, letter in the production correspondence or stage manager's report mentions her again. When I carefully re-viewed the archival video recording of a performance at the Royal Shakespeare Theatre and scanned all the production photographs, all I could find were images of two male gravediggers.

The glimpse I had caught of the gravedigger's daughter in the handwritten rehearsal notes was nevertheless enough to prompt an extended reverie about this character and her creation. I began to imagine the director

---

[1] 'Pragmatic Theater', *New York Review*, 23 September 1999.
[2] Rehearsal Note for *Hamlet* (dir. Ron Daniels), 19 August 1988, Shakespeare Centre, Stratford-upon-Avon.

of the production, Ron Daniels, yielding to the pressure of the RSC's female
actors clamouring for more speaking parts, however small, in the company's
productions of Shakespeare's plays.[3] I pictured him carefully sifting the
available roles in *Hamlet* and eventually settling on the role of the Second
Gravedigger as the least obtrusive speaking part that may be given to a
woman without 'endangering' the balance of the play – obviously, a female
Voltemand or, disastrously, a female Horatio would have created 'gender
trouble' (to borrow Judith Butler's evocative phrase) in suggesting that in
a country where Gertrude is queen, a woman could have a political role
beyond her choice of husband, or that Hamlet could feel genuine friendship
rather than sexual revulsion for a woman.[4] I then imagined the rehearsal:
the actor trying to give a body with a history to her character who, tellingly,
was no longer the independent 'Other' of the Second Quarto and Folio
speech headings, but whose identity was defined in relationship to the man
who has power over her. I dreamed up a scenario in which the director
tried to balance out his momentous decision to cast a woman in the role by
turning that role into a stereotype: the daughter who dutifully assists her
father in his job and brings him his 'stoup of liquor'. The reference to 'and
possibly a picnic for herself and her father' smacked of an afterthought, as
if the actor had asked for a sip of the liquor and had been told that if she
were well-behaved, she might get a bite of a sandwich instead.

Her presence at the end of the scene to 'tip the skull and bones back
into the grave and nail the trap lid onto the trap' I visualised as another
provisional and reluctant concession by the director who, I conjectured,
might by that time have realised that however inconspicuous the role of the
Second Gravedigger might have seemed to him at the outset, the casting of
a woman had inevitably en-gendered a new framework within which the
scene could be read. In this metatheatrical framework, in which cultural
meanings are generated through the use and appropriation of Shakespeare's
plays,[5] the modern woman's appropriation of the man's part found its
theatrical parallel in the healthy young gravedigger's daughter, the smutty,
intelligent working-class girl who is sensitive to social injustice, nailing
the trap lid over the over-refined body of her 'privileged' ancestor whom
playwright and fellow-characters have driven to marginalisation, insanity

---

[3] See Sarah Werner's chapter 'Punching Daddy, or the Politics of Company Politics', in her *Shakespeare and Feminist Performance: Ideology on Stage* (London: Routledge, 2001), pp. 50–68, for an account of the conflict between the RSC and its female members which came to a head with the creation of the RSC Women's Group in 1985.

[4] Judith Butler, *Gender Trouble: Feminism and the Subversion of Identity* (New York: Routledge, 1990), *passim*.

[5] Terence Hawkes, *Meaning by Shakespeare* (London: Routledge, 1992), pp. 1–10.

and premature death. Thus, in the margins of the play, I dreamed of an encounter in which, however tentatively, a modern young woman could meet her Shakespearean tragic equivalent, look at her drowned face in pity, bury Ophelia, wipe the dirt off her trousers and walk away perhaps to play Horatio in the next RSC production of *Hamlet*. And then, prompted by the ensuing silence about the gravedigger's daughter in the production documents, I pictured the director hastily changing the casting of the role, giving it back to a man before anyone could notice the implications of his early concession to the women of the RSC. I imagined a story of loss.

Introduction: filling the empty space

> I can take any empty space and call it a bare stage. A man walks across this empty space whilst someone else is watching him, and this is all that is needed for an act of theatre to be engaged.
>
> – Peter Brook[1]

> In the theatre, the body bears the brunt of performance; it is the material Shakespeare's text works on, works through. No body in the theatre is exempt – least of all, the spectator's. So how does the body play on Shakespeare's stage? What work does it do, and how can I account for it, bring it on stage within this text?
>
> – Carol Chillington Rutter[2]

Peter Brook, when defining the essential 'act of theatre', speaks of an empty space that is filled by a man walking across it. I want to combine this mental image of the man walking across the empty space with the image on the front of this book of a man pushing a woman down and out of the frame of the picture, creating an empty space. The man is Brian Cox as Lear, the woman Eve Matheson's Cordelia at the point when Lear disowns his daughter, effectively throwing her out of the play until her reappearance in act 4. The gap left by Cordelia is thereafter filled with Lear's story as the audience watches him walk across the empty space of the heath, filling it with his suffering, madness and new-found insight. It is through the expulsion of the alternative bodies and viewpoints of Cordelia and her sisters that Cox's Lear creates the empty space of the theatre – a theatre in which the 'traditional subject has been the male subject, with whom everyone must identify' and which, at least in Britain, is still predominantly run by (white) male artistic directors and board members.[3]

---

[1] Peter Brook, *The Empty Space* (London: MacGibbon & Kee, 1968), p. 9.
[2] Carol Chillington Rutter, *Enter the Body: Women and Representation on Shakespeare's Stage* (London: Routledge, 2001), p. xii.
[3] Sue-Ellen Case, *Feminism and Theatre* (Houndmills: Macmillan, 1988), p. 121. For the state of British theatres in the 1990s, see Sarah Werner, 'Notes on Sharing the Cake', in Lizbeth Goodman with

The project of this book is to find the moments at which the empty space of theatre is created in Shakespeare's tragedies and prevent Brook's generic man from walking across it. Instead, I will seek to fill out those spaces with narratives about how these gaps come to be, about the mechanisms that lead to the expulsion of some bodies from both playtexts and their critical reception, turning stories of loss and forgetfulness into remembrance and gain. It is the white male subject of tragedy who will be marginalised in this study and forced to make way for his gendered and racial Others. Whether they are the victims of the plot in being evacuated, mutilated or killed into silence or whether they are the objects of 'bemonstering' (Q *Lr* 4.2.64), by which I mean the projection of meanings onto a subject that turns it into an object, bodies that are marginalised in playtexts and literary criticism may come centrestage in performance and performance studies. There, these silenced, stigmatised, mutilated, erased bodies fill the empty spaces of our stages and screens, their textual absence compensated for by their physical presence. Performance challenges the erasure of Shakespeare's violated bodies and offers the attentive spectator alternative narratives, viewpoints and protagonists.

Like the opaque theatrical signs discussed by theatre semiotician Anne Ubersfeld, when these often silent figures fill the empty space of the stage or screen as iconic signs, their purpose and effect is to stimulate 'the spectator's own inventiveness', asking her/him 'to manufacture the relationship between the sign and its intelligibility, or its relationship to the world'.[4] The spectator is crucial to creating the meaning of these bodies in performance, a meaning that essentially arises out of the relationship between the bodies as signs and the contemporary 'world' of the spectator. In the theatre, Shakespeare's plays speak about the past in the present tense. Theatre is a medium in which meaning is created in collaboration between playtext(s), production team, physical and cultural context and spectator. It is in relationship to present concerns that Shakespeare's violated bodies can be made to mean in performance, and it is within the context of the present-day spectator's culture that they demand to be read. Precisely because these bodies are under threat of erasure within the playtexts, they become, like Desdemona, 'fair paper', blank pages/empty spaces onto which the interests, beliefs and anxieties of production teams and spectators can be projected (*Oth* 4.2). On stage and screen, Shakespeare's violated bodies

Jane de Gay (eds.), *The Routledge Reader in Gender and Performance* (London: Routledge, 1998), pp. 108–12.
[4] Anne Ubersfeld, 'The Pleasure of the Spectator', trans. Pierre Bouillaguet and Charles Jose, *Modern Drama* 25 (1982), 133.

become a barometer on which cultural changes of attitude can be registered as each generation makes them mean differently, using the same textual gaps to articulate ever-changing concerns. The life-expectancy of any one theatrical production, Peter Brook argues, is no longer than five years because 'Life is moving, influences are playing on actor and audience and other plays, other arts, the cinema, television, current events, join in the constant rewriting of history and the amending of the daily truth'.[5] Looking at Shakespeare's violated bodies in performance, then, means looking at ourselves and our recent past; each production a snapshot of the cultural climate that created it, each a 'mirror up to nature' that gives us a glimpse of our own cultural and political history (*Ham* 3.2.22).

TRAPPING THE MOUSE: WATCHING VIOLENCE IN SHAKESPEARE'S THEATRE

It is in *Hamlet*'s play-within-the-play that Shakespeare perhaps best displays his awareness of theatre's potential to reflect the concerns of its audience. At one remove from the plot of *Hamlet*, the 'poison[ing] in jest' (3.2.229) of the Player King stresses not only the theatrical illusion of his murder but even more so the referential *reality* of the represented violence: while *The Murder of Gonzago*, as adapted by Hamlet for the purpose of 'catch[ing] the conscience of the King', is a representation of Claudius's past murder and Hamlet's future revenge (2.2.601), it is also a portrayal of the real-life murder of the Duke of Urbino in 1538.[6] In Hamlet's view, the staging of the Player King's murder has the power to be both emotive and moral in its effect on the audience. At the same time, Hamlet's change of the title of *The Murder of Gonzago* to *The Mousetrap* is indicative of a more nasty side to the impact the representation of a murder may have on its audience. If a moral change is to be effected in Claudius, his conscience will have to be caught in Hamlet's trap – hardly a painless affair, as Hamlet's assertion that the play will make 'the galled jade wince' attests (3.2.237). Tragedy apparently not only represents an assault on the human body, but can itself be violent in its effect on the spectators. More than that, the context of *The Mousetrap* confirms Plato's worst fears about the power of represented violence to provoke violence, since Hamlet's irresolution about his revenge is momentarily forgotten as a result of watching the theatrical representation of the murder.[7] It is as a direct consequence of Hamlet's emotive response

---

[5] Brook, *Empty Space*, p. 16.   [6] Jenkins (ed.), *Hamlet*, p. 507.
[7] See the discussion of Plato in A. D. Nuttall, *Why Does Tragedy Give Pleasure?* (Oxford: Clarendon Press, 1996), pp. 4–6.

to the performance that he feels that he 'could . . . drink hot blood' (3.2.381) and that he attacks his mother with metaphorical daggers and kills Polonius with a literal sword.

As portrayed in *Hamlet*, then, the theatrical performance of an assault on the human body may be a political intervention that may lead to further action. In this, *The Murder of Gonzago/The Mousetrap* reflects a strongly topical concern in late Elizabethan England about the power of drama to change its audience's attitudes and move its members to political action and insurrection. If *Hamlet* was indeed completed in 1601, it would be surprising if the events of February 1601, when Essex's supporters paid the Chamberlain's Men to perform *Richard II* so as to prepare public opinion for Essex's rebellion, had not left a trace in the play.[8] After all, Augustine Phillips, a member of Shakespeare's company, even had to make a deposition to explain the Chamberlain's Men's involvement in the whole affair. Acted by the Chamberlain's Men, Hamlet's commissioning of a specific play from the repertoire of an established company of players with the aim of ascertaining Claudius's guilt in order to achieve a political upheaval must have struck Shakespeare's contemporaries as an almost imprudent affirmation of the political power of theatrical representation. Hamlet's textual and theatrical intervention, his addition of some lines to the play as well as his instructions to the actors in which he controls their movements, furthermore sets a precedent for modern appropriators and producers of Shakespeare's tragedies in showing how subtle changes to the way in which acts of violence are represented can make these acts speak directly to their audiences about contemporary political concerns.

Ultimately, however, *The Murder of Gonzago* is less a political play than a familial drama. Hence the stress on the Player Queen's unsustained protestations of affection for her husband, hence also Hamlet's specification that the murderer is 'nephew to the king' (3.2.239). To stress the dimension of usurpation is to forget that the only political motivation the audience(s) can ever discern in Lucianus is his taking off the sleeping king's crown and kissing it in the dumb show and Hamlet's commentary 'A poisons him i'th'garden for his estate' (3.2.255) – significantly, the play itself does not mention this motivation. The emphasis of the words in the fragment of the play is divided between the Player King's meditations on delay and the betrayal of the marital relationship by the Player Queen. The Player Queen's future infidelity is given as much prominence as is the murder of

---

[8] Jenkins (ed.), *Hamlet*, suggests that Rosencrantz's reference to a 'late innovation' (2.2.331) may well be an allusion to the Essex rebellion (pp. 470–2).

the king. The relationship between infidelity and murder is made crudely obvious in her lines *'None wed the second but who kill'd the first'* and *'A second time I kill my husband dead, / When second husband kisses me in bed'* (3.2.175, 179–80). True to Dympna Callaghan's observation that 'masculine transgressions are constructed in a way that frequently displace [sic] the blame and guilt onto representations of woman in the tragic narrative',[9] the guilt for the murder of the king is thus shown to be shared between the male murderer and the unfaithful woman, the possession of whose body comes to be almost synonymous with the possession of the crown. The intrigue takes place at a personal level, in which interactions between people, and especially between men and women, only secondarily come to stand for vaster political relationships, just as violence meted out on the human body comes to represent an assault on the body politic. In the old feminist adage, Hamlet's *Mousetrap* shows that the personal is always already political.

In its gendering of violence as male and the concomitant representation of femininity as the passive territory or obstacle that must be conquered by the male subject, *The Murder of Gonzago* would seem to be in line with the simple (if not simplistic) genderings of the 'mythical', archetypal text described by feminist critics. It is useful to outline these supposedly normative genderings here as a background against which Shakespeare's more complex and subversive genderings of violence may be set. In Teresa de Lauretis's words, 'the subject of the violence is always, by definition, masculine'. 'Woman', when not defined as 'an element of plot-space, a topos, a resistance, matrix and matter', takes the position of victim of the act of violence.[10] The paradigm identified by de Lauretis in 'high culture' texts has also been outlined by Carol Clover's analysis of modern horror films, showing how 'violence is en-gendered in representation':[11]

The functions of monster and hero are far more frequently represented by males and the function of victim far more garishly by females. The fact that female monsters and female heroes, when they do appear, are masculine in dress and behavior . . . , and that male victims are shown in feminine postures at the moment of their extremity, would seem to suggest that gender inheres in the function itself – that there is something about the victim function that wants manifestation in a female,

[9] Dympna Callaghan, *Woman and Gender in Renaissance Tragedy: A Study of* King Lear, Othello, The Duchess of Malfi *and* The White Devil (London: Harvester Wheatsheaf, 1989), p. 62.

[10] Teresa de Lauretis, *Technologies of Gender: Essays on Theory, Film, and Fiction* (Bloomington: Indiana University Press, 1987), pp. 43–4.

[11] de Lauretis, *Technologies of Gender*, p. 33.

and something about the monster and hero functions that wants expression in a male.[12]

Because, as de Lauretis explains, the '*construction of gender is both the product and the process of its representation*',[13] these insistent portrayals of violence as pertaining to 'masculinity' and victimisation to 'femininity' are a way of producing equivalent genderings in the social subjects who are meant to feel interpellated (in Althusser's sense) by such ideologically inflected representations.[14] As such, what passes for 'hold[ing] . . . the mirror up to nature' (3.2.22) may in fact be reactionary insofar as it works to 'naturalize sadistic violence as a fixture of masculinity'.[15] In fact, as Jill Dolan has provocatively suggested, not only the staging of aggressive and violated bodies, but *any* 'representation of bodies is . . . ideologically marked; it always connotes gender, which carries with it the meanings inscribed by the dominant culture'.[16] The stakes of any representation would therefore seem to be always already 'political' in the sense that representations seek to either consolidate or subvert the gender roles of their audiences.

A consideration of the on-stage audience's responses to *The Murder of Gonzago*, however, shows that the reactions of Hamlet, Gertrude and Claudius are both gendered and individual, and that the process of 'interpellation' is not quite as automatic as the theorists suggest. Claudius interrupts the performance, 'marvellous distempered . . . with choler' at the realisation that he is expected to identify with the perpetrator of the on-stage act of violence (3.2.292–5). He is the only member of the audience to be immediately aware of both the personal and political implications of what he has witnessed. He immediately asks Rosencrantz and Guildenstern to remove Hamlet from Elsinore and escort him to England. Having taken measures to protect his body politic from the threat implied by *The Murder of Gonzago*, Claudius then reacts to *The Mousetrap* as a body natural whose conscience has been 'caught'. What is noteworthy about his abortive prayer is that he conceives of his crime primarily in familial terms: it is 'A brother's

---

[12] Carol J. Clover, *Men, Women, and Chain Saws: Gender in the Modern Horror Film* (London: British Film Institute, 1992), pp. 12–13.

[13] de Lauretis, *Technologies of Gender*, p. 5, her emphasis.

[14] In Jeremy Hawthorn's gloss, Althusser's term describes the mechanism whereby 'individuals come to "live" a given set of ideological assumptions and beliefs, and to identify these with their own selves, by means of a process whereby they are persuaded that that which is presented *to* them actually represents their *own* inner identity or self'. *A Glossary of Contemporary Literary Theory* (London: Edward Arnold, 1992), p. 120.

[15] Clover, *Men, Women, and Chain Saws*, p. 226.

[16] Jill Dolan, *The Feminist Spectator as Critic* (Ann Arbor: UMI Research Press, 1991), p. 64.

murder' that he is trying to repent (3.3.38). Similarly, the excitement
Hamlet feels as a result of watching the play is expressed as a will to upbraid
his mother for her sexual infidelity and to revenge his father's murder rather
than Claudius's usurpation of the throne. Both men, then, are emotionally affected by the performance and identify with the male protagonist
who advances the action. In this production scripted by men (Hamlet,
the fictional original author of the play and Shakespeare) and acted by an
all-male company, the men in the audience find it easy (though, in the case
of Claudius, unbearably disturbing) to assume the position of the model
spectator constructed by the production.

Gertrude, on the other hand, sees the play with different eyes. For her,
as for the modern female spectator of Shakespeare's tragedies, it may be
problematic that the play is written and performed by men for a male model
spectator. Where Hamlet and Claudius see themselves reflected in Lucianus,
Gertrude's attention appears to be directed primarily at the only female
character in the tragedy, the Player Queen. If Gertrude chooses to identify
with the character, if she lets herself be interpellated by the play's staging
of gender, she will be coerced into a complicity with the male-authored
representation of the woman as inherently false and the cause of violence
and political unrest. She will have to forge a link between the actions
witnessed and her own life. This is the position which the production is
designed to make her adopt, as we can see from Hamlet's hopeful asides
'That's wormwood' and 'If she should break it now' (3.2.176, 219). Her
famous answer to Hamlet's question of how she likes the play – 'The lady
doth protest too much, methinks' (3.2.225) – predictably focuses exclusively
on the Player Queen, relating the character's actions to her own personal
experience of human interaction. Nevertheless, her response is remarkable
in two ways. Firstly, there is no sense in which the fact that the character
is impersonated by a boy actor stands in the way of her acceptance of the
representation as that of a 'lady'. Secondly, and more importantly here,
the response implies a critical distance on the part of Gertrude. Instead of
'breaking it now', as Hamlet hopes, Gertrude's defensive comment suggests
her determination to remain aloof and her refusal to play the part of the
guilty creature sitting at a play whose identification with the representation
of her sin is designed to make her 'proclaim [her] malefaction' (2.2.588).

Like the opposition between Hamlet's empathy for Hecuba in the Player
King's monologue and Polonius's judgment of the same performance by
purely aesthetic standards, the contrast between Claudius's and Gertrude's
modes of spectatorship in this scene is that between a response that is
empathic and involved (Hamlet and Claudius) versus one that is aesthetic

and distanced (Polonius and Gertrude). These two contrasting modes of response to the representation, whether in a description, in the visual arts or in performance, of an assault on the human body are mapped out in Elisabeth Bronfen's study of the representation of the female corpse. The choice facing the spectator of representations of violence is similar to that facing the spectator of Hodler's cycle of paintings of the terminally ill body of Valentine Godé-Darel, which Bronfen describes as follows:

> Should one assume the position of a morally involved spectator, treating the represented body as though it were the same as the material body it refers to, focusing, that is, on the question of reference and in so doing denying the representational aspect? . . . Or should one assume the position of the aesthetically involved specator [sic], distanced, disinterested, treating the representation of a dying body only as a signifier pointing to many other signifiers; judged on the basis of comparison with other signifiers (previous images in the painter's [or playwright's] oeuvre, in the image repertoire of his culture); foreclosing the question of the real?[17]

The key distinction in Bronfen's description is between the 'morality' of empathic spectatorship and the 'distance' of aesthetic spectatorship. What Bronfen does not allow for, however, is the possibility of an indifferent or sadistically excited response – types of response that become particularly relevant in the representation of Lavinia's brutalised body in *Titus Andronicus*. Bronfen also precludes strategic modes of viewing, whereby a spectator may actively choose to adopt one or the other mode of response for ideological/political reasons, modes of viewing in which it might be more 'moral' to distance oneself from the spectacle of the violated body.

This is, I would argue, what happens in *Hamlet*'s play-within-the-play, where Gertrude's distance from the representation displays an awareness that some spectators do not, and might deliberately not, react in the ways mapped out by the production. Indeed, the scene opens up the possibility for what reader and audience response critics have dubbed 'resisting' or 'negotiated' readings (as opposed to the 'dominant readings' proposed by the production). Shakespeare's representation of audience reactions to *The Murder of Gonzago* reveals a consciousness that differences in gender, moral sensitivity and personal experiences – and, I would like to add, class, race, sexuality and differing horizons of expectations – obviously lead to variant readings of a performance, however much all the sign systems used in its production may direct the spectator to adopt a specific subject

---

[17] Elisabeth Bronfen, *Over Her Dead Body: Death, Femininity and the Aesthetic* (Manchester: Manchester University Press, 1992), pp. 44–5.

position.[18] Present-day spectators and feminist critics can take Gertrude's 'incomprehension' further and actively choose to privilege particular clusters of theatrical signs to the detriment of others. Instead of looking at the perpetrator, we can look at the victim; even when the playtext prescribes silence for a violated body, our look can privilege that body over the talking bodies that surround it. As Christine Gledhill explains:

> It is necessary . . . for feminist criticism to perform a dual operation. In the first instance, the critic uses textual and contextual analysis to determine the conditions and possibilities of gendered readings. The critic opens up the negotiations of the text in order to animate the contradictions in play. But the feminist critic is also interested in some readings more than others. She enters into the polemics of negotiation, exploiting textual contradiction to put into circulation readings that draw the text into a female and/or feminist orbit . . . critical readings made under the rubric of negotiation offer . . . animations of possibilities arising from the negotiations into which the text enters.[19]

Negotiated readings deliberately seek out opaque signs, empty spaces, silences, marginalised sign-clusters and characters to offer alternative readings that work as far as possible *with* the object under analysis rather than against it, filling the 'empty' spaces with what is always already contained in them and what can be made visible with the help of a spotlight. The point of such negotiated readings is not only the recovery of invisible, lost, forgotten, marginalised stories, but also pleasure. Rather than be defeated by the frustration of not finding themselves interpellated by Shakespeare, whether in the playtexts or in performances, negotiating readers or spectators may '[reconceive] the struggle along different lines',[20] finding enjoyment in the contribution they make to the creation of meaning.

OBJECTS OF KNOWLEDGE: WRITING ABOUT PERFORMANCE

Crucially, I am directing the spotlight as much on the playtexts and the manner in which they circumscribe the empty spaces I seek to fill as on the performances in which actors literally reincorporate the violated, erased,

[18] See, for instance, Judith Mayne's chapters on 'Spectatorship as Institution' and 'Spectatorship Reconsidered', in her *Cinema and Spectatorship* (New York: Routledge, 1993), pp. 31–52, 53–76, and Sara Mills, 'Reading as/like a Feminist', in Sara Mills (ed.), *Gendering the Reader* (London: Harvester Wheatsheaf, 1994), pp. 25–46.
[19] Christine Gledhill, 'Pleasurable Negotiations', in E. Deidre Pribram (ed.), *Female Spectators: Looking at Film and Television* (London: Verso, 1988), pp. 75, 87.
[20] Jeanne Allen, 'Looking through *Rear Window*: Hitchcock's Traps and Lures of Heterosexual Romance', in Pribram (ed.), *Female Spectators*, p. 42.

stigmatised bodies in the body of the play. My premise is that Shakespeare's plays are works that live as much in their written/printed as in their performative re-productions and that they are therefore most fruitfully examined in both forms side by side. Looking at Shakespeare's violated bodies in performance – at representations of the rape, mutilation and murder of silenced Lavinia, the walking dead that people the court of Elsinore, the racially stigmatised bodies of Aaron and Othello, the stifled voice of Desdemona and the vilified and displaced female bodies that make way for the all-overwhelming suffering of Lear and Gloucester – allows me to return to language these silenced, objectified, stereotyped bodies by restoring them to the realm of critical discourse.

Writing about performance and considering performances alongside the printed playtexts they are based on, however, is fraught with difficulties of a theoretical nature, as performances and playtexts have distinct 'authors' (crudely: playwright versus performers) and represent two fundamentally different modes of textuality that stand in a complex relationship to one another. This is so even though both performances and playtexts can be subsumed under the names of 'the play' or 'the work' in Jerome McGann's view of 'the work as the entire complex of a culture's past and present encounters both with the text [the literary product as a purely lexical event] and the poem [the locus of a specific process of production and consumption]'.[21] Since, as textual critics of Shakespeare have long recognised, the problems pertaining to the textuality and authorship of Shakespeare's plays have their origins in the time of their creation, it is the past encounters with text and poem that I want to focus on here in order to arrive at a theorisation of our present encounters with the plays in contemporary performances. While it is possible to talk about performances without such a theoretical underpinning, far too much recent work in performance studies has simply assumed a common understanding of textual issues without clarifying these assumptions or providing a sound framework on which to base the analysis of performances. Performance theory itself has become the 'empty space' in Shakespearean performance studies that cries out to be filled.

The textual situation of *Romeo and Juliet* provides a good starting-point for such a theorisation. The play has come down to us in two distinct versions: the printed text of the 1597 First Quarto, *An Excellent conceited Tragedie of Romeo and Iuliet*, and that of the 1599 Second Quarto, *The Most*

---

[21] McGann as discussed by W. B. Worthen, *Shakespeare and the Authority of Performance* (Cambridge: Cambridge University Press, 1997), p. 14.

Excellent and lamentable Tragedie, of Romeo and Iuliet. The First Quarto, which is shorter than the Second Quarto by roughly one-third, has been classified by Pollard as a 'Bad Quarto' and has therefore until recently received but little critical attention. It is with the arrival of the New Textualist movement that the First Quarto has found defenders who go from claiming that it is a text which is probably closer to what was actually performed on the early modern stage than the Second Quarto, to asserting that the First Quarto is 'authorial'. Nevertheless, it is the Second Quarto, reprinted as the Third Quarto, which served as a copy-text for the 1623 First Folio as well as for most subsequent editions of the play.

From the very start, then, we have a multiplicity of texts, which all bear marks of textual corruption, competing for the status of *the* authorial version of Shakespeare's text – even though initially the author seems not to have been thought to be terribly important, since it is only in the Fourth, undated Quarto edition that in the middle of a print run the mention 'Written by W. Shake-speare' was introduced. As it happens, neither text can be said to be 'authorial' in the sense that its printing was officially sanctioned by Shakespeare himself (none of his plays was). Whereas the First Quarto, which contains traces of being a version prepared for the stage, derives its claim to authority not so much from the author as from the collaborative social institution of the theatre, the Second Quarto claims authority from a perceived closeness to what might be expected of the writer's own manuscript as well as from its connection with the First Folio. Both texts, I would like to argue, are worthy of critical attention, and the two texts should, as far as possible, be kept apart from each other.

From the point of view of a theorisation of performance, *Romeo and Juliet* is particularly interesting because one of the texts derives its 'authority' precisely from its connection with the theatre. What emerges from this brief outline of the textual situation of *Romeo and Juliet* is that, in the case of Shakespeare's plays in particular, Balz Engler is right in urging his readers to 'take seriously the collaborative nature of textuality – including not only authors and readers, but all those who have intervened between them (editors, printers, distributors, teachers, etc.), and its history'.[22] It might be useful to signal this awareness of the multiple 'authorship' of Shakespeare's texts by following John Rouse in adapting a phrase from Foucault and attributing the 'author-function' rather than the 'authorship'

---

[22] Balz Engler, 'Textualization', in Roger D. Sell (ed.), *Literary Pragmatics* (London: Routledge, 1991), p. 181.

of the plays to the historical person of William Shakespeare. This allows me to avoid the tedious putting of Shakespeare's name in inverted commas, which has the effect not only of questioning his sole authorship of the plays (which is legitimate), but also of implying a less productive doubt about Shakespeare's historical responsibility for the plays if not about his very historical existence. 'Author-function' can be seen as a space in the chain of communication of literary works which can be filled by a single person or several persons and institutions. The name which is designated as filling the author-function can thus be seen as a representative of the whole process of textual (re)production (composition, collaboration with the players, typesetting, printing).

John Rouse's appropriation of the term 'author-function' is as useful in relation to performance as in relation to the printed playtext(s). Rouse uses the term to describe

> the contradictory elaboration of discourse within the performance text: we all know, and usually murmur in passing, that this text is 'written' through a collaboration between those who control its various signifying systems (actors, designers, composers, etc.), but we 'legitimize' the text's authority by attributing it to the director . . . /Director/ has become that sign we use to inscribe that connotational consistency and interpretational purpose we propose to glimpse within and behind a 'weaving together' of the strands of the dramatic with those of the performance text.[23]

As a consequence, Rouse explains, there are two 'author-functions' involved in the production of a play: the function filled by the writer(s) and that filled by the producers (i.e. the whole team involved in creating a production) of a play. A modern production of a play by Shakespeare, as a consequence, can be seen as a site of negotiations between a modern group of producers and a text which has come down to them by tradition and which itself is, to a greater or lesser extent, the result of a collaboration.

Modern productions of Shakespeare's plays, then, could be described as 'diachronic collaborations',[24] a mixing of two historically quite distinct author-functions which together create the production, staging, or *mise en*

---

[23] John Rouse, 'Textuality and Authority in Theater and Drama: Some Contemporary Possibilities', in Janelle G. Reinelt and Joseph R. Roach (eds.), *Critical Theory and Performance* (Ann Arbor: University of Michigan Press, 1992), p. 147.

[24] Jeffrey Masten uses this term to designate 'the writing of several playwrights on a playtext at different times (revision) and the manifold absorption and reconstitution of plays and bits of plays by playwrights writing later'. 'Playwrighting: Authorship and Collaboration', in John D. Cox and David Scott Kastan (eds.), *A New History of Early English Drama* (New York: Columbia University Press, 1997), p. 378.

scène.[25] As defined by theatre semiotician Patrice Pavis, the *mise en scène* is 'an interpretation . . . bringing about a mediation between the original receiver and the present-day receiver'. It is 'an object of knowledge, a system of associations or relationships uniting the different stage materials, forged *in* performance'.[26] Pavis crucially situates the creation of a staging's meaning not only on the side of the production team (director(s), actors, designers, producers, technicians, stage hands, etc.), but more so on that of the spectator. 'Indeed', he writes, 'mise en scène, as a structural system, exists only when received and reconstructed by a spectator from the production.'[27] The *mise en scène* or production as an 'object of knowledge', then, is what the spectator or researcher can piece together in a *re*construction that is inevitably at a further remove from its object of analysis than is the reading of a printed text.

To distinguish between the different types of instability that characterise early modern printed texts in their multiplicity and contemporary productions in their elusiveness, Barbara Hodgdon suggests we refer to the former as 'playtexts'. The term, Hodgdon explains, is meant 'both to convey some sense of their indeterminacy and to differentiate them from other, more determinate, textual categories'. Her term for theatrical productions, on the other hand, is 'performance text', a deliberate apparent oxymoron that is designed to acknowledge 'the perceived incompatibility between the (infinitely) flexible substate(s) of a Shakespearean play and the (relative) fixity of the term "text"'.[28] The now widespread use of the term 'performance text' has come under attack by Douglas Lanier. He points out that the emergence of video technology, with the possibility of recording a performance and thus potentially creating 'a new monolithic and stable "text" – the ideal performance, recorded on tape, edited and reshaped in post-production, available for re-viewing' – represents a danger for performance studies:

If the central insight of performance criticism is that performance is radically contingent, open to historical and material pressures that may not outlast a performance . . . , the stability of the records from which we work may be false to the very historicity performance criticism seeks to address. The run of a play is marked by night-to-night differences that spring from chance, design, and serendipity,

[25] I tend not to use the term '*mise en scène*' when talking about theatrical production because in English, the term tends to be used technically to refer to the image within the cinematic/televisual frame as opposed to the *montage* or cutting between frames.

[26] Patrice Pavis, 'From Text to Performance', in Michael Issacharoff and Robin F. Jones (eds.), *Performing Texts* (Philadelphia: University of Pennsylvania Press, 1988), p. 96.

[27] Pavis, 'Text to Performance', p. 87.

[28] Barbara Hodgdon, *The End Crowns All: Closure and Contradiction in Shakespeare's History* (Princeton: Princeton University Press, 1991), p. 19.

differences that certainly shape reception and potentially reveal much about the performance process; yet the typical records of performance – promptbooks, set models, photographs, videotapes – tend to elide those differences, encouraging us instead to think of a given production as a self-consistent 'text'.[29]

To avoid the danger pointed out by Lanier, I suggest we draw a distinction between 'performance' and 'performance text'. The deliberate equivocation of Hodgdon's oxymoron needs to be disambiguated and fixed. I would use 'performance text' only to refer to the textualisation of an individual performance through the technical device of video. Archival video recordings, however poor their quality, do indeed function as Lanier's 'monolithic text'. On the other hand, I would like to reserve the term 'performance' for the physical realisation of the script (which is the text that emerges out of the collaborative efforts of director and company in rehearsal) at a specific historical moment.[30] Performance is characterised by its ephemerality, spontaneity, productive interaction between spectators and actors, and the subjectivity of its reception. It can be conferred 'textuality' only insofar as it is a message in a communicative chain and insofar as, from the point of view of its production, it fits with the etymology of the word 'text' as a weaving, an 'interlacing or entwining of any kind of material'.[31] Whereas the different sign systems used in the theatre are certainly interwoven to create a meaningful product, this product is importantly an *event* and not a fixed material object. In performance, production and reception of meaning happen simultaneously, and critically the distinction between the meaningful or intentional and the accidental remains blurred. Actors' charisma, the material conditions of the theatre building, audience moods and so on are all factors which, if taken as part of the 'text', stretch this term to the extent that it becomes too all-inclusive to be useful as a concept. In writing about performance, a physical, three-dimensional medium is flattened into two dimensions, leading inevitably to distortions and misrepresentations. Adapting Peter Novak's evocative description of the problems involved in talking about sign language, I could say that writing about performance is like dancing about architecture.[32]

[29] Douglas Lanier, 'Drowning the Book: *Prospero's Books* and the Textual Shakespeare', in James C. Bulman (ed.), *Shakespeare, Theory, and Performance* (London: Routledge, 1996), pp. 203–4.

[30] Richard Schechner describes the script as 'the interior map of a particular production' and as 'developed during rehearsals to suit a specific text as in orthodox western theater'. *Performance Theory*, revised and expanded edition (London: Routledge, 1988), pp. 85, 91.

[31] D. F. McKenzie, *Bibliography and the Sociology of Texts*, The Panizzi Lectures 1985 (London: The British Library, 1986), p. 5.

[32] Peter Novak, 'Shakespeare in the Fourth Dimension: *Twelfth Night* and American Sign Language', in Pascale Aebischer, Edward J. Esche and Nigel Wheale (eds.), *Remaking Shakespeare: Performance across Media, Genres and Cultures* (Houndmills: Palgrave Macmillan, 2003), p. 23.

Whereas individual performances are very difficult to write about from hindsight, since the critic has to rely on her or his individual memory as perhaps supported by notes hastily scribbled in a darkened auditorium, productions or *mises en scène* as a whole are slightly more tangible, though also more fragmented, as 'objects of knowledge'. Reconstructed self-consciously from a variety of sources, including personal memories and notes of individual performances, archival traces in the shape of video recordings, production photographs, reviews, promptbooks, set designs, lighting plots, rehearsal notes, the nightly reports of the stage manager during the run of a production and recorded comments made by members of the production team, productions can be discussed as an 'object of knowledge' only as long as the fragmentary and contingent nature of the evidence is acknowledged. The nature of the theatrical evidence and the subjectiveness of the approach preclude determinacy. It is therefore essential not to restrict the discussion of performances to 'thick' descriptions, that is, descriptions that seek to pad out fact with inferred or perceived motivations and aims and that, in the process, run the risk of glossing over the indeterminacies of their objects of analysis.[33] While 'thick' descriptions are important in that they render dry fact accessible, constructing a narrative out of fragments, I deliberately foreground the constructedness of my narratives by including, wherever possible, references to the documents (reviews, archival records, actors' memoirs, etc.) on which these pieced-together narratives are based. As in the writing of history, facts are often contradictory and may be compiled by individual researchers to create different narratives according to the relative weight given to different pieces of evidence in accordance with the researcher's ideological stance and political aims.

Arguably, the more stable textuality of film, video or DVD should allow for a more coherent, less consciously constructed, narrative. Because the performances recorded on film can be selected from a range of takes of the same scenes, which can be cut and altered in post-production, film is indeed, as Lanier suggested, as close as we can get to an 'ideal performance' or 'ideal text'. However, even films, video and DVD involve a certain multiplicity and instability of the text involved: films are increasingly accompanied by

---

[33] The term – coined by Gilbert Ryle in 'Thinking and Reflecting', *Collected Essays 1929–1968*, vol. II of his *Collected Papers*, 2 vols. (Bristol: Thoemmes Antiquarian Books Ltd, 1990), pp. 465–79 – has been appropriated in anthropology by Clifford Geertz, 'Thick Description: Toward an Interpretive Theory of Culture', *The Interpretation of Cultures: Selected Essays* (London: Fontana Press, 1993 [1973]), pp. 3–30. It has been very fruitfully used in Shakespearean performance studies by Barbara Hodgdon, *The Shakespeare Trade: Performances and Appropriations* (Philadelphia: University of Pennsylvania Press, 1998), p. xii, and by Carol Rutter, *Enter the Body*, p. xiii.

published screenplays that diverge to a greater or lesser extent from the finished product, Kenneth Branagh's *Hamlet* film exists in a long and a short version, and many films exist as both a studio cut and a director's cut. With the introduction of DVDs featuring commentaries by members of the production teams, interviews, scenes that were left out of the final cut and alternative takes, the textual multiplicity and instability of early modern playtexts finds a new form in the textual instability of film which is a function of the new technologies available. In the end, no amount of textual stability could ever compensate for the subjectivity and historical specificity of the researcher and her or his sociocultural context: films, like any other cultural 'text', have as many meanings as they have spectators.

FILLING THE EMPTY SPACE: SHAKESPEARE'S VIOLATED BODIES

While the fragmentary, unstable nature of playtexts, films and stage productions could be seen as a hindrance, I choose to see the gaps in the evidence, the discontinuities and the contradictions as so many empty spaces that ask to be filled with alternative narratives and viewpoints. In my critical practice, 'Shakespeare' designates the author-function of the playtexts (as partly mediated by modern editions), whereas the names of directors stand for their production teams. Where different members of the production team are 'pulling against each other', trying to create different meanings, my readings of these conflicts seek to highlight this fissure in the author-function and foreground the actor's authority over her/his own part of the production as yet another marginalised body to be pulled into the spotlight. Invoking Gledhill's notion of 'negotiated readings', these discontinuities are welcome in that they allow me to '[exploit] textual contradiction to put into circulation readings that draw the text into a female and/or feminist orbit'.[34] What I seek to achieve by reading playtexts and performances side by side is not a coherent stage history of each play I consider, but rather a cultural history of the reception of Shakespeare's violated bodies in performance as evident from a few representative, extreme or particularly telling examples that allow me to draw the texts into the four main overlapping orbits around which this book is organised.

Titus Andronicus, the play with which I begin, provides the structural foundation for my arguments throughout the book and, I will suggest,

---

[34] Gledhill, 'Pleasurable Negotiations', p. 75.

is also the structural foundation for Shakespeare's own exploration of key issues throughout his tragedies. Accordingly, the book evolves in a circular fashion, returning to *Titus* in every chapter to pick up on the different problems Shakespeare chooses to work over again in his later tragedies. Indeed, *Titus* could be said to be the 'richest' of the plays under consideration, as it contains the most extreme examples of self-conscious marginalisation, silencing and stigmatisation of characters and their instrumentalisation by the plot. In the first chapter, I choose to focus on the rape, mutilation and eventual murder of Lavinia. I argue that the rape, as a tragic representation of the nexus of power, gender and violence, has a contradictory position within the play, where it is both structurally central to the plot and paradoxically kept off-stage as an ob-scene, excessive spectacle that breaks through the boundaries of art and involves the spectator in its obscenity. In performance, the textual gap left by Lavinia's tongue-amputation is re-presented by the actor's body, just as the invisible rape is made visible through her mutilations. Reading productions of the play from Peter Brook's 1955 staging, via Julie Taymor's feature film *Titus* (1999) up to the post 11 September Kaos touring production, I show how stagings of the play deal with, and often replicate, the obscenity of Lavinia's sexual, vocal and physical erasure both on- and off-stage, reflecting cultural attitudes towards gender and violence in the process. The key case study here is Antony Sher's attitude towards the role of Lavinia as an 'empty space' as evidenced both in his performance of Titus in Gregory Doran's 1995 South African production and in his appropriation of the character in his novel *The Feast*. Rather than read the fate of Lavinia as an unequivocal narrative of loss, my work on novel, diaries, biographies, playtext and performances alike foregrounds the resistance of both character and performers to their silencing, stressing the structural relationship between Shakespeare's earliest revenge tragedy and the modern rape-revenge films analysed by horror film theorist Carol Clover. Lavinia's silencing, I will argue, is a reaction to the verbal threat she poses, and her determination to be revenged contributes to the tragedy's reversal of the traditional gendering of violence as Revenge (both character and concept) is gendered female.

As Lavinia's silenced body is arguably instrumentalised as a theatrical property during the six scenes in which she appears after her mutilation, the dead and not-yet-quite-dead bodies that crowd the stage in *Hamlet* are equally under the threat of being treated as objects. In the second chapter I will discuss the ways in which, in recent productions of *Hamlet*, the corpses of Old Hamlet (in the guise of his Ghost), Polonius, Ophelia and Yorick have challenged their objectification and laid claim to our attention to them as subjects. *Hamlet*'s dead and not-yet-quite-dead bodies emerge as 'improper properties' that threaten to break out of their circumscription within fiction into a disconcerting reality. Linking this attention-grabbing of *Hamlet*'s promiscuous corpses to the instability of the play's three-text corpus, my argument revolves around the ways in which the ambiguities of the body of the play are replicated in the ambiguities of its bodies. In particular, the uncertainties surrounding Old Hamlet's Ghost as a theatrical sign relate back to Shakespeare's representation of Lavinia's mutilated and raped body as a broken-up sign that can be read as a metonymy for the (semiotic) disruption of the entire body politic. *Hamlet*'s not-yet-quite-dead bodies, then, in their instability as theatrical signifiers, are symptomatic of the semiotic breakdown that prevents Hamlet from proceeding with his revenge. The chapter concludes with a discussion of Yorick's skull as the 'improper property' *par excellence*, a property that, in its excessive significa-tion, becomes in its late-twentieth-century incarnations the embodiment of *Hamlet*'s paradoxical familiarity and ever-increasing elusiveness.

In 'Murderous male moors: gazing at race in *Titus Andronicus* and *Othello*', the return to the concerns of *Titus* is threefold: it revisits the play's 'Othering' strategies in the characterisation of Aaron, its portrayal of semiotic disruption as the cause and/or effect of physical violence and its erasure of the outspoken female in favour of the portrayal of the male hero as, to anticipate Lear, 'more sinned against than sinning' (F *Lr* 3.2.60). As the chapter's title indicates, the early tragedy's representation of racial difference is set side by side here with Shakespeare's portrayal of Othello in an attempt to tease out not only the divergent attitudes towards race in the two tragedies but also to think through the problems facing modern interpreters. The chapter begins with a discussion of Théophile Gautier's mid-nineteenth-century account of the black actor Ira Aldridge's perfor-mance of King Lear in whiteface, using this example and the comments of black actors and academics to evaluate the different casting choices avail-able for the roles of Aaron and Othello. A separate section considers the changing attitudes towards the casting and representation of Aaron in the twentieth century, revisiting the productions discussed in the first chapter and looking at them not through the lens of gender but through that of race. From there, the chapter will move on to a consideration of the semiotics of race in *Othello*, investigating how the playtexts complicate Othello's black-ness as a theatrical sign by suggesting that there may be a difference between the blackness of the hero's skin and the fairness of his mind. I argue that it is this semiotic uncertainty, as exploited by Iago, that leads to Othello's murder of Desdemona. In the second half of the play, Desdemona becomes the epitome of the opaque theatrical sign that invites the projection of meaning onto her body as an empty space or 'fair paper . . . / Made to write "whore" upon' (*Oth* 4.2.72–3). Using Orson Welles's erasure of Suzanne Cloutier's Desdemona in his film of *Othello* as a starting-point, I conclude with an investigation of how Desdemona's rejection of such projection and her assertion of semiotic coherence competes with Othello's claim to heroism in the murder scene. The scene provides an ideal point of comparison as it is the site where a production's attitudes towards race and gender tend to pull the interpretation in opposing directions. Key productions that have remained influential either because they were conceived as feature films or because they have subsequently been taped for television allow me to trace the fluctuating attitudes towards the performance of racial difference and gender.

King Lear, the last play I consider in this book, also represents the end of my ability to engage in pleasurable negotiations. Faced with the evacuation of Cordelia from the plot and the 'bemonstering' of her sisters that leave them irredeemably impossible as points of identification in the second part of the play, I choose not to fill the empty space left by Lear's daughters. Instead, the fourth chapter concentrates on describing the mechanisms whereby the play's female characters, as well as its 'secondary' male characters, are marginalised and/or instrumentalised so as to amplify Lear's suffering, making it, in A. D. Nuttall's words (but in a different sense than his), a work that 'does not please; it hurts too much'.[35] The play, I argue, is centred on the punitive infliction of suffering not only on the characters, but also on its audience. More than in previous chapters, I am here concerned with emptiness: the feelings of emptiness and powerlessness I am left with as a pointlessly resisting spectator; the gaps of the play's performance history as the blinding of Gloucester – arguably the central scene in which gender roles are negotiated around an act of spectacular physical violence – is elided, rewritten, restaged without being able to prevent its demonisation of Regan. Thinking through different performance choices and acting styles, I use the productions directed by Nicholas Hytner in 1990 and Richard Eyre in 1997–8, in conjunction with Kathleen McLuskie's 1985 essay on 'The Patriarchal Bard', to argue that a possible compromise that might help resolve the problems the play poses for a modern female spectator could be to create a stylistically discontinuous production whose fragmentary nature might help expose the 'empty space' at the heart of

---

[35] Nuttall, *Why Does Tragedy Give Pleasure?*, p. 100.

the play. In a return to the concern with the broken-up theatrical sign in the other three tragedies, the chapter closes on an examination of the nexus of gender, speech and sight and the tragedy's last-minute cancellation of its revenge structure in its final focus on Cordelia's unresponsive, unreadable body. I end on a feeling of loss – not Lear's loss of Cordelia, but my loss of alternative viewpoints and protagonists.

CHAPTER ONE

Titus Andronicus: *spectacular obscenities*

The video cover for Christopher Dunne's 1998 'new cult/horror classic!' video of 'William Shakespeare's savage epic of brutal revenge *Titus Andronicus*' features a graphic picture of a grim and bloody Lucius holding up the facial skin of Alarbus, whose flayed head, eyeballs horrifically exposed and mouth wide open, is falling towards the viewer in the foreground. The reverse of the tape (not to speak of its content) is similarly crude, with inset stills of gloomy Tamora, crazed Titus in a chef's outfit, Titus about to butcher one of Tamora's sons and the bloody heads of Chiron and Demetrius on a platter. A little drawing of a chopped-off hand with cut-off fingers lying over a bloody sword is preceded by a description of *Titus Andronicus* as 'A tale of timeless relevance and depth, yet a bizarre and exotic indulgence in the horrific imagery of humankind's inhumanity to itself . . . TORTURE, DISMEMBERMENT, MURDER, CONSPIRACY, DEMENTIA, CANNIBALISM, INFANTICIDE and more!'

Dunne's 'Shakesploitation' video, in its extremeness, raises some of the most important questions that I am seeking to address.[1] Its very excess of violence highlights the relative restraint of Shakespeare's playtext, which selects specific acts of violence for on-stage display while others are hidden from view. If Titus can chop off his hand on-stage and Hieronimo, in Kyd's roughly contemporary play *The Spanish Tragedy*, can bite off and spit out his own tongue, why is the playtext so reluctant to portray the process of Lavinia's mutilation? Dunne, predictably, shows no such restraint where the mutilations of his near-nude Lavinia are concerned, but it is highly significant that he nevertheless chooses not to portray her rape, which takes place off-screen. The list of atrocities on Dunne's video cover does not mention rape, nor does the cover include a still of Lavinia, who within the video disappears after she is found by Marcus and only reappears to

---

[1] I borrow this term from Lorn Richey, as quoted in Richard Burt, 'Shakespeare and the Holocaust: Julie Taymor's *Titus* is Beautiful, or Shakesploi Meets (the) Camp', *Colby Quarterly* 37:1 (2001), 85.

be killed in the final massacre. Does that make her rape and dismembered figure the '. . . and more!', the unspeakable and ultimately unrepresentable excess of violence promised by the blurb? If the mutilated Lavinia is so easily elided in Dunne's video, in whose favour does she disappear? What are the implications for performance of the textual gap left by Lavinia's erasure? What are its implications for literary criticism?

'ARISE AND LOOK UPON HER': LOOKING AT THE UNREPRESENTABLE AND WRITING THE UNSPEAKABLE

Almost at the centre of *Titus Andronicus* lies the rape of Lavinia, a tragic representation of the nexus of power, gender and violence that has profound resonances today. An early exchange in the play bears witness to the uncomfortable semantic slippage whereby, in *Titus Andronicus*, 'rape' may refer as much to the theft of one man's property by another as to a sexual assault. The debate recalls the play's historical specificity, the fact that it was written at a time when the sexual and gendered nature of the crime of rape was gradually acknowledged in legal definitions that challenged its former legal status as mainly a property crime, thus ending centuries of conflation of the *raptus* of clandestine marriage with non-consensual sexual violation.[2] In the confrontation between the brothers Bassianus and Saturninus, the definition of 'rape' is angrily debated, while the contested property, Lavinia, stands silently by:

> SATURNINUS Traitor, if Rome have law or we have power
>   Thou and thy faction shall repent this rape.
> BASSIANUS 'Rape' call you it, my lord, to seize my own,
>   My true betrothed love, and now my wife?
>   But let the laws of Rome determine all;
>   Meanwhile am I possessed of what is mine. (1.1.408–13)

Later in the play, rape as abduction is replaced by the sexual violation perpetrated by the Andronici's enemies, and Lavinia's voluntary silence about her *raptus* is brutally forced upon her through the amputations of tongue and hands that accompany her rape. The rapists' double intention of satisfying sexual desire and wreaking revenge on the male Andronici prefigures late twentieth-century debates about whether rape is the expression of sexual desire or of power, showing it to be an effect of both: a sexualised technique of warfare. Rape in Shakespeare's tragedy is thus both personal and

---

[2] Lorraine Helms, '"The High Roman Fashion": Sacrifice, Suicide, and the Shakespearean Stage', *PMLA* 107 (1992), 557.

political, a claiming of the woman's body as sexualised enemy territory to be conquered.

Although the rape is structurally central to the play, in that it is the act of violence that motivates more than any other the horrific revenge of the Andronici, it is paradoxically hidden from sight, becoming an act, to appropriate Sidney's phrase, 'Whose presence absence, absence presence is'.[3] Titus' statement that his 'bowels cannot hide [Lavinia's] woes' (3.1.231) and Lavinia's insistent physical presence on-stage suggest the inability of protagonist and play to contain the impact of her injuries. At the same time, the actual rape, while contained in the body of the play, takes place off-stage, is figuratively concealed within the body of Titus and literally hidden inside that of Lavinia. As the off-stage rape acquires a central importance and symbolic presence, the elision of the rape in the play-text and the subsequent textual silence of the rape victim is made up for, in performance, by the actor. Whereas in the study, reading *Titus Andronicus* means reading Titus' grief in response to the textual gap left by his daughter's violation, in the theatre, the mutilated rape victim is insistently kept before the audience's eyes for six scenes. The actor's body re*presents* the absence of words. Watching *Titus Andronicus* therefore means watching Lavinia. In the theatre, the Andronici's scripted reactions to Lavinia expose their *inability* to respond appropriately to her physical and mental needs. What the playtext decorously conceals, the performance shockingly reveals. It is indicative of the shocking indecorum of Lavinia's body in performance that Eugene M. Waith felt that, in the scene where Lavinia is discovered by her uncle, her presence is an impediment:

For the Ovidian description of Lavinia to work as it might work in the *Metamorphoses* an even greater freedom is required. A physical impersonation of the mutilated Lavinia should not block our vision . . . We have the description which almost transforms Lavinia, but in the presence of live actors the poetry cannot perform the necessary magic.[4]

If readers and spectators feel frustrated by Marcus' struggle to come to terms with/find the terms for Lavinia or are momentarily checked in their effort to attach a metaphorical meaning to her ravaged body, that

[3] Sir Philip Sidney, *Astrophel and Stella*, sonnet 60.
[4] Eugene M. Waith, 'The Metamorphosis of Violence in *Titus Andronicus*', *Shakespeare Survey* 10 (1957), 47–8. Waith's 1957 article had a great influence on the critical appreciation of *Titus* in the second half of the twentieth century. In his later *Patterns and Perspectives in English Renaissance Drama* (London: Associated University Presses, 1988) however, Waith revised his opinion and described 'the discrepancy between what we see on the stage and what Marcus says as a kind of double vision' (p. 142).

is precisely because the theatrical function of Lavinia's continual presence is to disconcert. Her body acts as a grim reminder of violence and the need for revenge while remaining, at the most irreducible level, an icon of the body in pain as described by Laura Tanner and Elaine Scarry: a human being who has been thrust 'into the status of uncontestable [sic] embodiment'[5] and whose physical condition literally cannot be translated into words. 'Physical pain', Scarry explains, 'actively destroys' language insofar as it 'bring[s] about an immediate reversion to a state anterior to language, to the sounds and cries a human being makes before language is learned'. Physical pain is also linguistically disabling because it 'has no referential content. It is not *of* or *for* anything. It is precisely because it takes no object that it, more than any other phenomenon, resists objectification in language.'[6] Rape and the physical pain it causes are both invisible and inarticulable; rape does not necessarily leave any physical evidence on the body of the victim (at least in the theatre, where forensic examination is impracticable). While Lavinia's hand- and tongue-amputations do write 'rape' onto her body through a metonymical displacement of her wound (making the implicit explicit elsewhere) and an intertextual evocation of the Ovidian myth of Philomela, these amputations are also the incarnation of the 'unspeakab[ility]' of the wrongs sustained by the Andronici (5.3.125). By intertextually and metonymically pointing to the victim's invisible rape, the mutilations put into visual signs what is unutterable both within the playtext and in Waith's 'disembodied' allegorising critical discourse.

It is the literary aspect of Lavinia's violation, its association with inter-textuality and rhetorical tropes, that constitutes the greatest challenge to an 'embodied' consideration of her rape as an act of physical cruelty per-petrated by men on the body of a woman. The incisions in Lavinia's flesh open her up not only to the most empathically 'embodied' responses – her brother Lucius collapses on the ground at the sight of her (3.1.65) – but also to the most aesthetically detached readings of her figure as an emblematic representation of concepts that are extraneous to her character. In a striking contrast with Titus' on-stage hand-amputation, which stresses the act of cruelty and the immediate physical suffering of the victim, the tragedy's strategy of withholding the process of Lavinia's dismemberment from view focuses the audience's attention on the *result* of the amputation, the 'lopped' figure of Lavinia as a *fait accompli*. As a consequence, mutilated Lavinia is

---

[5] Laura E. Tanner, *Intimate Violence: Reading Rape and Torture in Twentieth-Century Fiction* (Bloom-ington: Indiana University Press, 1994), p. 4.

[6] Elaine Scarry, *The Body in Pain: The Making and Unmaking of the World* (Oxford: Oxford University Press, 1985), pp. 4, 5.

available for interpretation not so much as a suffering subject of violence, but as an object: an object of contemplation for her uncle Marcus, an 'objective correlative' for Titus' grief, an 'object' the sight of which figuratively 'kills' Lucius (3.1.65). This objectification is consolidated in the imagery associated with her, exposing her to metaphorical readings that politicise her body and trope her out of the state of painful embodiment into the realm of discourse. Marcus' infamous 'bubbling fountain' and 'conduit' images (2.3.23, 30) can be read as attempts to render her wounds 'speakable' through metaphoric distancing. The images translate the gruesome and physical into the aesthetic and verbal in an endeavour to contain the violence at the same time as the excess of the speech, in terms of both rhetorical elaboration and length, exposes the inappropriateness of his response.

While Marcus' metaphorical 'translation' of pain into poetry, however inadequate, is relatively innocent and apolitical (if interpreted as part of his effort to come to terms with both his and his niece's human suffering), the playtext contains clusters of images that politicise Lavinia as 'Rome's rich ornament' (1.1.55) in ways that work to gloss over, sublimate and ultimately negate her physical pain and humanity. Having lost the 'sweet ornaments' of her hands as a result of Demetrius and Chiron 'thrash[ing] the corn' of her chastity (2.3.18; 2.2.123), Lavinia is visually and metaphorically linked to the 'scattered corn' of the body politic that Marcus, at the end of the tragedy, promises to 'knit again . . . into one mutual sheaf, / These broken limbs into one body' (5.3.69–71). The danger in following through these image-clusters is that, as Jocelyn Catty points out, '"Political" readings (or writings) of rape . . . – that is, readings that privilege these functions of rape – can mask the power-relationship between the sexes upon which rape is always based and which it enforces'.[7] In modern-day critical interpretations that see Lavinia's body as representing 'the violation of Rome and of all civilized value',[8] as 'a grim image of the dangers of sexuality',[9] as a reminder of 'the right of the people to consent to the authority of the monarch',[10] or, yet more abstractly, as figuring 'the deflowering of the chaste poetic word, the private possession of the lyric-narrative poet, when it encounters the "barbarities" of the public theater and suffers the mauling of a raucous

[7] Jocelyn Catty, *Writing Rape, Writing Women in Early Modern England* (Houndmills: Macmillan, 1999), p. 10.

[8] Albert Tricomi, 'The Aesthetics of Mutilation in *Titus Andronicus*', *Shakespeare Survey* 27 (1974), 17.

[9] David Willbern, 'Rape and Revenge in *Titus Andronicus*', *English Literary Renaissance* 8 (1978), 173.

[10] Sid Ray, '"Rape, I Fear, Was Root of Thy Annoy": The Politics of Consent in *Titus Andronicus*', *Shakespeare Quarterly* 49 (1998), 22.

audience',[11] Lavinia's suffering is sublimated and the issues of gender and power that lie at the heart of her rape are obscured. By thus privileging the allegorical at the expense of the literal, such readings turn the most starkly physical presence on-stage into a pure conceptualisation.

What the problematic allegorisation of Lavinia in both playtext and critical discourse highlights is the sheer strain Lavinia and the tragedy's violence in general put on language. Pure emblematisation is no less offensive than the opposite 'excessive violence' of the stage direction in act 2 scene 3 with its 'deliberate catalogue'[12] of '*Enter . . .* LAVINIA, *her hands cut off and her tongue cut out, and ravished*' which, in its explicit display of the opened-up female body, borders on sadistic pornography. How can one write about the play's 'horrors' – a favourite word among critics and reviewers and one that conveniently glosses over what it refers to – without being either crude or euphemistic? How can one talk about the raped and dismembered Lavinia without being as obscenely meticulous in one's enumeration of her visible and invisible wounds as is the stage direction, without squeamishly taking refuge in metaphors as do her male relatives, without allegorising her out of her pain as do political interpretations or without sadistically distancing oneself from her through the use of humour in a way that would align the commentator with her rapists and torturers? On the surface, for instance, a remark like Giles Gordon's about the resemblance, in the 1987 RSC production directed by Deborah Warner, of Sonia Ritter's Lavinia to 'a tragic piglet after her mutilation' may well appear funny.[13] But the reviewer's distancing strategy, in which the humorous simile simultaneously deprives the character of her humanity and, by implication, her appeal to the reader's sympathy, is ultimately tasteless, cruel and only one step away from some of the entries by eminent scholars in the *Titus Andronicus* limerick contest 2000, whose organisers disingenuously apologised for the noticeable 'preponderance of Lavinia limericks'.[14]

The crucial point here is not so much that all of these modes of response (graphically descriptive, aesthetically distanced, allusive, allegorising, humorous) are improper, but that Shakespeare thrusts obscenity upon readers, spectators and characters alike. The raped Lavinia is *ob-scene*, literally 'off, or to one side of the stage', in that her mangled, leaking, open body

---

[11] James L. Calderwood, *Shakespearean Metadrama: The Argument of the Play in* Titus Andronicus, Love's Labour's Lost, Romeo and Juliet, A Midsummer Night's Dream *and* Richard II (Minneapolis: University of Minnesota Press, 1971), pp. 32–3.
[12] A. C. Hamilton, '*Titus Andronicus*: The Form of Shakespearian Tragedy', *Shakespeare Quarterly* 14 (1963), 201.
[13] Giles Gordon, 'Mortality Explored', *London Daily News*, 13 May 1987.
[14] <http://www.bardcentral.com.tituslims.html>, 28 April 2002.

forces into our view 'that which is just beyond representation'.[15] If, as Lynda
Nead in her study of the female nude suggests, the function of art is to
contain and regulate the unstructured, inherently excessive and transgressive female body through style and form, making it suitable for aesthetic
judgment and contemplation, the obscene is the site where this aesthetic
framework is ruptured in what effectively constitutes an aggression on the
viewer. 'Art', Nead writes, 'is being defined in terms of the containing of
form within limits; obscenity, on the other hand, is defined in terms of
excess, as form beyond limit, beyond the frame of representation.'[16] The
'quiet, contemplative pleasure' of high art is, in obscenity, replaced by the
'excited arousal' and the 'incentive to action' that characterise non-artistic
forms of representation – whether the arousal to action be the on-stage
collapse of Lucius and the Andronici's determination for revenge, the off-
stage spectators' nausea and sense of outrage or the literary critics' desire to
expunge this excessive and grotesque play from the body of Shakespeare's
work.[17] Explicating the art historian Kenneth Clark's distinction between
the artistic and the obscene, Nead proposes that 'As soon as an image
becomes "an incentive to action" it is expelled from the realm of art
and creativity and enters the inferior and corrupted domain of documentary, propaganda and pornography. In this domain there is no imaginative
escape from the real, and the viewer becomes motivated and disturbed rather
than lifted into aesthetic contemplation.'[18] Waith's objection to Lavinia's
on-stage presence can thus be read as a frustration with the obscenity that
stands in the way of his attempted imaginative escape from the 'reality'
of her mangled body. In the obscene figure of dismembered and violated
Lavinia, Shakespeare displays the unspeakable and unrepresentable in a
manner that leaves the viewer or reader hardly any way of responding ade-
quately without replicating and potentially even reinforcing the obscenity
of her representation. Lavinia's violation thus *involves* the audience: while
the incisions in her body open her up to the spectators' voyeuristic gazes,
her obscene on-stage presence renders outside observation (whether visual

---

[15] Lynda Nead, *The Female Nude: Art, Obscenity and Sexuality* (London and New York: Routledge,
    1992), p. 25. See also Olivier Pot, 'Le Problème de l'obscénité à l'âge classique', *XVIIe siècle* 173 (1991),
    403–36.
[16] Nead, *The Female Nude*, p. 20.
[17] There is a fitting irony in the fact that one of the most recent scrupulous scholarly attempts to
    establish the authorship of *Titus Andronicus* resulted in the conclusion that the play is probably
    the result of a collaboration between Peele, who is held responsible for the relatively innocuous
    first act, and Shakespeare, who is mainly responsible for the remainder of the play, including rape
    and mutilations. MacDonald P. Jackson, 'Stage Directions and Speech Headings in Act I of *Titus
    Andronicus* Q (1594): Shakespeare or Peele?', *Studies in Bibliography* 49 (1996), 134–48.
[18] Nead, *The Female Nude*, p. 27.

or verbal) obscene. Titus' promise that he will '*wrest* an alphabet' (3.2.44; emphasis added) from Lavinia's signs – a verb that implies forceful usurpation and perversion of meaning – is indicative of the violence that is always already involved in attempting to speak of and for Lavinia.

At the same time as the playtext thus problematises the verbalisation of Lavinia's violation, exposing the violence and obscenity that accompany both representation and response, it also implies that speaking about the violence and finding the words of which Lavinia is deprived is desperately important to the characters as non-allegorical human figures. Repeatedly, the playtext insists on the fact that even inadequate expression gives more relief than silence: Marcus feels the urge to 'rail . . . to ease [his] mind' (2.3.35) and Lavinia eventually breaks through her enforced silence with the help of a staff – although even at this point the unutterability of rape is conveyed by her use of the Latin word *stuprum*. Titus, too, when pleading for the lives of his condemned sons, acknowledges the need to speak even in the absence of an interlocutor: 'yet plead I must, / And bootless unto them' (3.1.35–6). His remonstrance to Lucius to 'arise and look upon' Lavinia counts for us as well (3.1.66): where speech is disabled, looking must replace reading. After the rape, it is Lavinia's gestures that speak for her: 'Hark, Marcus, what she *says* / I can interpret all her martyred *signs*' (3.2.35–6; emphases added). It is the modern actor and performance team who fill the gap left by the Shakespearean playtext. And it is in reading performance that I can attempt to tell Lavinia's story: 'to wrest' in the *OED* sense of 'emit or utter, esp. with difficulty', a mode of writing that acknowledges inadequacy while seeking to overcome it.

OBSCENE REPRESENTATIONS: (UP)STAGING LAVINIA . . . AND MORE!

Possibly the most 'obscene' representation of Lavinia can be found not in Christopher Dunne's 'low culture' horror video of the play, but in Antony Sher's novel *The Feast*. Written by an established Shakespearean actor with a reputation as a visual artist and author, and concerned with the issues of artistic expression, sexual orientation and political repression, the novel has 'high culture' aspirations. Sher tells the story of an actor/director by the name of Felix who returns to his African home after the collapse of a dictatorship. His search for the girlfriend of a boy who was murdered in police custody – a crime to which she is the only witness – leads him into a surreal museum-tent. In it, transgressive human bodies are featured as exhibits, classical monsters in that these bodies 'offer striking similarities to

categories to which they are not related, blurring the differences between
genres, and disrupting the rigorous order of nature'.[19] While ostensibly
framed as 'art', the monstrous bodies on display obscenely explode that
framework: 'giants, dwarfs, hunchbacks, Siamese twins, a real one-eyed
cyclops, and others, some with signs above them – Our Own Elephant
Man, the Bird Woman, the Inside-out Child'.[20] At the farthest end of the
tent, 'under a sign that read[s] "The Nightmare"', Felix and his companions
find 'a young woman . . . curled on a mattress, dressed in a short nightgown.
Her hands and feet were missing.' Felix's party soon realise that her tongue
has also been amputated:

> '*Ai kipenzi*', Kaz said to the girl. 'You are in hell, ehh?, isn't it? But why – *why* –
> did they have to do this thing as well?'
>   The girl shrugged in her odd, peaceful way, while Zikki answered for her:
> '"Why"? For this reason, this one, this, this, here, now! She's the witness – *Zeuge,
> ja?* – but she can't tell us nothing!'
>   'Oh, yes she can', said Felix stepping forward, a bizarre idea surfacing through
> his shock and queasiness. 'D'you think if . . . ? None of you know *Titus*, do you?,
> because . . .'
>   'Titus?' said Charlie. 'Who finished building the Colosseum? The Emperor
> Titus Flavi –'
>   '*Titus Andronicus*!' Felix said impatiently. 'Shakespeare's Titus. The daughter
> Lavinia, is, sort of . . .' He gestured apologetically towards the girl.[21]

In an odd replication of the 'and more!' on Dunne's video blurb that
promises what it elides, the excess of Lavinia's suffering remains unspoken
in the allusive 'sort of . . .' with which Felix's explanation peters out. What
happens next is sadly predictable: Felix gets the girl to draw the story of
her rape and mutilation and to write the identity of the boy's killer in
the sand. When she is no longer of use as a witness, his friend Charlie
whips out his mobile phone, rings for a helicopter and has her trans-
ported to the hospital, never to appear again in the novel. Lavinia, here,
is explicitly represented as a monstrous *spectacle*, an object for contemplation and amusement for her depraved audience who, 'As they reached each
new exhibit, . . . began giggling'.[22] Deprived of agency (she has an 'odd,
peaceful way'), this complacent female trunk is the very opposite of Shakespeare's active Lavinia who runs after her nephew in order to get hold of
his copy of Ovid. Exposed to the inquisitive gazes of her questioners, Sher's

[19] Marie-Hélène Huet, 'Monstrous Imagination: Progeny as Art in French Classicism', *Critical Inquiry*
17 (1991), 719.
[20] Antony Sher, *The Feast* (London: Little, Brown and Company, 1998), p. 94.
[21] Sher, *Feast*, p. 97.   [22] Sher, *Feast*, p. 95.

Lavinia-figure briefly becomes a combination of a pornographic exhibit and anti-government propaganda, provoking the key responses of excited arousal and incentive to action that Nead identifies with the obscene. But where, in Shakespeare's tragedy, the obscenity persists, disrupting aesthetic containment and spectatorly detachment till the last scene in an insistent reminder of the character's human suffering, Sher's Lavinia is crudely instrumentalised by his plot. Her suffering is negated by the very clinical action which air-lifts her out of the plot into a hospital.

What can possibly justify this textual violation of Lavinia and the seemingly pointless one-upmanship of the foot-amputation in Sher's novel? Whereas Shakespeare's outdoing of Ovid in the hand-mutilation is part of the pervasive use, within the play, of classical pre-texts of violence, no such argument can be used to defend Sher's momentary appropriation and outdoing of Shakespeare. The explanation for this textual aggression, I want to suggest, lies in a desire, on the part of the author, to definitively (and violently) contain Lavinia's spectacular body. The roots of this desire can most likely be found in South African expatriate Sher's ambitious project, barely three years before the publication of his novel, to star as Titus in a 'South African' production of *Titus Andronicus* directed by his long-term partner Gregory Doran. It is easy to see the parallel, in Sher's fictional protagonist's journey home, to the post-Apartheid theatrical return to South Africa of the actor–director team of Sher and Doran. Contrary to the impression conveyed by *Woza Shakespeare!*, the diary Sher and Doran jointly published in 1996, their Johannesburg staging of *Titus Andronicus* was fraught not only with the acknowledged '*wilderness* of problems' in the rehearsal stage,[23] but also with a hostile critical and popular reception, leaving the Market Theatre in Johannesburg near financial collapse. Under attack from all sides, the last straw for the team of star actor and director seems to have been the attempt by Jennifer Woodburne, the production's Lavinia, to thoroughly understand and embody the raped and dismembered Lavinia.

Even though Doran and Sher obviously meant to keep the published account of their conflict with Woodburne humorous, the strains that marked the production and led to Sher's novelistic 'revenge' on Lavinia are obvious to anyone looking at the video recording of the production alongside *Woza Shakespeare!* and *The Feast*. As part of her research into her role, the Doran/Sher diary tells us, Woodburne interviewed a man whose hand had

[23] Gregory Doran and Antony Sher, *Woza Shakespeare!* Titus Andronicus *in South Africa* (London: Methuen, 1996), p. 152.

been chopped off and sewn back on. She moreover visited a hospital (the tame real-life version of Sher's amoral museum-tent), where she met a patient whose lack of a tongue rendered him incapable of preventing himself from salivating – a feature that became crucial in her interpretation of Lavinia and which resurfaces in *The Feast*, where the Lavinia-figure keeps 'throwing back her head to swallow her saliva'.[24] This research, focusing on real-life male amputees, was the sort of preparation for a role Sher approved of and appropriated for the preparation of his own role as well as for his portrayals of mutilation in his novel.

Woodburne's investigations into the effects of the violence on Lavinia as a woman, on the other hand, are ridiculed in the diary as 'OTT' – over the top.[25] Woodburne apparently consulted her doctor about the possible effects of Lavinia's double rape and was told that Lavinia might well be pregnant. When Gregory Doran objected to Woodburne's idea of Lavinia's progressively visible pregnancy, the following happened during a rehearsal of act 4 scene 3, the scene in which Titus orders his followers to shoot arrows bearing messages to Astraea:

GREG: 'Jennifer, why are you squirming like that while they're speaking?'
JENNIFER: 'Well, you remember I asked if I could be pregnant?'
GREG (GUARDED): 'Yeees . . . ?'
JENNIFER: 'And you said no.'
GREG: 'Yeees . . . ?'
JENNIFER: 'Well, I went back to the doctor, and said, "My director won't let me be pregnant, so now what do I do?" And he said, "Well, if there was any chance of your rapists having a sexually transmitted disease . . . ?" And I interrupted and said, "There's *every* chance!" And he said, "Well, then she might miscarry . . ."'
GREG: 'Yeees . . . ?'
JENNIFER: 'Well, that's what I'm doing with the squirming. I'm miscarrying.'
ME [ANTONY SHER] (SPLUTTERING): 'What . . . ? What . . . ? While I'm busy acting my bollocks off . . . doing all my poignant Don Quixote acting, she's over on the other side of the stage having a *miscarriage*?!'
    Greg and I look at one another, then Greg says, 'Which one of us should remind her that, as written, Lavinia isn't even in this scene, and that if she doesn't keep very, *very* still, she could find herself taken out of it again?'[26]

Sher's spluttering exclamation revealingly links being upstaged to emasculation and sets up an opposition between 'bollocks' and 'miscarriage' that

[24] Sher, *Feast*, p. 97; Woodburne's research is detailed in Doran and Sher, *Woza Shakespeare!*, pp. 81–3 and 143–4.
[25] Doran and Sher, *Woza Shakespeare!*, p. 144.   [26] Doran and Sher, *Woza Shakespeare!*, pp. 144–5.

casts the conflict of star actor and director versus supporting actor in gendered language. The physical excess of Woodburne's on-stage miscarriage is opposed to Sher's cerebral art in the contrast between *having* a miscarriage and *acting* Quixotically.

What the 'bollocks versus miscarriage' episode highlights is the radical readjustment of focus that occurs when the playtext of *Titus Andronicus* is performed and the textual absence of Lavinia (Doran is right in pointing out that the playtext does not include her in this scene) is filled with the 'excessive' physical presence of the actor. The star role in the playtext clearly belongs to the actor playing Titus, and this is obviously how Doran perceived it when he wrote:

Shakespeare piles horror upon horror. Titus has to deal with the sentencing of his sons, the mutilation of his daughter, the pointless loss of his hand and then the spectacle of his sons' heads being presented to him. It is as if Shakespeare challenges himself by pushing his characters to the limits of human endurance to explore how the human psyche deals with trauma.[27]

To Doran (and, I daresay, to Sher), the human psyche explored by Shakespeare is coterminous with Titus, whose suffering subsumes and absorbs the individual plights of his family members in a way that anticipates Lear's all-encompassing torment. Sher's appropriation of the isolation and suffering portrayed in the playtext for himself as Titus and for his partner as the beleaguered director is vividly illustrated in his drawing, in *Woza Shakespeare!*, of himself and Doran standing in the middle of a 'wilderness of sea' – an image that in the playtext applies jointly to Titus and Lavinia.

But this elision of Lavinia is only viable within the published diary and the novel. On-stage, Titus' verbal primacy is almost inevitably contested by the visual impact of his daughter. This is especially true when Lavinia is played by an actor like Woodburne, who refused to allegorise her character and insistently brought Lavinia's body into play: her embarrassment at being unable to use her hands to stop her tongueless salivating, her gynaecological troubles following her double rape, her difficulties swallowing food and consequent refusal to eat. Instead of seeing Lavinia as an abstract fiction, Woodburne's research grounded her in reality, in the bodies of the victims whose photographs covered her dressing-room mirror to the extent that she could hardly see herself, submerging her own identity in the violated bodies she was so anxious 'to do justice to' in her performance.[28] Doran's threat of taking Woodburne/Lavinia out of the 'Astraea' scene (at this point

---

[27] Doran and Sher, *Woza Shakespeare!*, p. 150.   [28] Doran and Sher, *Woza Shakespeare!*, p. 199.

in the diary, fictional character and actor have become indistinguishable in their physical threat to Sher's primacy as Titus) unless 'she' keeps 'very, *very* still' amounts to a silencing of the actor that duplicates the violent silencing of the character within the play as a directorial gesture.

It is the more remarkable, in view of this threat, that Woodburne's Lavinia, in the video recording of the production, is *loud*: apparently inspired by the tongueless patient who kept talking even though he could no longer be understood, Woodburne's Lavinia groans, sobs, giggles and shrieks through the production. The spectators are made to watch and listen to her 'empty' bleeding and salivating mouth uttering those primal pained sounds which, more than the deepest silence, emphasise the destruction of language that accompanies her rape. In the scene from which she was almost cut out, it is even possible to see, in Woodburne's performance, a thematisation of her conflict with the director/star team: while the men are busy shooting off their arrows, Lavinia is stumbling about upstage, trying to attract their attention through her signing. Nobody notices her, and she eventually sits down on a centrestage beer crate: if she does not get the attention of the Andronici, she does end up getting that of the audience. In spite of Doran's and Sher's interventions, Woodburne manages to 'squirm' Lavinia's body out of the margins of the stage and into the centrestage spotlight. Even when ignored by her family (and perhaps the more so *because* she is ignored), Woodburne's Lavinia is an active subject who resists allegorisation.

It is particularly jarring, therefore, that in a production whose director insisted that his staging was 'certainly not presenting allegory',[29] the staging of the two scenes that frame the off-stage rape slips from a realistic mode of representation that is in tune with Woodburne's performance choices to a symbolic mode. True enough, Shakespeare's playtext itself is subject to a double reading in which emblematic and naturalistic modes of interpretation co-exist. Nevertheless, in a production that stages all other acts of violence (including Titus' hand-amputation) realistically, the decision to distance the violence of Lavinia's rape and mutilation through stylisation is incongruous. After Bassianus is stabbed with Chiron's and Demetrius' butterfly knives, Woodburne's Lavinia aggressively pleads with Tamora to be killed, screaming until Chiron grabs her and stops her mouth by kissing her. Suddenly, out of nowhere, we hear a little dance tune. Lavinia, held in a dance position, goes limp and puppet-like in Chiron's arms while he licks her face. The 'rape waltz', as the tune was referred to by the production

[29] Doran and Sher, *Woza Shakespeare!*, p. 179.

team,[30] is heard again two scenes later, when Lavinia re-enters on her own, dancing to the music in a trance, her hair down, her hands bound into stumps, and a lipstick smear symbolising the absent tongue. In the video, the image of her numbed dance is superimposed with shots of Chiron and Demetrius savagely miming her violation on a shop-window dummy while taunting her. They cut into the dummy's mouth, pull off its hands, and eventually Demetrius repeatedly stabs it between its legs with his knife. While this may sound more brutal than the gap left by Shakespeare's relegation of the rape off-stage, the combination of explicit sexual violence and displacement onto a substitute body actually has the effect of containing the violence: as Michael Billington astutely observed, the 'appalling violence towards Lavinia' is in this production 'minimised by being perpetrated on a shop-window dummy'.[31] It is only in the later scenes, when Woodburne's body shakes off the trance of symbolism and emerges in its alarming vulnerability, that the horror of her mutilation has its full impact.

The stylisation of Lavinia's rape in Doran's production can be seen as the legacy of the first, and most influential, major production of *Titus Andronicus* in the second half of the twentieth century. The casting of Laurence Olivier and his wife Vivien Leigh as Titus and Lavinia in Peter Brook's 1955 Shakespeare Memorial Theatre production could have promised a balance between Titus' verbal and Lavinia's physical prominence. In fact, Brook's cuts to the text and his decision to stylise the production, and in particular the part of Lavinia, had the opposite effect. Following a realistic staging of the build-up to the rape, which saw Leigh's Lavinia violently dragged off-stage by her rapists, the entrance stage direction for Lavinia after her rape was, famously, visualised symbolically. Leigh's artistically dishevelled hair signified her rape while the streamers flowing down from her wrists and mouth symbolised the blood flowing from her amputated limbs.

In the playtext, Marcus at this point launches into a 47-line mournful poetic description of his niece's ravaged body, so that the previously fetishised female body ('Rome's rich ornament' (1.1.55)) is held up for the audience's contemplation, showing the inadequacy of Marcus' words and exposing the violence behind his and the rapists' Petrarchan imagery. The rapists' conception of their love-object as a doe to be hunted easily blends violence and affection in its objectification and dehumanisation of the woman, and their endorsement of the misogynist cliché 'She is a woman,

---

[30] Doran and Sher, *Woza Shakespeare!*, p. 177.
[31] Michael Billington, 'A Brutal Sort of Interrogation', *Guardian*, 14 July 1995.

Illustration 1: Vivien Leigh as the raped and mutilated Lavinia in Peter Brook's 1955
RSC production of *Titus Andronicus*

therefore may be won' codes femininity as inherently sexually available (1.1.583), defining gender difference in terms of the subject's 'rapability'.[32] Now Lavinia's lips are not 'rosed' because of their freshness but because of the blood that stains them, and her sweet ornamental arms have been shown to be 'branches' indeed, since they easily lend themselves to being chopped off (2.3.24, 18). The woman whose initial ornamental beauty invited just the type of 'fetishistic scopophilia' in its viewers that Laura Mulvey has described for the representation of women in classic Hollywood cinema, 'build[ing] up the physical beauty of the object, transforming it into something satisfying in itself',[33] is in this scene relentlessly held up to the same onlookers who are now forced to acknowledge that the obscene spectacle of violence before them is provoked by the very ideology that informs their own fetishising gaze. The scene's very length and static nature parody the fetishising representations of femininity in classic cinema and theatre where the woman's 'visual presence tends to work against the development of a story-line, to freeze the flow of action'.[34]

By cutting Marcus' speech and stylising Lavinia's wounds, Brook purged the scene of its obscenity and its indictment of the violence that underlies the fetishising gaze. When Antony Sher asked Janet Suzman (herself a Lavinia in Trevor Nunn's 1972 RSC production) about her memories of this moment in Brook's staging, she said that 'The whole audience gasped' not because, as Sher supposed, the sight of Lavinia 'was so shocking', but 'because she was so beautiful!'[35] Again and again, what reviewers and eyewitnesses of the production remember is the ethereal beauty of the stage image. Even when, like Jan Kott, they mention Lavinia's suffering, their compassion is couched in the language of aesthetics: 'What is left is just the eyes, the flutter of veiled hands, the figure, the walk. And how can she walk; how can she look! How much suffering she is able to convey just by bending

[32] Lynn A. Higgins and Brenda R. Silver, 'Introduction: Rereading Rape', in Lynn A. Higgins and Brenda R. Silver (eds.), *Rape and Representation* (New York: Columbia University Press, 1991), p. 3.

[33] Laura Mulvey, 'Visual Pleasure and Narrative Cinema' (reprinted from *Screen* 16:3 (1975), 6–18), in her *Visual and Other Pleasures* (Bloomington: Indiana University Press, 1989), p. 21. Although Mulvey's application of these concepts has been criticised for her assumption of a passive monolithic spectator and her presupposition of an identity between Hollywood cinema and patriarchy, as well as for her deterministic use of psychoanalysis, I find her distinction between and definitions of 'fetishistic scopophilia' and 'voyeurism' (which I will apply to *Othello* in chapter 4) both valid and useful even though I would be reluctant to endorse the psychoanalytical framework they are based on. For a critique of Mulvey, see Mayne, *Cinema and Spectatorship*, pp. 48–52.

[34] Mulvey, *Visual and Other Pleasures*, p. 19. A Shakespearean example of this fetishising gaze that holds up the narrative flow is the moment in which Romeo sees Juliet for the first time.

[35] Sher and Doran, *Woza Shakespeare!*, p. 218.

her body, by hiding her face.'[36] Instead of revealing obscenity, Brook's aesthetic/symbolic staging of the raped Lavinia as an icon reinforced the fetishistic scopophilia of the viewers – far from being an incentive to action and preventing an imaginative escape from the reality of Lavinia's injuries, Leigh's Lavinia never stopped being 'something satisfying in itself'. 'She looked', wrote Noël Coward, 'lovely throughout, regardless of ravishment and her tongue being cut out and her hands cut off. Her clothes and hair-do were impeccable and her face remained untouched by tragedy.'[37] This Lavinia was no Bakhtinian grotesque body, a body whose invaded orifices and leaking wounds could be read as a critique of the violence inherent in the drive to discipline the female body and turn it into a work of art. Instead, Brook's stylisation imposed the control associated with the 'classical body', creating in Leigh's statuesque figure and her aestheticised, neatly tied-up and beribboned mutilations

> an entirely finished, completed, strictly limited body . . . That which protrudes, bulges, sprouts, or branches off (when a body transgresses its limits and a new one begins) is eliminated, hidden, or moderated. All orifices of the body are closed. The basis of the image is the individual, strictly limited mass, the impenetrable façade.[38]

It was by thus negating the grotesqueness and obscenity of Lavinia's body, by 'judiciously' cutting Marcus' speech, Lavinia's indecorous chase after her nephew, the disturbingly suggestive images of her holding her father's hand and a staff in her mouth, and her involvement in the final revenge[39] – by reducing Lavinia's time on-stage and imposing an aestheticising framework on her presence – that Brook managed to convey the 'dark flowing current out of which surge the horrors, rhythmically and logically related' which resulted in what he called 'the expression of a powerful and eventually beautiful barbaric ritual'.[40] His production's particular rhythm and especially its ritualistic *beauty* could only exist at the expense of Lavinia's obscenity and her grounding in reality.

However, Brook's classical control over Lavinia's textual and theatrical body and Olivier's efforts to rein in his manic-depressive wife's sexuality and social behaviour underwent a serious challenge of which audiences

[36] Jan Kott, 'Shakespeare – Cruel and True', in Philip C. Kolin (ed.), Titus Andronicus: *Critical Essays* (London: Garland, 1995), p. 398.

[37] Quoted by Anthony Holden, *Olivier* (London: Weidenfeld and Nicolson, 1988), p. 299.

[38] Mikhail Bakhtin, *Rabelais and His World*, trans. Helene Iswolsky (Bloomington: Indiana University Press, 1984), p. 320.

[39] Daniel Scuro, '*Titus Andronicus*: A Crimson-Flushed Stage!' in Kolin (ed.), *Titus Andronicus*, p. 403.

[40] Brook, *Empty Space*, p. 95.

seem to have remained unaware. Brook's drastic textual cuts and stylisation of Lavinia had left Leigh, whose ambition was to match her husband in the classical repertoire, very little to work with. Whether as a result of her frustrated artistic ambition, her mental illness or her exasperation with her husband's attempts to control her, Leigh's off-stage sexual escapades and manic behaviour were, during the production's European tour, increasingly complemented by on-stage unruliness. Several anecdotes suggest that Leigh's apparently impassive performance of the silenced and partly veiled Lavinia concealed furious whispered attacks on her husband that seem to have been aimed at undermining his performance as the grieving Titus. During a matinée in Belgrade, says one biographer, 'Vivien eyed Titus's wailing misery. Quite audibly she pronounced, "You cunt!"'[41] Alexander Walker, too, quotes a cast member recalling:

I've been on [the stage] with Vivien when she would swear under her breath, 'You shit, you shit' . . . and Larry would continue to spout the most marvellous poetry and then at the end of it whisper, 'Fuck you, fuck you . . . I remember Vivien appearing with a swollen eye one day, saying she'd been bitten by a mosquito. Someone had hit her, I thought.[42]

Whether or not the allegation of marital violence to restrain Leigh was justified, these back-stage accounts do suggest that Olivier was as threatened by Leigh's desire to throw him off balance as Sher was by Woodburne's attempt to do justice to Lavinia. In the instance, Olivier and Brook seem to have won the contest: the production is remembered for its daring direction and its magnificent, eloquent Titus, whereas Leigh's Lavinia is fixed in theatrical memory as the beautiful, passive icon of suffering that Brook designed her to be.

If Brook's distancing approach to the rape, and *Titus Andronicus* in general, was almost the only way the play could be rehabilitated in the 1950s in the eyes of a British audience reluctant to acknowledge the play's violence as 'Shakespearean', the situation dramatically changed following the RSC's 'Theatre of Cruelty' season of 1963–4 and the publication, in 1975, of Susan Brownmiller's seminal study *Against Our Will: Men, Women, and Rape*.[43] Alerted to the political implications of rape and its cultural representations, aided by cinema's increasingly explicit portrayal of acts of violence and against the background of Artaud's vision of a theatre 'that

---

[41] Jesse Lasky Jr with Pat Silver, *Love Scene: The Story of Laurence Olivier and Vivien Leigh* (Brighton: Angus & Robertson, 1978), p. 248.
[42] Alexander Walker, *Vivien: The Life of Vivien Leigh* (London: Orion, 1994), p. 303.
[43] Susan Brownmiller, *Against Our Will: Men, Women, and Rape* (London: Secker and Warburg, 1975).

had the power to disturb the spectator to the depths of his being, to make him confront the ugliness and evil within himself without the uplift associated with the Aristotelian concept [of catharsis]',[44] the playtext's obscenity was no longer something to be elided but rather an element that had to be appreciated as an intrinsic component of the tragedy. Feminist thought increasingly insisted on the fact that representing rape 'cannot be a neutral activity':[45] since it creates its object (both the woman-as-victim and the act of violence) as a cultural and artistic reality, the representation of rape runs the risk of naturalising violence as male and victimisation as female. Portrayals of violence as pertaining to 'masculinity' and victimisation to 'femininity' were now seen as a way of producing equivalent genderings in the social subjects who are meant to feel interpellated by such ideologically inflected representations.

It is within this intellectual and cultural climate that Deborah Warner, the first woman to direct the play for a professional British theatre company, directed Sonia Ritter's Lavinia for the 1987 RSC production in the intimate space of the excitingly new Swan theatre.[46] Under Warner's guidance, the play remained uncut and was treated as entirely trustworthy for the first time in its modern stage history. As a result of the company's close attention to the playtext, Sonia Ritter's Lavinia gained a prominence no Lavinia had achieved before her on the British stage, a prominence which was increased as the production matured and the company seems to have realised the importance of the rape within the play. Whereas in the Swan season of 1987 Chiron stopped Lavinia's mouth and dragged her off the stage to be raped, in the Barbican season of the following year Chiron additionally put his hand under Lavinia's dress and seemed to lift her up with his hand inside her, tossing her up and down to the accompaniment of her frightful cries. Lavinia's return after the rape, on the other hand, remained fairly consistent throughout the run. Preceded by Demetrius and Chiron, who, giggling, crawled on-stage in a cruel imitation of their maimed victim, Lavinia painfully pulled her body into the spotlight by her elbows. Her stumps, her hair and her once-golden dress were caked in mud (mud, during the first four acts, being the production's substitute for blood). As the rapists collapsed on the ground laughing hysterically, she raised herself

[44] Sally Beauman, *The Royal Shakespeare Company: A History of Ten Decades* (Oxford: Oxford University Press, 1982), p. 274.
[45] Catty, *Writing Rape*, p. 22.
[46] Joyce Green MacDonald gives a helpful account of Warner's career and her production of *Titus Andronicus* in 'Women and Theatrical Authority: Deborah Warner's *Titus Andronicus*', in Marianne Novy (ed.), *Cross-Cultural Performances: Differences in Women's Re-Visions of Shakespeare* (Urbana and Chicago: University of Illinois Press, 1993), pp. 185–205.

up, attempted to walk past them and fell down between them. Demetrius grabbed one of her stumps and waved it about to illustrate her 'scrawling', ridiculing her inability to speak. Meanwhile, Chiron spat in Lavinia's face, evoking for me, in a very personal reaction that had more to do with my recent reading than with possible directorial intention, the custom of publicly spitting at and urinating on unruly, talkative women in the early modern *charivari*, the ritual silencing and shaming of so-called 'scolds'.[47] This reminder was the stronger for the fact that the uncut text had allowed Lavinia to speak all her fifty-eight lines, twenty-two of which contain more or less direct insults to her interlocutors, leading to a characterisation of Lavinia as, at crucial moments, mockingly outspoken and confident.

Warner's (probably inadvertent) introduction of a *charivari* element into the rapists' treatment of their victim opened up a new reading of the rape and mutilations: no longer a 'straightforward' result of the aggressors' sexual desire, I could interpret the violence towards Lavinia as the result of a collective endeavour to silence and control her. More than simply the gratification of male desire and the exercise of power over an enemy faction, Lavinia's rape, through the visual association with the ritual humiliation of the *charivari*, could here be understood as a punishment for her outspokenness and her alleged promiscuity as the 'changing piece' who had abandoned Saturninus for Bassianus (1.1.314). The production had not shied away from the implication of sexual knowledge in Lavinia's innuendoes about Tamora's 'experiments' (2.2.69), and the character's assertive sexuality had been clearly established by her obvious complicity in her abduction and preference for Bassianus. Even Lavinia's declaration, following her wedding night, that she has been 'broad awake two hours and more' (2.1.17) – a line that is often read as indicative of 'a kind of disengagement . . . which is accompanied by an abjuration of sexuality'[48] – had been rendered by Sonia Ritter as a frank declaration of sexual interest.

By allusively representing the rape and mutilations as a means of controlling Lavinia's potential transgressiveness, Warner tapped a rich vein that exposed the playtext's *critique* of the male characters' pervasive urge to restrain Lavinia and control her freedom of speech and action. The efforts by the Brook/Olivier and Doran/Sher teams to restrain their respective Lavinias can, in the light of this, be seen as extratextual perpetuations of the drive to control Lavinia that are ironically unaware of the playtext's exposure of

---

[47] See Lynda E. Boose, 'Scolding Brides and Bridling Scolds: Taming the Woman's Unruly Member', *Shakespeare Quarterly* 42 (1991), 178–213.

[48] Mary Laughlin Fawcett, 'Arms/Words/Tears: Language and the Body in *Titus Andronicus*', *English Literary History* 50 (1983), 266–7.

the violence inherent in such control. The brutality of Lavinia's rape and maiming, the obscenity of Marcus' attempts to aestheticise her suffering and the repeated moments of incomprehension that show the Andronici baffled by Lavinia's signs and Lavinia resisting (mis)interpretation stress the cruelty inherent in the urge to repress Lavinia's sexuality and self-expression. Behind the Andronici's eloquent outrage at Lavinia's mutilation there is a discreet counter-current of suggestions that her brutal silencing is the consequence of her vocal and sexual assertiveness. It is worth remembering, at this point, that Lavinia's marriage to Bassianus takes place against her father's will and command – a defiance of parental authority that her brother Mutius pays for with his life and a shaming of his family that Titus never explicitly forgives her for.

The Andronici's laments over the loss of Lavinia's hands and tongue, accordingly, betray a contradictory attitude towards Lavinia's speech. This is particularly clear in Marcus' overly elaborate periphrasis with which he describes Lavinia's tongue-amputation:

O, that delightful *engine* of her thoughts,
That *blabbed* them with such pleasing eloquence,
Is torn from forth that pretty hollow cage
Where, like a sweet melodious bird, it sung
Sweet varied notes, enchanting every ear.
                    (3.1.83–7, emphases added)

Behind the ostensible praise of Lavinia's sweet melodiousness and spontaneous articulateness, there is a regretful insinuation that Lavinia's silencing may be justified, however much he enjoyed her 'pleasing eloquence'. It appears unlikely that, as Alan Hughes's commentary to the New Cambridge edition asserts, 'blabbed' here 'is free of the implication that she spoke too much, or inappropriately'.[49] The conjunction of 'blab', which means 'To talk indiscreetly about what should be kept secret, to reveal or betray secrets' (*OED*) – the main sense in which Shakespeare used this word in all its occurrences in his plays – with 'engine', which could in the sixteenth century refer to either a tool or any offensive weapon, points in a different direction: underlying the main thrust of Marcus' monologue of wistful praise of Lavinia's voice, there seems to be a counter-current suggesting that Lavinia's speech was both indiscreet and offensive in revealing her thoughts which would have been better kept secret. This interpretation is substantiated by Aaron's use of two synonyms of 'blab', 'tattle' and 'babble', when referring to the midwife and her 'long-tongued, babbling gossip' friend the nurse (4.2.170, 152), both of whom he kills in order to prevent their indiscreet speech. Lavinia's silencing is representative of a larger drive to control women's speech in the tragedy, a drive which culminates in the moment when Tamora, who claims the power to make 'both ear and heart obey [her] tongue' (4.4.98), is silenced by being fed a mouthful of son pie. What lies just beyond representation but can be obscenely glimpsed behind Marcus' aestheticising rhetoric is his condoning of the gruesome regulation of Lavinia's speech and body, a control which culminates in her murder at her father's hands.

The first production to stage Marcus' speech in its entirety, Warner's staging was also the first to call attention to the disturbing ambivalence of Lavinia's (male) relatives towards her self-expression. Donald Sumpter's Marcus was unmistakably empathic in his stunned and pained reaction to the mutilated Lavinia, whom he approached like a traumatised animal before finally catching her in his comforting arms. But his laboured rhetoric was insufficient to transform the muddied, mauled, trembling body of his niece into an aesthetic object of contemplation. Neither his, nor later Titus' confident claims to be able to speak for Lavinia were successful in this staging. Ritter's performance stressed both Lavinia's ongoing resistance to attempts to limit her self-expression and the frustrations she had to deal with when her signs were 'wrested' away from her intentions. The production made a big point out of Titus' misinterpretation of Lavinia's thirst as meaning that 'she drinks no other drink but tears' (3.2.36–7).[50] It empha-sised her expressiveness in the scene of Titus' hand-amputation as well as, crucially, her determination to communicate the story of her rape in spite of her father's initial dismissal of her choice of reading matter. This Lavinia did not allow viewers to establish any easy equivalence between femininity and victimisation but rather stressed the desire and ability of the traumatised rape victim to survive and seek revenge. If Vivien Leigh's Lavinia could be summed up in the static beautiful image of the streamers flowing from her wounds after the rape, Sonia Ritter's performance was encapsulated by the frustrated stamp that accompanied her Lavinia's realisation that Titus was unwilling or unable to understand her description of the rapists.

Nevertheless, Ritter's powerfully assertive performance in the scenes fol-lowing her rape was ultimately not sufficient to rival Brian Cox's eloquence as Titus. In Cox's view, his character's all-encompassing suffering absorbed

[50] Brian Cox, '*Titus Andronicus*', in Russell Jackson and Robert Smallwood (eds.), *Players of Shake-speare 3: Further Essays in Shakespearian Performance by Players with the Royal Shakespeare Company* (Cambridge: Cambridge University Press, 1993), p. 182.

Lavinia's pain to become the central, unbearable, focus of grief in the production. 'When [Titus] opens himself... to Lavinia's pain', Cox later wrote,
'it's too much, too shocking. It was not for nothing that audiences could
not always take it: when members of the audience left the performance
it was not, I think, because of the horrors of the play; they left because
of the man's grief.'[51] In fact, the spectators who left the theatre *did* leave
because of the 'horrors of the play' – this can be gleaned from the nightly
reports written by the production's stage managers. But Cox was right in his
assessment insofar as they left or fainted not at the sight of Lavinia after her
rape, but at the moment at which, just a few feet away from the audience,
Aaron cut Titus' hand off with a cheese-wire. Although it was the homely
suggestiveness of the hand-amputation and not Titus' grief that proved
to be unbearable for successive audiences, again and again, and in terms
that are strongly reminiscent of the Sher/Doran diaries, Cox's account of
the production portrays Lavinia and Sonia Ritter as supporting characters whose main function was to buttress his own performance of mental
and physical pain. It does not seem to occur to him that audiences might
be more appalled at Lavinia's inarticulate agony than at Titus' eloquent
grief.

A similar attitude is apparent in Julie Taymor's 1999 *Titus*, the only
feature-film of the play and, as such, probably the production that will
have the greatest impact on the play's perception in the early twenty-first
century. The film bears traces of its long gestation period, from Taymor's
1994 stage production for the Theater for a New Audience in New York to
her filming of the play in 1998. During this time, Taymor was exposed to
the news coverage of the gruesome machete-dismemberments, mass-rapes
and sexual mutilations of the Rwandan civil war. She eventually filmed the
Coliseum scenes for *Titus* in Croatia only two months before a renewed
flaring-up of the Balkans conflict,[52] using members of the Croatian police
academy for Titus' mud-caked soldiers. (The film's Aaron, Harry Lennix,
sardonically remarked in his DVD commentary that these men 'have a
history of being much more than adorable'.) This proximity to actual
conflicts in which rapes were perpetrated on a large scale as a method
of warfare and nation-building put the Shakespearean rape in a modern
context within which it had to be perceived both as a personal, sexual crime
and as a political act and expression of power.

---

[51] Cox, '*Titus Andronicus*', p. 182.
[52] Eileen Blumenthal and Julie Taymor, *Julie Taymor: Playing with Fire* (New York: Harry N. Abrams,
1999), p. 36.

Illustration 2: Video-still of Lavinia (Laura Fraser) on a tree-stump in Julie Taymor's 1999 film *Titus*. The camera-angle emphasises her literal and metaphorical elevation

More than the political context, however, what informed Taymor's portrayal of Lavinia were previous cinematic and cultural portrayals of femininity and metaphorical rape. Staying true to her reputation as an artist who deliberately and self-consciously absorbs 'popular' and 'high' culture in her work, Taymor explicitly modelled the fetishised, inaccessible Lavinia of the play's beginning on the elegant aloofness of Grace Kelly. By contrast, the defiled and brutally sexualised Lavinia of the rape was patterned on 'the famous image of Marilyn Monroe standing over a subway grate and holding her blowing dress down' – an image which, to Taymor, 'seemed an apt modern iconic parallel adding to this scene of humiliation and rape'.[53] Disturbingly, the association with Monroe codes Lavinia both as a victim of male exploitation and as 'available' and 'asking for it' in the ambiguous sense in which 'ravish' can refer both to the male act of rape and the female condition of being 'ravishing'.[54] It is no coincidence that this is the word that was used by a reviewer of Taymor's stage production, who wrote that 'Miriam Healy-Louie is simply ravishing as Lavinia'.[55] Standing on a charred tree-stump in the midst of a muddy nightmare landscape of rotting trees, and taunted by the boys who, excited by their own violence, childishly 'moon' at her, Laura Fraser's Lavinia in the film is both exquisitely beautiful and horribly defiled.

[53] Julie Taymor, *Titus: The Illustrated Screenplay, Adapted from the Play by William Shakespeare* (New York: Newmarket, 2000), pp. 181, 184.
[54] 'As Gravdal explains, the literal signification of "ravish" presupposes a male subject, but in the figurative sense it is the female who is ravishing, who causes the male to be "carried away" and who is responsible for any ensuing sexual acts. This semantic phenomenon gives rise to a useful rhetorical tool, whereby rape is "erased behind the romantic troping of ravishment".' Catty, *Writing Rape*, p. 14.
[55] David Kaufman, 'Robobard', *Village Voice*, 22 March 1994.

As in her stage production, Taymor's staging of Marcus' voice-over monologue upon his discovery of his mauled niece, even though it is radically
shortened in the film, stresses the playtext's exploration of the violence that
hides behind the fetishising gaze:

> By placing the bloodied, ravished Lavinia on a truncated column [in the stage
> version] while Marcus looks up at her from a distance, a physical metaphor was
> created that represented their entire life's relationship. She, the once-perfect god-
> dess, is now a tree whose limbs have been lopped off, helpless, unable to get down
> from her pedestal.[56]

The visual allusion to Degas's ballerina similarly explores the potential
defilement of the female body that accompanies its glorification in high
art.[57] These concerns are also apparent in the camera-work and editing.
By alternating shots of stunned Marcus with shots of the disturbingly
beautiful figure of Lavinia, Taymor's film explores the playtext's morbid
fascination with and metaphorical beautification of the maimed female
body. The film thus prevents any simplistic response: Lavinia is simultaneously an icon of damaged femininity and defiled idolisation (Grace
Kelly/Marilyn Monroe), an emblem of the mutilated Roman body politic
(relating her to the sculpted feet and hands that litter Taymor's Rome)
and, on the most literal level, a brutally mauled, traumatised rape victim.
The spectator is torn between compassion and aesthetic pleasure, between
a gut-reaction of horrified identification with the rape victim and an
intellectual response identified with her uncle's and the film's attempts to
read her wounds metaphorically. No less than in the final banquet scene, of
which Taymor said that it 'highlights the way we create art out of violence',
the representation of the raped Lavinia interrogates art's (and the media's)
capacity simultaneously to expose violence and gloss over it by showing the
'exquisite beauty in the ugliness and the torture'.[58]

   This exploration of beauty and horror and the attempt to strike a balance between the focus on Lavinia's individual, gendered suffering and the
overall plot is typical of Taymor's approach to the character. The decision
to metaphorically represent the rape elided in the playtext in a flashback
as Lavinia is frantically writing the names of her rapists in the sand was a
result of Taymor's awareness that 'when a woman has to testify at a rape trial
she is re-experiencing the rape'.[59] Significantly, however, and in a return

---

[56] Blumenthal and Taymor, *Playing with Fire*, p. 190.   [57] Taymor, *Titus*, p. 181.
[58] Stephen Pizzello, 'From Stage to Screen', *American Cinematographer* 81:2 (2000), 73, 66.
[59] Maria DeLuca and Mary Lindroth, 'Mayhem, Madness, Method: An Interview with Julie Taymor',
    Cinéaste 25:3 (2000), 30.

to Brook's technique of stylisation, Taymor decided that her portrayal of
Lavinia's rape should be distanced to prevent it from falling into what she
calls 'the trap of utter realism. There is a danger in the literal and graphic
portrayal of an image such as Lavinia's dismemberment. It is easily too
grotesque and horrific, and can upstage the larger event.'[60] Not only did
she soften the graphic impact of Lavinia's stumps by replacing the missing
limbs with twigs and later equipping her with wooden prosthetic hands,
but she couched the victim's nightmarish re-experiencing of her rape in
one of the film's allegorical 'Penny Arcade Nightmares' that form a parallel
directorial commentary on Shakespeare's playtext. Clearly, as in all other
interpretations discussed so far, the representation of Lavinia's individual
plight is ultimately not allowed to compete with 'the larger event', the
political and tribal conflict of Romans and Goths and the central grief of
Anthony Hopkins's Titus.

It is only in a recent British stage production of *Titus Andronicus*, directed
by Xavier Leret for Kaos Theatre in 2001–2, that Lavinia's suffering was
not subsumed under Titus' vocal grief and the politics of the play. What
this stunning production exposed, better than any critical reading could
do, was that in spite of – or perhaps because of – the brutal silencing of
Lavinia, Shakespeare in this early tragedy does not necessarily privilege
the male over the female hero. If anything, his consistent portrayal of
the inadequacy of language in the face of such violence lays greater stress
on physical expressions of suffering than on attempts to verbalise pain.
Rehearsed at the time of the terrorist attacks on New York and Washington
on 11 September 2001, and destined to tour a Britain supposedly at war
against terrorism and an Israel torn by the conflict with Palestinian fighters
and under the constant threat of suicide bombers, this production was all
too aware of the violence inherent in 'civilisation' and of the relevance of
the play for its specific historical moment.

The production also started from the premise that nobody is exempt
from violence. Lavinia, in particular, was treated by the company as central to the action. The production's Titus, Lee Beagley, in striking contrast
with Sher and Cox, described Titus' and Lavinia's suffering as equivalent
in depth but different in expression: whereas Titus works through his grief
linguistically, Lavinia works through hers physically. Jane Hartley, the production's Lavinia, pointed out that it is her elopement with Bassianus that
sets the action in motion and that the revenge at the end belongs to both
her and Titus. Leret, too, insisted on Lavinia's centrality as the motivating

---

[60] Blumenthal and Taymor, *Playing with Fire*, p. 226.

Illustration 3: Video-still of Lavinia (Jane Hartley) entering after her rape in Xavier Leret's 2001–2 Kaos Theatre production of *Titus Andronicus* (promotional video by Louise Teal)

force behind the second half of the play. In order to represent the full horror of the rape that triggers the spiral of revenge, Leret and his cast uncompromisingly refused to 'poeticise' the representation of Lavinia. In striking contrast to Taymor, Leret insisted that 'the danger of poeticising is that you're not really telling the story of the horror'.[61]

The result was the most obscene (in Nead's definition of obscenity as 'excess' and 'form beyond limit, beyond the frame of representation') portrayal of Lavinia's rape I have ever witnessed. Jane Hartley's Lavinia was very much a present-day woman – lively, assertive, fond of her father, but also willing to cross him by finding a sexual partner of her own choice. The giggle that accompanied her statement that she had been wide awake left no doubt as to her enjoyment of her wedding night, and the assurance and sarcasm with which she later confronted Tamora at no point suggested weakness or a predisposition to victimisation. Chiron only managed to kill Bassianus because Demetrius was holding the screaming Lavinia, who repeatedly attacked her tormentors and was even involved in a brief, ferocious fight with Tamora. Tamora's involvement and her condoning of her sons' sexual violence against Lavinia – they groped under her skirt and suggestively licked their fingers when they revealed their intention to rape her – made the rape a demonstration of power and revenge on her part as much as a gratification of sexual drives for the sons. Tamora's contempt for Lavinia's pleas brought to the fore a will to humiliate, hurt and control that transcended gender. In both women's attempts to police and

[61] Private conversations with Lee Beagley, Jane Hartley and Xavier Leret, 23 February 2002.

denounce each other's sexuality what was at stake was power rather than sex. Sexual assault (slander or rape) was clearly an instrument of political domination, recalling the fact that the accusation of slander or scolding, in early modern England, was most commonly levelled by women against other women in an attempt to exert control over their behaviour and sexuality, even at the expense of perpetuating the double standard that regulated their lives.[62] When Lavinia's mouth was stopped by Chiron pushing his finger into it, the image powerfully conveyed the equivalence between rape and tongue-mutilation, between silencing and sexual regulation that, in Warner's staging, had been suggested by the evocation of the *charivari*.

Lavinia returned onto the white-tiled stage – the design was inspired by the idea of a morgue or torture chamber – with her clothes bloodied and torn and her back to the audience. She dragged herself along the back-stage wall, her mouth leaving a long smear of blood on the gleaming tiles. When she turned around, the spectators were confronted with the sight of bare arms hacked off below the elbow (no bound hands, muddy rags, twigs or streamers here) and, most harrowing, of her skirt ripped open to reveal her naked crotch from which blood was still dripping down along the legs. In the intimate space of the Riverside Studio 3, it was no longer possible to dissociate the violation of the character from that of the actor, to pretend that our very act of watching the actor's brutalised and sexually exposed body did not in some way make us complicit in her violation. The defensive mechanism whereby audiences remind themselves that 'this is only fiction' was disabled by the 'uncontestable embodiment' (to re-use Tanner's phrase) of the actor's violated body which foreclosed aesthetic distance. The sight was too horrifying to watch, and yet the production had, from the very beginning when the captive Goths and Aaron, wrapped only in blankets, had been displayed within a window, represented cruelty as a spectacle. Framed by the window as if by a television screen, violence – whether the exposure of the captives, the dead body of Bassianus, the near-hanging of the beaten-up Aaron or the capture of Chiron and Demetrius – was insistently spectacularised, questioning the audience's pleasurable investment in the show of violence. When Chiron, in bloody underwear, and the nude Demetrius, with blood dripping from his genitals and smeared over his chest and hands, followed Lavinia on-stage to taunt her, their mockery was sickening. Audience members held their hands before their mouths,

---

[62] See Laura Gowing, 'Language, Power and the Law: Women's Slander Litigation in Early Modern London', in Jenny Kermode and Garthine Walker (eds.), *Women, Crime and the Courts in Early Modern England* (Chapel Hill: University of North Carolina Press, 1994), pp. 26–47.

in stunned silence, and started gagging as Lavinia seemed to choke on the blood in her mouth.[63] Marcus' monologue did nothing to relieve the horror, the discrepancy between his poetry and the sight of Lavinia being excruciatingly obvious. The performance in no way allowed spectators to retreat into aesthetic distance but provoked the most immediate form of empathy possible in the audience's replication, through their speechless gagging, of Lavinia's predicament – the feeling of intractable disgust arising from the deep moral seriousness of the production.

The outrage and dismay of the audience members, their compulsive need to talk about what they had witnessed in the interval, the desire of some not to return for the second half of the play, all bore witness to this obscene spectacle's excess, its aggression on the viewer, its incentive to action, but also its seriousness. If theatregoers did giggle in the second half of the play, where Leret played up the farcical potential of the retaliatory violence, what was striking in the portrayal of Lavinia's rape was the refusal to play the scene for its potential humour. As reviewer Anna Shepherd observed, 'The production [could not] be described as enjoyable' even if the 'ridiculous plot leaves itself open to a few jokes . . . There's a limit to the amount of laughing you can do when there's a young girl wandering about the place with her arms and tongue cut off.'[64] All audience members I talked to agreed that the most upsetting act of violence was not the chopping off of Titus' hand (carried out with a machete, the hand being projected across the stage with a squirt of blood), but Lavinia's rape. Yet there was no sense that Lee Beagley's impressive Titus had been upstaged; it was rather that he never seemed to consider his pain to be superior to Lavinia's, so that father and daughter were united in their fellow-suffering. The response of two female drama students in particular was telling: they were debating about whether or not to miss the second part of the performance, not because they did not think the production was excellent, but because they felt unwilling to 'take more'. On the other hand, since they did not know the plot, they were eager to know where the story was heading and asked me to outline what was going to happen. When I told them that the play would end with the Andronici's revenge, they decided to stay: they wanted to watch the rapists die. Put off by the spectacle of violence, what they were craving was further violence.

---

[63] Both the lighting technician at the Riverside Studios and Jo Carr, Kaos's producer, confirmed that audiences could be seen gagging night after night, especially at the moment when Lavinia struggled to take her father's hand (returned inside a bloodied transparent plastic bag) into her mouth. Private conversation, 23 February 2002.

[64] Anna Shepherd, 'A Bloody Night with Titus', *Kenilworth Weekly News*, 8 February 2002.

SWEET REVENGE: THE GENDER OF VIOLENCE

Quite unconsciously, these bloodthirsty young women confirmed the structural affinity of *Titus Andronicus* with the modern rape-revenge film (a subgenre of the 'slasher movie'), in which a surfeit of violence inflicted on the female rape victim in the first half leads to an enjoyment of her revenge in the second half. The archetypal nature of this narrative structure, with its concomitant demand for flexible audience identification with both masochistic ('female') and sadistic ('male') subject positions, is elucidated in Carol Clover's seminal study of the modern horror film. Clover argues that, in the rape-revenge genre, violence in the first part of the narrative is felt to be painful, with the audience (both male and female) identifying with the 'passive' victim. A reversal takes place in the second part, where the audience is invited to identify sadistically with the perpetrator in her revenge and the violence conveys an exhilarating sense of power and liberation. Crucially, in this reversal, the female revenger assumes the traditionally 'male' subject position of the 'active' aggressor and, in her literal or symbolic castration of her assailant(s) 'will become as directly or indirectly violent as her assailant'.[65] Insofar as 'the center of gravity of these films lies more in the reaction (the revenge) than the act (the rape)',[66] such narratives arguably avoid the risk of naturalising victimisation as female and aggression as male and instead present these subject positions as flexible. The point that is stressed in the end, and the point that the drama students were so determined to see, is the reversibility of gender roles in which the rapists become the victims of a (sexual) assault at the hands of the empowered woman. Shakespeare's playtext, in its self-conscious use and elaboration of the archetypal rape-revenge plot of Ovid's tale of Philomela, reveals an attitude towards gender and violence that is far more subtle and flexible than its preoccupation with the male world of Rome and its victimisation of its female characters might initially suggest.

The most obvious way in which the normative gendering of violence as male is challenged in *Titus Andronicus* is through the characters' persistent invocation of literary precedents or pre-texts that authorise acts of violence and Lavinia's appropriation of the pre-text of Philomela to justify her own revenge. The weight of tradition makes of 'Roman rites' Roman *rights* (1.1.146), rendering custom indistinguishable from law. Romans and 'barbarians', women and men alike are ruled by the mythological past.

---

[65] Clover, *Men, Women, and Chain Saws*, pp. 49 and 123.
[66] Clover, *Men, Women, and Chain Saws*, p. 154.

The characters are so caught within the confines of literary precedent, even when looking for excuses, that Chiron and Demetrius quite ridiculously

> seem to believe that they will prevent Lavinia from writing down the crime and their names simply by correcting the error in the crime in the book [the *Metamorphoses*] . . . Amazingly, however, their plan almost works because Shakespeare's Lavinia is as dependent on books as they are.[67]

But Lavinia is the first character in this play who manages to break out of the precedent to which she has been forced to conform: she refuses to submit to her aggressors' pre-text (the amended myth of Philomela) according to which she should remain silent and unnoticed. Instead, she pursues her nephew in search of that same patterning text in order to appropriate it, take control over it and turn it into her family's pre-text for taking revenge. It is Lavinia who, through her determination to finally publish the rape of which norms of female modesty forbid her to speak (2.2.173–4), breaks away from the disempowering structure of precedent which has kept her family inactive up to that point. The ungainly breach of decorum of Lavinia running in pursuit of her nephew gives emphasis to her relatives' inertia and her own frantic desire to overcome her physical limitations and provide her family with the text and the words that will allow them to proceed to their revenge. Without Lavinia's appropriation of her patterning text, in itself a precedent for the Andronici's overreaching of their enemies in their own devices (5.2.143), Titus would not then be able to perform their revenge.

It is noteworthy that the text Lavinia 'quotes' insists on the rape victim's determination to publicise her rape and revenge it. Crucially, the tale of Philomela ends with the victim's triumph over her tormentor, her survival and re-acquisition of her tongue in her metamorphosis into a nightingale. This constitutes an implicit rejection of 'shame culture' as described by cultural anthropologists, within which the rape victim's 'physical condition determines her status' and in which, regardless of the victim's refusal to collaborate in the rape, her 'pollution . . . [can] be removed only by death'.[68] Instead, Lavinia acts according to the rules of a 'guilt culture', in which revealing the identity of her rapists and making clear that she was not complicit in the act (as her mutilations testify) should warrant their punishment and her survival. Carolyn Williams explains that, within guilt

---

[67] Grace Starry West, 'Going by the Book: Classical Allusions in Shakespeare's *Titus Andronicus*', *Studies in Philology* 79 (1982), 73–4.
[68] Carolyn D. Williams, '"Silence, like a Lucrece Knife": Shakespeare and the Meanings of Rape', *Yearbook of English Studies* 23 (1993), 94–5.

culture, attention is focussed 'on the victim's mind. Her utterance is crucially important. Lack of consent defines the rape . . . Her ability to tell her
story afterwards vindicates her honour.'[69] Lavinia's choice of pre-text, in
Golding's 1567 translation,[70] tellingly emphasises the victim's rejection of
shame culture and her desire to *speak* ('bewray', 'blase') and find the means
of attaining vengeance:

> Yea I my selfe rejecting shame thy doings will bewray.
> And if I may have power to come abrode, them blase I will
> In open face of all the world . . .
> . . .
> Great is the wit of pensivenesse, and when the head is ract
> With hard misfortune, sharpe forecast of practise entereth in.
> (6.694–6, 6.734–5)

How much Titus himself leans on Lavinia's guilt culture pre-text is also
obvious, not least in his use of the Ovidian recipe for son pie. When Tamora
and her sons come to him in disguise, his wording of 'how like the empress'
sons they are' (5.2.64) reveals that he has identified with Progne, Philomela's
sister, at the moment when she realises how to revenge Philomela and, looking at the rapist's son, exclaims 'Ah, how like thou art / Thy wicked father'
(6.787–8). His identification with the role of Progne, and consequently his
full endorsement of Lavinia's pre-text, is even made explicit when he tells
Chiron and Demetrius that 'worse than Philomel you used my daughter, /
And worse than Progne I will be revenged' (5.2.194–5). One cannot avoid
the implication that when Titus cuts the rapists' throats – a deed performed
by Philomela in Ovid's tale – he acts as a substitute for Lavinia who cannot
do this herself. By the same token, holding the bowl between her stumps is
the closest she can come, in her present state, to killing the rapists herself,
conforming closely to the rape-revenge plot structure.

This structure of identification, in which Titus, in his revenge, adopts
a cross-gender identification with Progne, leaves to Tamora the role of
Tereus the rapist – a parallel which is, once more, reinforced by an intertextual allusion to Golding's Ovid.[71] Tamora's cross-gender association with
Tereus points back to her heavy involvement in the rape, complicating any
attempt to reduce it to 'simply' an effect of male desire. In a play in which

---

[69] Williams, 'Silence', 95.
[70] The quotations from Golding's translation of Ovid refer to the edition by W. H. D. Rouse, *Shake-speare's Ovid: Being Arthur Golding's Translation of the Metamorphoses* (London: Centaur, 1961).
[71] Titus' 'Whereof their mother daintily hath fed, / Eating the flesh that she herself hath bred' (5.3.60–1) is an echo of Golding's 'King *Tereus* sitting in the throne of his forefathers, fed / And swallowed downe the selfe same flesh that of his bowels bred' (6.824–5).

the visual element is strongly foregrounded, we see Tamora trying to stab Lavinia with a poniard, for which she willingly lets her sons substitute rape. This visual equivalent of rape is complemented by the fact that, in speaking of 'the honey *we* desire' (2.2.131, emphasis added) – a line that is often emended to 'the honey *ye* desire' – Tamora identifies with her sons' lust.[72] What is more, the prospect of her sons' 'deflowering' of the 'trull' seems to sexually excite her, so that she goes off to 'seek [her] lovely Moor' (2.2.190–1). Tamora is then associated with Tereus precisely because she occupies an equivalent position within the play, because she has refused to acknowledge her 'womanhood' and has taken on the 'male' subject position of the aggressor.

The play, however, does not let its spectators settle into too easy an association of violence with the transgression of gender boundaries. Instead, the association of *both* Titus and Tamora with the mythological revenger Hecuba shows, as Emrys Jones suggests, 'Shakespeare's usual firm grasp on the ethical principle of reciprocity. Tamora at this moment is to Titus what Titus is later to be to her.'[73] On the other hand, Titus' identification with a female character's desire for revenge fits in with numerous other invocations of pre-texts in the play which ultimately point to a tendency to gender revenge and violence as female. Even the Latin tags from Seneca's *Hippolytus* point towards female vindictiveness (Phaedra) as the cause for male dismemberment (Hippolytus). So does Tamora's pre-text for threatening Bassianus, whom she identifies with Actaeon, the huntsman dismembered by his dogs for having offended Diana. Her repeated association with Semiramis is a further instance of this pattern, as is Aaron's subliminal identification with a Gorgon when rejecting Tamora's advances in favour of violence. There is then in the use of these allusions a consistent association of violence and revenge with female classical precedents, which are used as role models by both male and female characters in the tragedy. Evil deeds may be as black as Aaron's face, but Revenge is a woman.

COVERING UP THE EVIDENCE: EUTHANASIA OR MURDER?

It is the more striking, in view of the play's rape-revenge plot that invites identification with the female revenger, and its use of the Philomela myth that provides a precedent for the survival of the revenging rape victim, that Lavinia's prominence in the revenge and, yet more pervasively, her

---

[72] Robert S. Miola, '*Titus Andronicus* and the Mythos of Shakespeare's Rome', *Shakespeare Studies* 14 (1981), 88.
[73] Emrys Jones, *The Origins of Shakespeare* (Oxford: Clarendon Press, 1977), pp. 104–5.

potential will to survive, are generally suppressed by the tragedy's modern interpreters. The violence of Titus' abandonment of Lavinia's choice of Philomela's precedent in favour of a pre-text according to which she is to be killed is evident, in the playtext, from the fact that Titus has to 'wrest' his 'pattern, precedent, and lively warrant' in order to make it fit his situation (5.3.43). In fact, Livy's Virginius kills his daughter to *prevent* her rape, and not, as Titus intimates, because Virginia had been 'enforced, stained and deflowered' (5.3.38).[74] Lavinia's last-minute betrayal by her father and her murder can, then, be read as the culmination of the silencing and violent disciplining of her transgressing body that began with her rape and dismemberment. It appears that, in order to obtain revenge, Lavinia has to adhere to guilt standards and, since it does not seem to have occurred to Titus that rape might be the 'root of [her] annoy' (4.1.49), to tell her father about the rape. Her father, then, makes the knowledge about her rape public in order to justify their revenge. In a final tragic reversal, the fact that the rape – and hence the family's shame – has been made public necessitates the killing of Lavinia. True to the precepts of shame culture, Titus kills Lavinia to purge his own honour and sorrow: 'Die, die, Lavinia, and thy shame with thee, / And with thy shame thy father's sorrow die' (5.3.45–6). The playtext represents Lavinia as trapped by social structures that punish her self-expression even when it is designed to vindicate her chastity and her family's honour.

What never ceases to amaze me about Lavinia's death is the sheer endorsement Titus receives from critics and performers alike for his wresting of her into another myth which prescribes her destruction. In spite of the obvious unsoundness of Titus' pre-text, and regardless of Saturninus' condemnation of Lavinia's murder as 'unnatural and unkind' (5.3.47), modern interpretations have a tendency to support Titus' murder of his daughter. It is as if everybody were secretly relieved to be rid of the obscenity her mangled body forces on us, as if there existed a conspiracy to refigure murder as euthanasia or assisted suicide. From the critics' point of view, this takes the shape of claims like the following: 'Titus's action can be viewed as a substitute for the suicide she cannot manage alone',[75] or: 'His killing of Lavinia is a private act, a commitment to a personal relationship'[76] or even: 'The murder is shown as an act of love to which Lavinia gives her

---

[74] See Carolyn Asp, '"Upon Her Wit Doth Earthly Honor Wait": Female Agency in *Titus Andronicus*', in Kolin (ed.), *Titus Andronicus*, p. 341.

[75] Williams, 'Silence', 107.

[76] Robert Johnson, '*Titus Andronicus*: The First of the Roman Plays', in T. R. Sharma (ed.), *Essays on Shakespeare in Honour of A. A. Ansari* (Meerut, India: Shalabh, 1986), p. 85.

tacit consent.'[77] How can Lavinia's consent (or lack of it) be anything but 'tacit'?

If critics sideline Lavinia's crucial role in the revenge and never seem to envisage a Lavinia who is taken by surprise by Titus' decision to kill her after all, directors seem to go to even greater lengths to counter the rape-revenge structure's emphasis on the female revenger's survival and to flesh out Lavinia's 'tacit consent' to her death. Peter Brook opened the way for his successors not only by eliding Lavinia's involvement in the revenge, but also by directing Leigh's Lavinia, in the highly formal final banquet scene, to stand up to signal her readiness for the ritual of her killing. In response to her signal, Titus crossed the stage to join her. He first kissed and then stabbed her on the second 'die' of line 45, which had been changed to 'Lavinia, die, die, and thy shame with thee'.[78] Arguably, since the Quarto text of the play (which is supposedly 'printed from Shakespeare's working manuscript')[79] contains no stage direction to indicate at which point Titus kills Lavinia, the placement of the action should be evident from the text. To make the killing coincide with Titus' 'Die, die', so as to take an increasingly bewildered Lavinia by surprise, would be consistent with the type of deictic pointing towards the violent act which is typical of this play. Brook's emendation of the line meant that Titus had the time to address and kiss Lavinia before killing her, giving her time to welcome her death. Titus' second line was cut, hence removing for the benefit of a modern audience the implication of a selfish motive. Instead, he showed his affection for Lavinia by gently laying her down on the dinner table and closing her eyes before proceeding with his revenge. Thereafter, the focus shifted entirely towards Roman politics. Shakespeare's ending is remarkably long and 'messy', in that it intermingles a political coup, personal mourning and judicial condemnation in a way that stresses the inextricability of private and public concerns in the tragedy. In an attempt to gloss over the ambiguities that surround the struggle for leadership till the very end of the play, Brook cut all private elements from the concluding lines and made sure that Lucius did not perform the murder of Saturninus himself. Having remained literally aloof from the violence that left dinner guests and hosts slumped over the table, Lucius, on the balcony above the stage, was quickly and elegantly declared emperor. No condemnation of the 'barbarians' or last homage to Lavinia and Titus

---

[77] Maurice Charney, *Titus Andronicus* (London: Harvester Wheatsheaf, 1990), p. 118.

[78] Promptbook for *Titus Andronicus*, dir. Peter Brook, Shakespeare Memorial Theatre, 1955, Shakespeare Centre, Stratford-upon-Avon.

[79] Jonathan Bate, 'Introduction', in Jonathan Bate (ed.), *Titus Andronicus*, The Arden Shakespeare (London: Routledge, 1995), p. 97.

was allowed to disturb this neat restoration of the tragedy to patriarchal order.

Brook's lead in suggesting Lavinia's consent to her killing and in 'cleaning up' Shakespeare's ending was followed by nearly all subsequent directors, including those who did not seek to diminish Lavinia's role in the revenge. While Trevor Nunn, seventeen years later, did allow Janet Suzman's Lavinia to be present for the murder of her rapists (though she did not actively collect their blood but stood before them to watch them die), he eventually outdid Brook's support of Titus in the final scene. Whereas Brook had, almost pointedly, only emphasised Titus' love for Lavinia, whose impassive face did not imply any reciprocity, Nunn directed Suzman to show her character's affection for Titus at the point of her death, making her obviously desirous of being put out of her misery. Essentially the same approach to the murder was adopted by Jane Howell in her 1985 BBC/Time-Life adaptation for television. Anna Calder-Marshall's Lavinia does not seem to relish her task of assisting her father in the butchering, but her complicity with him is evident in her killing, which is portrayed as loving euthanasia – Lavinia here even provides Titus with the knife with which he then stabs her. Although the Lavinia of Silviu Pucarete's stage production for the National Theatre of Craiova (Romania) which toured Europe extensively in the 1990s had been a coolly determined participant in her revenge, she, too, was apparently yearning to die in the final scene, eagerly nodding in approval of Saturninus' answer and smiling at her father when he covered her head with a white cloth and cut her throat. In Julie Taymor's film, the darkly excited gleam in Lavinia's eyes as she approaches with the bowl in her prosthetic hands is, to a large extent, cancelled out by the director's choice to set the butchering in the kitchen in which Titus lost his hand. This structural rhyme makes of the scene a revenge for his own hand-amputation rather than Lavinia's rape and dismemberment.[80] Even Xavier Leret's staging emphasised Lavinia's happiness at the moment of her death, allowing her movingly to take leave of her relatives before Titus stabbed her in the stomach. Significantly, however, in this production, the audience's desire for revenge had been gratified and the female gendering of violence had been acknowledged in a scene that showed Lavinia defiant in her confrontation of her tormentors, exultant at their capture, eager to assist in their killing and distressed only when their blood squirted not only into the metal bucket she held in her mouth but also across her face. In a final

---

[80] For a fuller discussion of Howell and Taymor that reads Taymor's film in the context of the 'honour killings' perpetrated on rape victims during the Balkans war, see my 'Women Filming Rape in Shakespeare's *Titus Andronicus*: Jane Howell and Julie Taymor', *Etudes Anglaises* 55:2 (2002), 136–47.

acknowledgement of the importance of Lavinia, in the last scene her body was not, as in most other productions, left to lie unobserved in a corner of the stage. Instead, she died on the centrestage table, where Marcus and Lucius assisted her in her final spasms. It was Lavinia whom Titus reached out to as he sat dying, with his back to the audience, while the lights dimmed. As this brief survey shows, again and again, with minor variations, Lavinia's murder is staged as an assisted suicide.

Only two productions, Warner's and Doran's, are worth singling out for their more ambivalent treatment of Lavinia in the final act of the tragedy. Whereas all her predecessors had, in different ways, striven to attenuate the revenge on the rapists and, in particular, Lavinia's involvement in their slaughter, Deborah Warner was the first director to work with, rather than against, the rape-revenge structure of the play. Not only did she not shy away from exposing the discrepancy between the obscene spectacle of the 'trimmed' Lavinia and the aestheticising rhetoric of her uncle, showing, in the reactions of rapists and relatives, the relation between her violation and the socially sanctioned silencing of unruly women, but she deliberately emphasised the play's capacity to disturb and involve its viewers. Brian Cox gives a remarkable account of audience dynamics at the moment of the butchering of the rapists, in which Ritter's keen Lavinia was fully involved:

I was aware, as I played the scene with the boys, that members of the audience were thrilled that I had them, thrilled as I gripped their heads to expose their throats, thrilled at the revenge. The scene plays on certain yearnings in people, which is legitimate, truthful, and honest – and frightening . . . We had held back in the production from showing much blood but here blood was spilled, unstintingly. To the horror, and to the delight, of the audience the blood of Demetrius and Chiron gushed into the bowl held between Lavinia's stumps . . .[81]

If Cox's account is typically self-centred, it is nonetheless a surprisingly powerful testimony to the play's (and production's) successful manipulation of audience identification. Like the drama students in Leret's audience, Warner's spectators, who had a tendency to faint or leave the theatre at the sight of the Andronici's victimisation, seem to have experienced a reversal and actively craved graphic violence in the second part of the play. Warner's production, with its direct addresses to the audience as the Roman people in the opening and closing scenes of the play, turned the spectators

[81] Cox, '*Titus Andronicus*', pp. 186–7; see also Robert Smallwood, 'Director's Shakespeare', in Jonathan Bate and Russell Jackson (eds.), *Shakespeare: An Illustrated Stage History* (Oxford: Oxford University Press, 1996), p. 183.

into witnesses of and accomplices in the violence. The stage manager's reports, which create a correlation between audiences that are '[very] good squeamish value', actual injuries happening on-stage and the quality of the performance ('Quite a slick show otherwise'), bear witness to the truth of Warner's assertion that she '"wanted it to hurt", to "find ways of making it unbearable", "of making the audience scream out that they could not take any more"'.[82]

While this emphasis on audience identification with the revenge and on provoking the audience into strong reactions, combined with Ritter's 'resisting' Lavinia, created an ideal forum for a staging of her murder *as* a murder, the production in the end went along with Titus in his substitution of shame for guilt. Under the pretext of love, murder was once more staged as euthanasia: Titus brought the golden-veiled Lavinia forward to his seat and, sitting down, made her sit on his lap. She remained catatonic as he pulled off her veil and invoked the 'pattern, precedent, and lively warrant' for killing her. Sorrowfully, he spoke his last lines to her and paused once more before suddenly breaking her neck with an audible crack. With Ritter's Lavinia insensible to what was happening around her, the focus was shifted from her reaction to her killing to Titus' manner of performing the killing, which, in its pained reluctance, ultimately eschewed the accusation of a selfish motive. Brian Cox remembers that the method of killing Lavinia was based on the idea that 'this classic image of parent and child, was also an image of vulnerability and of potential brutality'. In a diminishing simile that is indicative of his attitude towards Lavinia, Cox also reveals that, crucially, what is at issue in her death is a breach of trust: 'You could do incredible damage . . . when they are that close, trusting you as a little child, a little animal, might trust you . . . The whole of the creation of Titus came from that one image of a man sitting in a chef's outfit with a little girl on his knee, about to break her neck like a chicken.'[83] Although Cox's performance stressed his sorrow at having to put Lavinia out of her misery, in Warner's production Lavinia's catatonia, for the first time, emphasised not her complicity in her killing, but Titus' initiative and sole responsibility for the act.

In marked contrast with Ritter's actively revengeful Lavinia, Woodburne in Gregory Doran's production portrayed Lavinia as someone for whom

---

[82] In particular, stage manager's reports for 25 April 1987 (Swan Theatre) and 30 September 1988 (The Pit, Barbican Theatre). Dominique Goy-Blanquet, 'Titus Resartus: Deborah Warner, Peter Stein and Daniel Mesguich Have a Cut at *Titus Andronicus*', in Dennis Kennedy (ed.), *Foreign Shakespeare: Contemporary Performance* (Cambridge: Cambridge University Press, 1993), p. 41.

[83] Cox, '*Titus Andronicus*', p. 177.

every act of violence, including revenge, was deeply traumatic in making her live through her own brutalisation again. Standing beside Titus and looking down at her gagged and bound assailants, Woodburne's Lavinia was shaking and salivating uncontrollably. Titus brusquely yanked her before her rapists to point to her missing hands and tongue. Whereas Caius and Publius seemed excited at Titus' detailed description of the revenge, Lavinia was clearly shocked. Instead of collaborating with Titus when he cut the rapists' throats, she remained on the floor, shaking violently all the while. She finally crawled off on her own, screeching in distress. When she reappeared for the banquet, she was still determined to distance herself from her father's revenge. She pathetically reached out to the son pie as Titus carried it in and threw herself on it, screaming, when the unsuspecting Marcus was handed a thick slice. To calm Lavinia down, Titus kissed her head comfortingly and seized her firmly in his arms while Tamora continued to gulp down huge mouthfuls of pie. To the accompaniment of the jingling 'rape waltz', Titus rocked Lavinia, imploring her to die. There was no visible violence apart from a slight twitching as, in Doran's description, 'Titus suffocate[d] her in his embrace and she slip[ped] quietly to the floor. It [was] all over almost before anyone ha[d] noticed.'[84]

Typically, for this production, the rationale behind Lavinia's refusal to get involved in the revenge came not from the playtext, but from Woodburne's research on the behaviour of rape victims, as a result of which she decided that 'Lavinia would be traumatised by having to face her attackers and is not only reluctant to assist her father in their slaughter, but repulsed by it. She is so revolted that she rejects her father. It is a rejection he cannot comprehend.'[85] Ironically, it was Woodburne's objection to the gendering of violence as female in the rape victim's revenge that led to the only production in which Titus could be seen to kill Lavinia with obviously selfish motives. Her murder, however gentle, was not only clearly figured as Titus' desperate attempt to regain control (both physical and emotional) over Lavinia, but it was staged as a silencing of a voice that simply would not die down in spite of the tongue-mutilation. Moreover, in the musical reprise of the 'rape waltz', Titus' murder of Lavinia was linked to her rape, so that, in a final twist to the 'bollocks versus miscarriage' conflict, the murder that finally put an end to Woodburne's upstaging of Sher was troped as a sexual crime. Sher's rationalisation of the murder to his fellow-actors, to whom he explained that Lavinia 'is a sick dog . . . [who] needs to be put down',

[84] Doran and Sher, *Woza Shakespeare!*, p. 177.   [85] Doran and Sher, *Woza Shakespeare!*, p. 176.

takes no account of the complexity created by the invocation of the rape at the point of Lavinia's death. In a staging that had consistently attempted to deny Lavinia her 'voice', that had attempted to aestheticise her obscenity through stylisation and that had tried to freeze her into a Vivien Leigh-type icon of beautifully wounded femininity, violence was obviously gendered male.

CHAPTER TWO

'Not dead? not yet quite dead?': Hamlet's unruly corpses

> I began with the desire to speak with the dead.
>
> – Stephen Greenblatt[1]

I begin this chapter not with a Greenblattian desire to speak with the dead, but with a desire to look at them. *Hamlet*, Carol Rutter writes, 'is crowded with male bodies presented in all stages of post-mortem recuperation, from ghost-walking Hamlet to fresh-bleeding Polonius to mouldering Yorick to Priam of deathless memory'.[2] What, I want to ask, is the function of *Hamlet*'s corpses and revenants within the tragedy? How are these dead or not-yet-quite-dead bodies represented on stage and screen – what do they mean and how are they (dis)played? When a human body 'plays dead', in Rutter's evocatively ambiguous phrase,[3] does it remain passive? When it is used by the other actors as a theatrical property – a 'stage requisite, appurtenance or accessory' in the *OED*'s concise definition – does its humanity push it from the position of accessory or object to that of principal or subject? Certainly, the fact that, in 1990, Estelle Kohler, who was playing Goneril in Nicholas Hytner's RSC *King Lear*, was replaced by a 'body double' for her performance of Goneril's corpse because she had a recurring cough suggests that, when the live play the dead, the dead run the risk of coming back to life in disturbing, often involuntarily humorous ways.[4] Attila Kiss, in his comparison of *Titus Andronicus* and *Hamlet*, concludes that 'if we examine [the latter] in terms of the relation between spectacular image and word, *Hamlet* already signifies the emergence of the dominance of *discourse* over the conspicuous presence of the desemioticized body'.[5] Far from concurring with his view, I want to read *Hamlet*'s corpses

---

[1] The famous opening sentence of his *Shakespearean Negotiations: The Circulation of Social Energy in Renaissance England* (Berkeley: University of California Press, 1988), p. 1.

[2] Rutter, *Enter the Body*, p. 28.   [3] Rutter, *Enter the Body*, pp. 1–2, 16–18, *passim*.

[4] Stage manager's report, 6 May 1991.

[5] Attila Kiss, *The Semiotics of Revenge: Subjectivity and Abjection in English Renaissance Tragedy* (Szeged: *Acta Universitatis Szegediensis de Attila József Nominatae* Papers in English and American Studies 5, 1995), p. 63, his emphasis.

as an elaboration of the semiotics of the body, and specifically of Lavinia's body, in Shakespeare's first tragedy. Human bodies used as props may become improper properties, objects that challenge their status and may well upstage the living; visual, embodied commentaries that have the potential to undercut the verbal and sideline the play's verbose hero.

OFELIA'S NECROPHILIA — CORPSES AND CORPUS

At the end the dead sit upright on their steel thrones, their staring, sightless eyes gazing straight out at the audience, appearing to survey some terrible catastrophe that has taken place in the auditorium. It makes you want to shut your eyes and hide.[6]

It makes me want to open my eyes and look. Lyn Gardner's description of the final tableau of Red Shift's 1999 touring production of *Hamlet: First Cut* – a staging of the 1603 Quarto text directed by Jonathan Holloway – is telling in its evocation of the visceral force of this production's deployment of dead bodies. It is as if, in attempting to resuscitate the First Quarto and restore it to the Shakespearean corpus in the theatre, the company had had to dig up not only the play but also its corpses, multiplying them, displaying them as erotic objects and creating a disconcerting equivalence between the desire to resurrect a neglected playtext and the necrophiliac's erotic investment in dead bodies. The sheer multiplicity of the dead men and women walking, sitting and lying in this production could be read as a metaphor for the textual promiscuity of *Hamlet* as a play existing in at least three distinct textual versions. It aptly troped modern criticism's and performance practice's (perverted) relation with *Hamlet*, the interpreters' tendency to exhume one or another of the play's textual instantiations and, in their appropriation of it, reject the competing texts as so many rotting corpses that must be hidden from sight. Rather than argue for the predominance of one playtext or another, I will in what follows treat all competing texts of *Hamlet* – modern performances no less than early modern playtexts – as integral parts of the *Hamlet* corpus. *Hamlet*, after all, is a body of work whose multiple textual forms and competing meanings intriguingly replicate the questions of interpretation that surround and are posed by its protean young hero (look here upon this text and on this . . .).[7]

[6] Lyn Gardner, '*Hamlet: First Cut*', *Guardian*, 13 September 1999.
[7] See also Laurie Maguire's elaborate conceit of the Prince as editor and textual collator in '"Actions That a Man Might Play": Mourning, Memory, Editing', *Performance Research* 7 (2002), 66–76.

Before the corpses invaded the stage in Holloway's production, the play's most important walking corpse shone through his absence. Surrounded by a cloud of smoke and the unnerving cries of seagulls and roar of jet engines, the armed watches saw an invisible ghost in the strong pool of light that one of them directed at the back of the audience with his torch. Was the Ghost but a figment of their imagination? And if yes, what was to be made of the watches' obvious desire to see what was not there, to talk with the dead? Later, in the second battlements scene, the Ghost did appear in the flesh, dispelling the audience's doubts about his actual existence. At the same time, however, doubts were literally multiplied as instead of a single Ghost three figures in combat uniform with muffled heads marched on-stage from the left. Horatio's flashlight eventually picked out a fourth uniformed figure on a raised part of the set on the right. When the light hit the Ghost's face, a slight shock accompanied the recognition that this was the face of the usurping King (played by Guy Oliver-Watts), implying the affinity between the dead and the living, the legitimate king and his usurper. One brother dead but walking, the other alive but shortly to be made a ghost of. Both simultaneously there and not-there in the actor's polysemic body, creating a 'flickering effect', an 'ontological oscillation' in which the spectator was disturbed by flashes of alternative meanings, neither of which could be seized on with absolute certainty.[8]

What I like to think of as the 'promiscuity' of dead bodies and Ghosts in this production – in the sense of both indiscriminate multiplicity and sexual charge – was exacerbated as the play progressed. Doubling of roles turned into trebling as Oliver-Watts reappeared as the Player King, enacting first the revenger Pyrrhus and then the murder victim in the play-within-the-play. The more roles Oliver-Watts took on, the more his body and voice came to stand for indeterminacy, for an in-between state in which he was both alive and dead, both murderer and his own victim, both 'theatrical' (as the characters acted by the Player King) and 'real' (as their equivalents within the play). The staging deliberately emphasised the actor's uncanny proliferation by multiplying his presence in the play-watching scene: not only was he present on-stage as the King (Claudius) watching the spectacle, but the device of presenting *The Mousetrap* as a film – a flicker of coloured lights reflected on the courtiers' faces, accompanied by a cinematic soundtrack – allowed him to be present also as the disembodied

---

[8] See Brian McHale's discussion of Roman Ingarden's 'opalescence', explained as the type of ambiguity in which, according to Ingarden, 'two different worlds are struggling for supremacy, with neither of them capable of attaining it', in *Postmodernist Fiction* (London: Methuen, 1987), p. 32.

voice of the Player King. The ghostly presence of two uniformed muffled figures witnessing the scene from the wings completed the multiplication of bodies and meanings by evoking Old Hamlet's Ghost, playing on the spectators' memory of the second Ghost scene to project Oliver-Watts's features onto the hooded heads.

This identification of the muffled soldiers with Old Hamlet was, however, disrupted in the closet scene, where the polysemy of these bodies was extended to embrace Corambis (the First Quarto's equivalent of Polonius) as well. Played by Tim Weekes, the only black actor in the company, Corambis concealed himself by standing behind a plastic sheet that was draped over one of the four hollow steel obelisks that made up the impressively versatile set. Hamlet stabbed him through the sheet, which, as it slipped off the obelisk, revealed Corambis, face contorted in pain, while from behind the obelisk a previously invisible muffled soldier dropped to the floor. When Corambis's Ghost hit the floor, Weekes's facial expression grew bland and he walked off-stage. He reappeared two scenes later, in uniform and hooded, alongside three more muffled soldiers. The four dead men leant against the four upright obelisks as, to a Kate-Bush-type high-pitched rendition of 'He is dead and gone', mad Ofelia (played harrowingly by Rachel Nicholson), 'tarted up' and in a short pink skirt, sensuously rubbed herself up against each corpse in turn, 'wrapping her legs round them and pushing her face into their necks – a horridly graphic necrophiliac embrace and the closest she could ever manage to a loving relationship.'[9] Reaching the fourth corpse, she started when she recognised her father's black hand. She pulled off his hood and began to sob, clinging disconsolately to his impassive body.

Her erotic relationship with the dead was carried over into her next mad scene. Here the obelisks were laid down flat on the stage, bottom ends facing the audience as four gaping holes. Their surfaces served as an upper stage on which Ofelia stood with the King, Gertred and Laertes while the four dead bodies marched past, holding photographs of who they were when alive before them. Ofelia collected the pictures and redistributed these 'herbs' to her appalled on-stage audience. As she sang the Valentine song, the corpses sank feet first into the obelisks that thus became four graves. Ofelia knelt down over the grave of her father, reaching down to him while he and all the other dead men reached up to her, stroking her arms as she devotedly caressed her father's.

---

[9] Peter J. Smith, '*Hamlet: First Cut*, Directed by Jonathan Holloway for Red Shift, The Bull, Barnet, London, 4 December 1999, Mid Stalls', *Cahiers Elisabéthains* 57 (April 2000), 132.

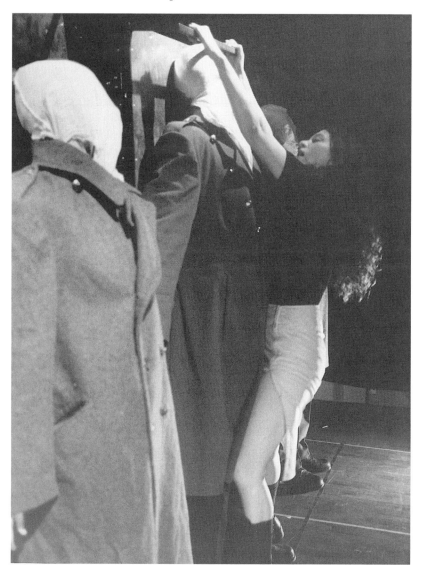

Illustration 4: Mad Ofelia (Rachel Nicholson) sensuously rubbing herself against the upright muffled Ghosts in *Hamlet: First Cut*, dir. Jonathan Holloway, Red Shift, 1999

If Ofelia's selection of Corambis's corpse out of a number of 'identical' dead bodies could be read as yet another instance of the production's metatheatrical reflection on its selection of one 'dead' text to revive in preference to another (Weekes's skin colour adding an extra layer of significance in that his body *was* a signifier of stigmatised alterity), her mad scenes also added to the multiplicity, interchangeability and erotic charge of the not-yet-quite-dead bodies in the production. 'Playing dead' here meant staying alive, interfering with the stage action and insisting on personal remembrance in a way that gave added prominence to the parallels between Hamlet's and Ofelia's dead fathers. Nor was the uncanny presence and duplication of revenants over with this scene: Ofelia eerily played the cello during Gertred's account of her drowning, and both she and her father reappeared as the Second and First Clowns in the graveyard scene, where the dead girl helped dig her own grave. In a production in which dead bodies were deployed in such an insistent fashion, the fact that the doubling of roles was obviously motivated by the small size of the cast was ultimately irrelevant when weighed against the power of this uncanny resuscitation of Ofelia in her own grave. In the purgatorial cityscape shaped by the builders' drills and the roar of traffic on the soundtrack, she had apparently been reunited with her father and found some semblance of peace before their union was disrupted by the arrival of Hamlet and her funeral cortège. As her lover and brother fought over her dead body, both she and Corambis/ First Clown helped restrain Laertes – an otherworldly family reunion and gripping image of the hold of the dead over the living.

In the duel scene, the balance of the play finally tipped entirely in favour of the dead. Once Gertred (in accordance with the First Quarto's portrayal of her as suspicious of Claudius following the closet scene) had knowingly drunk the poison destined for her son, Ofelia reappeared upstage with her cello. Gertred's death was marked by a freezing up of the action, with Ofelia playing and singing her high-pitched, chilling version of the Valentine song as Gertred went to sit on her steel throne, from which she stared into the audience. The same eerie interruption of the action marked the deaths of Claudius, Laertes and Hamlet. Then Corambis walked on and sat down on the last empty throne, creating the disconcerting tableau of staring corpses that made Gardner want to hide. In the midst of the ensuing silence, the racket of a helicopter announced Fortinbras's arrival. Standing in front of the assembly of corpses, Fortinbras's combat outfit closed the circle of the play's plot by evoking, one last time, the uniformed Ghost of Old Hamlet. The performance ended with the ghostly Fortinbras pointing his gun at

Horatio's head before the sudden blackout 'killed' this last survivor of the
tragedy as well.

If nothing else (and it did much more), Holloway's striking interpretation
of the First Quarto text brought into focus both the prominence of not-
yet-quite-dead bodies in *Hamlet* and the play's generic affiliation to revenge
tragedy. Far from the Romantic conception of the hero as an introverted
man with a repulsion for violent action, Peter Collins's boyish Hamlet,
described by John Thaxter as 'a wide-eyed Wittenburg student with a flick-
knife in his back pocket and a stomach for vengeance',[10] 'hardly ha[d]
much time for introspection as the affairs of state and stage proceed[ed]
apace'.[11] This was a production that was centred not on contemplation
but on a more involved type of remembrance in which Hamlet no less
than Ofelia sought to commemorate their fathers' deaths by reviving them,
whether through Hamlet's theatrical restaging of his father's murder or
through crazed Ofelia's necrophilia (revealing Shakespeare's anticipation of
the macabre eroticism that would mark later revenge tragedies – Vindice's
fetishisation of Gloriana's skull in *The Revenger's Tragedy* and the perverted
love Middleton's Tyrant lavishes on the Lady's corpse in *The Maiden's
Tragedy* spring to mind). Far from 'denounc[ing] the revenge theater and
all its works with the utmost daring',[12] this production presented *Hamlet*
as a play firmly endorsing the values of and embedded within the genre of
revenge tragedy.

As such, its deployment of dead bodies demanded to be read within
that tradition, against the background of Andrea's Ghost and Horatio's
hanged and stabbed corpse in Kyd's *The Spanish Tragedy* and as a sequel
to Shakespeare's own deployment of mutilated bodies and body parts in
Titus Andronicus. The syntax of revenge in both these generic predecessors
of *Hamlet* requires that the wounded body – whether dead like Horatio's or
not-yet-quite-dead like Lavinia's – be displayed on-stage as a reminder, for
both audience and the revenger(s), of the crime to be revenged, a *memento
vindictae* rather than a *memento mori*. As John Kerrigan points out, *The
Spanish Tragedy* centres on 'the relationship between memory and revenge'

---

[10] John Thaxter, 'Politics, Thrills and Revenge', *Stage*, 16 September 1999.
[11] Charles Godfrey-Faussett, '*Hamlet: First Cut*', *Time Out*, 26 January–2 February 1999.
[12] René Girard, 'Hamlet's Dull Revenge', in Patricia Parker and David Quint (eds.), *Literary Theory /
Renaissance Text* (Baltimore: Johns Hopkins University Press, 1986), p. 283.

that is literally incarnated in Horatio's 'corpse, a surrogate ghost to whet his purpose should it ever blunt, and the gory napkin, a memento to be carried near his heart'.[13] Rather than see Horatio's corpse as a surrogate ghost, however, I want to invert Kerrigan's statement and suggest that Old Hamlet's Ghost in Shakespeare's tragedy is a surrogate corpse. The Ghost is an insubstantial and therefore insufficient substitute for the wounded, neither quite live nor yet entirely dead-and-buried body on which revenge is predicated in *The Spanish Tragedy* and *Titus Andronicus*. Set against the background of its generic predecessors, *Hamlet*'s Ghost and the problematic corpses that populate the play can be seen as an elaboration of Shakespeare's engagement with the syntax and semiotics of revenge in *Titus Andronicus*.

The starting-point in both plays is an attack on the body politic, as emblematised by the mutilation of Lavinia in *Titus* and the murder of the King in *Hamlet*, which must be restored through violent retributive action. In semiotic terms, Lavinia's body can be described as a referent, a physical presence (Tanner's 'uncontestable embodiment') for which within the world of the play there is no appropriate signifier until she reveals that the concept 'rape' should be attached to her body. The mutilation of the Roman body politic is thus accompanied by a disruption of the linguistic and theatrical sign, a feature that is strikingly apparent not only in Lavinia's symbolic tongue-amputation, but equally so in the play's 'wresting' language. Words in *Titus Andronicus* are violently misinterpreted, obscenely punned on, disjoined from their meanings and wilfully ignored.[14] As long as the linguistic sign is thus disrupted and Lavinia's wounds are not interpreted correctly, action is unsuccessful and Titus' words remain ineffectual. Within the logic of the play, then, revenge is predicated not only on the presence of Lavinia's mutilated body as a physical piece of evidence and reminder of the crime to be revenged, but also on the correct naming of that body's wounds and the concomitant restoration of disrupted language. Only once Lavinia has given a name to the crime and its perpetrators is the power of language restored – as emblematically represented by the conjunction of words and weapons in Titus' missive to Tamora's sons – and Titus finally able to plot their revenge. Only now can he seize on Lavinia's maimed body as the

---

[13] John Kerrigan, *Revenge Tragedy: Aeschylus to Armageddon* (Oxford: Clarendon Press, 1997), pp. 175, 174.

[14] Peter Sacks comments on 'the inability of language [in *Titus Andronicus*] to afford a certain kind of transparency or efficacy, as though the passage from word to referent, or from speaker to auditor, were always being blockaded, or worse, interrupted'. Peter Sacks, 'Where Words Prevail Not: Grief, Revenge, and Language in Kyd and Shakespeare', *English Literary History* 49 (1982), 591.

catalyst and justification for his revenge in the same way that Hieronimo in Kyd's tragedy uses the 'show' or 'spectacle' of his son's theatrically displayed cadaver to vindicate his revenge (*Sp Tr* 4.4.89).

Old Hamlet's Ghost, in contrast to the nameless referent constituted by Lavinia's body, can be described as an iconic sign for an absent human being. The Ghost who tells the story of the corruption of his body is, Horatio maintains, itself an 'illusion' (1.1.130), an 'apparition' (1.2.211) – a point made obvious by Holloway's staging of the first Ghost scene in which the watches and Horatio directed their spotlight and eyes at an invisible figure. Even when, as in Holloway's second Ghost scene, the Ghost is embodied by an actor, within the fiction it nevertheless has no physically present referent, so that 'Doubt and uncertainty surround every appearance of the Ghost'.[15] When Horatio tells Hamlet about the Ghost, his description of it is based on uncertainty and ambiguity. It is 'a figure *like* [Hamlet's] father' that he *thinks* he saw, and he is unsure about its very movements: 'Yet once *methought* / It lifted up it [sic] head and did address / Itself to motion *like as it would* speak' (1.2.199, 189, 215–17; emphases added). Even in Horatio's strongest assertion of the Ghost's identity as Hamlet's father, there is an ambiguity: 'I knew your father; / These hands are not more like' does not point to identity so much as to mirror-image resemblance (1.2.211–12).[16] Hamlet himself acknowledges this fundamental problem of interpretation in his doubtful address to the 'questionable shape' of the Ghost (1.4.43). When he finally names the apparition, it is evident that even naming is here an uncertain interpretative choice: 'I'll call thee Hamlet, / King, father, royal Dane' (1.4.44–5).

Although the Ghost is thus accepted by Hamlet as a sign for an absent referent (the body of his father), the sign remains problematic since what it refers to is neither the decaying corpse lying in a grave nor the body of the king as it was on the day of his murder. Rather, the Ghost refers to an *anterior* reality. The guards and Hamlet all insist on the apparition being 'fair and warlike' (1.1.50), wearing 'the very armour he had on / When he th'ambitious Norway combated' thirty years prior to old Hamlet's death (1.1.63–4). It would then seem that the Ghost is, more precisely, the *signified*, the *concept* of 'Hamlet, King, father, royal Dane'. No single term can encompass all the diverse identities – individual, political, familial – of the apparition which collapses past and present, bringing the origin of Fortinbras's attempt at

---

[15] Nigel Alexander, *Poison, Play and Duel: A Study in* Hamlet (London: Routledge and Kegan Paul, 1971), p. 30.

[16] See Valeria Wagner, 'Losing the Name of Action', in Mark Thornton Burnett and John Manning (eds.), *New Essays on* Hamlet (New York: AMS Press, 1994), p. 149.

retrieving the lands lost by his father side by side with the narrative that will prompt Hamlet's revenge on Claudius. What Holloway's Ghost and its three spectral doubles in their multiplicity and polysemy brought into play was precisely such a disruption of the theatrical sign in which one body could stand for many characters and a number of bodies could stand for a single character. Hamlet's singling out of one Ghost among four as his father had the same quality of uncertain interpretative choice and projection as that conveyed by his spread-betting approach to naming the Ghost in the playtexts.

If Holloway stressed the indeterminacy of the Ghost, his polysemy and the element of interpretation that informs Hamlet's interactions with his father's 'spirit', Matthew Warchus's 1997 RSC modern-dress staging explored the implications of the perception of the Ghost as a disembodied concept, as Hamlet's abstract memory of the dead king. In the playtexts, all witnesses to the apparition describe the Ghost in terms of their individual perception of the king when he was alive. The Ghost seems to stand for what everyone who sees it remembers of the king during his lifetime, so that his memory establishes a continuity between death and life, past and present, enabling the strange grammatical construction 'so like the King / That *was and is* the question of these wars' (1.1.113–14, emphasis added). It is this connection with the past and Hamlet's mournful memories of his father that were poignantly explored by Warchus's controversial interpretation which Michael Billington judged to be 'one of the most exciting main-house Stratford productions in years' because it did not 'just cut the play' but 'totally re-aligned it'.[17]

Seizing on the ability of film to re-present the past through the literal projection of an iconic sign that stands for an absent referent, Warchus taught the old mole some new tricks. He opened his interpretation of the tragedy with the image of Alex Jennings's Hamlet holding the urn containing his father's ashes while black-and-white 16mm footage of Old Hamlet playing with his toddler son flickered on a screen behind him. Described by Richard Edmonds as 'a master stroke uniting the memories of a dead king with a living son in a most potent way',[18] this silent scene of memory, loss and absence set the stage for the brash forgetfulness of Denmark's courtiers in the extravagant wedding party that subsequently erupted onto the stage. Amidst the merriment of the dancing couples and the spectacle of Gertrude's and Claudius's prolonged public kiss, the

---

[17] Michael Billington, 'Get Shorter', *Guardian*, 10 May 1997.
[18] Richard Edmonds, 'Hamlet in the Shadows', *Birmingham Post*, 10 May 1997.

melancholy Prince seemed the only dignified figure and entirely justified
in resisting his suave uncle's shouted order to think of him as a father.
Coming so shortly after the intensely intimate scene of Hamlet's filial
remembrance and mourning, the court's oblivion appeared more 'common'
and indecorous than drunken Hamlet's shouted declaration to the stunned
party that 'The funeral bak'd meats / Did coldly furnish forth the marriage
tables' (1.2.181). In the midst of the festivities, 'amid champagne, fireworks,
balloons and bridesmaids',[19] the Ghost (Edward Petherbridge) appeared
in a smoking jacket as yet another unobtrusive, albeit eerily pale, party
guest. The fact that only Horatio and Hamlet could see the Ghost highlighted their remembrance and the others' guilty forgetfulness. At the same
time, Hamlet's frantic behaviour in trying to follow the apparition motivated Ophelia's bewilderment and Polonius's prohibition of further contact between the lovers while stressing the girl's inability to empathise with
Hamlet's loss.

When the Ghost reappeared in the closet scene (set here in the conjugal bedroom), he was once more associated with Hamlet's memory and
Gertrude's guilty oblivion. Following the First Quarto's stage direction
that significantly requires the Ghost to enter the room '*in his night gowne*'
(Q1 SD 1551), the Ghost here appeared in his dressing gown over a pair of
elegant pyjamas. While in the Ghost's first appearance in the flesh Warchus's
textual and temporal rearrangement had made the playtexts' call for armour
irrelevant, substituting the elegant figure of a statesman at an official function for that of the warrior king, here he observed the stage direction's call
for the image of a father and husband joining his family in the private
space of the closet. The fact that in all playtexts Gertrude, unlike her son,
cannot see her husband in this scene is symptomatic of her unwillingness
or inability to remember him. Here, Diana Quick's frightened Gertrude,
kneeling on the marital bed, stared unseeingly through the mournful figure
of the Ghost who had sat down beside her – the disturbing image of oblivion made more distressing by Hamlet's despondent question 'Do you see
nothing there?' (3.4.132), which provoked a denial by a Gertrude desperate
to see but ultimately lacking in faith.

Hamlet's and its Ghost's emphasis on remembrance and faith in the
absence of physical evidence, substituted for by the 'questionable shape' of
the Ghost, constitute Shakespeare's greatest intervention in the syntax of
revenge. Instead of being able, like Hieronimo and Titus, to rely on the
certainty about the crime and the need for revenge that is warranted by

[19] Robert Butler, 'Warchus Puts His *Art* into His *Hamlet*', *Independent on Sunday*, 11 May 1997.

Illustration 5: Gertrude (Diana Quick) unable to see the Ghost (Edward Petherbridge) in Matthew Warchus's 1997 RSC production of *Hamlet*

the physical presence of murdered Horatio's corpse and Lavinia's ravaged body (as well as Titus' stump and his sons' severed heads), Hamlet has to remember his father. The plot requires him to believe unconditionally in the account of the murder given by a Ghost who is suspended between death and life, heaven and hell, visibility and invisibility – an emblem of the condition of being 'disjoint and out of frame' that characterises not only language, but the realm of Denmark as a whole (3.2.300, 1.2.20). The ambiguities surrounding the Ghost can be read as the origin of the tragedy's all-pervasive uncertainty, which Kenneth Muir bravely undertook to quantify by counting 'more than 250 questions in the course of the play and many speeches of argument and discussion'.[20] The relatively straightforward movement from physical evidence to action in *The Spanish Tragedy* and *Titus Andronicus* is portrayed in *Hamlet* as a mediated relationship via remembrance and faith that must compensate for the lack of physical evidence and consequent doubts of the hero.

[20] Kenneth Muir, 'Imagery and Symbolism in *Hamlet*', *Etudes Anglaises* 17 (1964), 360.

Seen within this context, Hamlet's delay can be explained as an effect of the absence of physical proof, the lack of referents to match the signifier 'murder' and the signified 'Ghost'. As in *Titus Andronicus*, what seems at stake during the first part of the play is the reuniting of the disjoined components of the sign without which, according to the oddly proto-Saussurean logic of these plays, effective language and action are apparently impossible. Hamlet's re-presentation of his father's murder in the play-within-the-play can therefore be read as a mnemonic device meant not just to trigger the memory of the murderer, but also to create a referent for Hamlet's artificial, second-hand memory of his father's murder. The canny doubling of roles by Holloway and Warchus, who both used the same actor to play the Ghost and the Player King, allowed their productions to foreground this attempt to 'flesh out' the Ghost in the play-within-the-play. In Warchus's staging, this 'doubling secured the connection between *The Mousetrap* and Hamlet's memories, especially since the Ghost in this production . . . seemed almost certainly an image from Hamlet's anguished mind (and the timid Horatio's suggestible imagination)'.[21] Hamlet dares 'take the ghost's *word* for a thousand pound' only once he has *seen* his father's murder (3.2.280–1; emphasis added), for that 'word' has, for a fleeting moment, acquired the wholeness it lacked. Only now can the hero attempt, however disastrously, to move to action, stabbing the man he mistakes for Claudius in his mother's closet. In doing so he creates the first 'human prop' of the play and the first piece of genuine physical evidence of a crime to be revenged.

POLONIUS'S DANCE OF DEATH: AN INTERLUDE

In the closet scene, Hamlet harangues his mother against the background (or, more rarely, the foreground) of Polonius's freshly stabbed body which remains on-stage throughout the scene. Even though Polonius is incontestably dead and physically present in the scene, his body remains oddly elusive and alive in this revenge tragedy that challenges the rules of the genre and in which murder victims in particular have a tendency to refuse to die. The laughs that frequently greet not only the Ghost's solemn commands from the 'cellerage' at the beginning of the play, but also Hamlet's incongruous declaration 'I am dead, Horatio' at its end, are only two examples

---

[21] Cynthia Marshall, 'Sight and Sound: Two Models of Shakespearean Subjectivity on the British Stage', *Shakespeare Quarterly* 51 (2000), 356.

of this often comical resistance to death in the tragedy.[22] But whereas these moments are only potentially comical, Polonius's death, albeit deadly serious in that it provides the turning-point in the plot in which Hamlet the revenger of his father becomes the object of another son's revenge for the murder of his own father,[23] is deliberately scripted as a comic interlude which disconcertingly frames the serious confrontation of Gertrude and Hamlet. Beginning with Hamlet's pun on 'a rat' which may refer at once to Polonius's squeals, his treacherous nature, his foolishly self-destructive move of drawing attention to himself, and possibly even to the popular association of arrases with rats and rat-shaped seals of quality on the fabric,[24] Polonius's comic turn does not even end with his unceremonious exit from the stage when Hamlet 'lug[s] the guts into the neighbour room' (3.4.214). Instead, it is carried on into Polonius's imaginary afterlife, in which he is eaten by a 'convocation of politic worms' (4.3.20), has travelled to heaven, is stowed somewhere on the way up to the lobby, buried in hugger-mugger and finally revived, as in Holloway's staging, in Ophelia's songs and mad commemoration. It is as if dead Polonius's co-existence with the Ghost in the closet scene provoked a sort of double-act in which the spectral King plays the straight man to his bungling courtier's stooge and neither man is allowed to rest in peace. In some ways, Polonius emerges as the more 'perturbed spirit' of the two (1.5.190).

The scene for Polonius's comical interlude is set already in the run-up to *The Mousetrap*, in which death is theatricalised and the distinction between reality and fiction is challenged. In Ron Daniels's 1984 and 1989 productions for the RSC, the link between the two scenes was made particularly clear by the fact that Hamlet mimed killing Polonius when mockingly referring to Brutus' 'brute part . . . to kill so capital a calf' in the Capitol (3.2.104). In 1984, Daniels hid Polonius behind a translucent upstage curtain for the entire 'closet' scene in an apparent attempt to contain the scene's comic potential and the hazard of dying Polonius upstaging Hamlet and Gertrude during the roughly 140 lines of dialogue (depending on the playtext) in which the protagonists manage to ignore him. This spared Daniels the indignity of having to stage what I always think of as the 'Polonius dance'. As exemplified by Warchus's production, this dance is a delicate piece of choreography that involves Polonius deftly staggering out of the arras and across the stage in order to decorously collapse out of sight and danger

---

[22] The archival video recording of Ron Daniels's 1984 RSC production contains a particularly loud and general laugh at Hamlet's (Roger Rees's) dead-pan announcement of his own demise.

[23] See Barbara Everett, '*Hamlet*: A Time to Die', *Shakespeare Survey* 30 (1977), 120.

[24] Ian Gadd, 'The Rat and Hamlet's Arras', *Notes and Queries* ns 44:1 (1997), 61–2.

behind the centrestage bed. (This is more elegantly accomplished in films, where the selective eye of the camera almost invariably chooses not to show Polonius during the mother-and-son dialogue and the appearance of the Ghost.) But while it was successful in containing Polonius's comic potential, Daniels's decision to conceal the body was the catalyst for a no less disconcerting series of ambiguities. In fact, the appearance of the Ghost from behind the brightly lit curtain where the audience knew Polonius lay created a moment of uncertainty as to whether this revenant was the King or his courtier. The hesitation was carried over into the next scene, in which Claudius, wearing a night-gown almost identical to his ghostly brother's, also appeared from behind the same curtain. The result was a morphing effect in which Polonius 'dissolved' (the cinematic term seems the most appropriate) into Old Hamlet and finally Claudius, thus including Hamlet's future victim in Rutter's group of 'male bodies presented in all stages of post-mortem recuperation'. Polonius, in 1984, was 'contaminated' by the Ghost's semiotic uncertainty and the interpretative problem it poses, his invisible body functioning both as an indirect *memento mori*, a warning of Claudius's impending death, and as an illustration of Hamlet's insistence that 'Your fat king and your lean beggar is but variable service – two dishes, but to one table' (4.3.23–4).

In 1989, on the other hand, Daniels bravely decided to exploit the scene's potential absurdity while containing it by concealing Polonius under Gertrude's bedcovers on the prominent bed. Clare Higgins's imperious Gertrude did not seem to appreciate the officious old man's intrusion and was therefore already nervy and irritated when Mark Rylance's Hamlet tentatively entered the room and confronted her with quiet intensity. Their encounter was, therefore, fraught from the very outset, and Gertrude broke into sobs even prior to Hamlet pulling out the dagger in which he tried to show his mother the reflection of her face. Her shrill scream at the sight of the weapon caused Polonius to attempt to free himself from the covers and crawl out of the bed. Hamlet leapt onto the bed, further entangling his victim in the sheets, and stabbed him repeatedly and violently while his mother, beside the bed, went on screaming and sobbing uncontrollably. Once Polonius stopped moving, Hamlet let go of his body, which rolled off the bed into the shadows at the side of the stage to perform the finishing flourish of the 'Polonius dance'. The killing was thus at once central (on the bed) and effaced (under the covers and later in the shade). Hamlet's vest and the sheets on the bed on which the major part of the dialogue between Hamlet and Gertrude took place were so bloody that the spectators could at no point entirely forget about the killing they had witnessed. The rehearsal notes testify to the effort that went into creating this effect: not only do they specify the use of a bowl full of stage blood 'attached to the bed head for Polonius' murder', but a later note suggests that Hamlet was additionally 'bloodied between blocks 8 + 9 i.e. after dragging the body around'.[25]

The audience's attention was firmly riveted on the bloodied sheets when Hamlet, in an expression of profound sexual disgust, picked them up and tried to force his mother to sniff them so as to demonstrate to her how much she was deprived of her sense of smell if she could ignore 'the rank sweat of an enseamed bed' (3.4.79, 92). The result was the startling visual irony of the son accusing the mother of the pollution of a bed that was visibly more polluted by his murderous frenzy than by his mother's promiscuity. The Ghost's intervention at this very moment, comfortingly seizing his unseeing and unfeeling wife from behind, further reinforced Hamlet's point about his mother's lack of senses and created a 'poignant' and '[u]nforgettable' image of 'Russell Enoch's Ghost embracing Gertrude on the bed, and sadly stealing away when she fails to see him'.[26] The audience's uncomfortable laugh at the end of the scene, when Hamlet bitterly laughed at his doggerel rhyme about the grave knave and tucked his mother into the bloody sheets, was symptomatic of the spectators' continued awareness of Polonius's murder and the discomforting ironies this awareness provoked. Although the 1984 production had the merit of not featuring a bed in the closet scene, and therefore of steering clear of the implications of incest that have been hanging like a Freudian curse over the play's performance history ever since Olivier's 1948 film,[27] the 1989 interpretation, with its appropriation of the Oedipal bed only to thwart audience expectations by having Polonius killed inside it, was far more powerful in its impact on the viewers.

In fact, a strong case can be made for keeping Polonius even more firmly in focus than did Daniels's second RSC production. Alan Dessen points out that the scene potentially affords a visual irony in which Polonius's corpse, merely through its presence, can undercut Hamlet's verbose condemnation

---

[25] Rehearsal notes for 22 March and 25 August 1988, Shakespeare Centre, Stratford-upon-Avon.

[26] Paul Lapworth, 'Daniels' Hamlet a Degree off Balance?', *Stratford Herald*, 5 May 1989, and Irving Wardle, 'Barbarous but Unforgettable Assault', *The Times*, 28 April 1989.

[27] James R. Simmons Jr traces the appearance of the bed back to John Gielgud's 1936 production, but it was only given overtly Freudian overtones by Olivier in response to his conversations with psychoanalyst Ernest Jones. '"In the Rank Sweat of an Enseamed Bed": Sexual Aberration and the Paradigmatic Screen *Hamlets*', *Literature/Film Quarterly* 25:2 (1997), 113. See also Lisa S. Starks, 'The Displaced Body of Desire: Sexuality in Kenneth Branagh's *Hamlet*', in Christy Desmet and Robert Sawyer (eds.), *Shakespeare and Appropriation* (London and New York: Routledge, 1999), pp. 160–78, and Philip Weller, 'Freud's Footprints in Films of *Hamlet*', *Literature/Film Quarterly* 25:2 (2000), 117–25.

Illustration 6: Hamlet (Mark Rylance) in bloodied vest and pyjamas, the Ghost (Russell
Enoch) and Gertrude (Clare Higgins) in Ron Daniels's 1989 RSC production of
Hamlet – Polonius remains invisible

of his mother and point to the hero's own unseeing hypocrisy: 'if Polonius'
body, suitably bloodied, is in full view during those one hundred and
forty lines and if Hamlet, for even part of the time, is waving a bloody
sword, an image of a Pyrrhus-like revenger is juxtaposed with his accusa-
tions against Gertrude for *her* crimes and not-seeing'.[28] This was exactly
what was achieved by Peter Brook's beautifully minimal and innovative
'adaptation' *The Tragedy of Hamlet* in 2000–1, which aptly validated its
director's statement that the tragedy 'is like a crystal ball, ever rotating. At
each instant, it turns a new facet towards us and suddenly we seem to see
the whole play more clearly.'[29]

One of the old facets that appeared more clearly here was the easy co-
existence of comedy and tragedy in Shakespeare's plays. Like the disturbing
mixture of humour and violence in the last act of *Titus Andronicus*, a

---

[28] Alan C. Dessen, *Elizabethan Stage Conventions and Modern Interpretations* (Cambridge: Cambridge
University Press, 1984), p. 154.
[29] Peter Brook, 'Come, Begin . . .', Programme for *The Tragedy of Hamlet* for The Young Vic Theatre
Company in association with The Tara Ulemek Foundation, Young Vic, London, 2001.

dramatic technique which Brian Cox described as 'get people to laugh, and then kick them',[30] Brook's staging stressed the capacity of what is often seen as 'cheap' comedy to give greater depth to the tragedy – comic 'relief' in the sense of contrast and three-dimensionality rather than a lessening of anxiety. (Brook's *Tragedy of Hamlet*, in this respect, represents the director's radical reassessment of the usefulness of comic elements in tragedy and his development away from the severe excision of humour that characterised his 1955 *Titus Andronicus*.) In the *Mousetrap* scene, already, a potentially comic moment added depth to Claudius's realisation of the import of the play when the Player King, instead of dying, rose, turned, looked at Claudius and started at the recognition of his 'real' murderer. The Player King's refusal to die prepared the way for Polonius's resilience at the end of the closet scene. There, the arras was represented by a cloth that Bruce Myers's Polonius held up in front of him and that fell over his head when Adrian Lester's Hamlet stabbed him in a terrifyingly intense moment. Polonius collapsed and remained lying in the same place throughout Hamlet's fraught dialogue with Gertrude, a spotlight on his corpse making sure that he was never entirely out of the audience's focus. His comic revival occurred when Hamlet, at the end of a profoundly serious and moving scene which had seen the Ghost hesitate in his departure to hear Gertrude say that she could neither see nor hear his presence, returned his attention to Polonius's body. He got hold of the corpse, lifted it up and used it as a puppet with which he mimed the old courtier's foolish prating – a truly funny conclusion that conveyed not so much the Prince's mockery as his gauche expression of affection for Polonius. This bitter-sweet moment prepared the scene both for the humorous elusiveness of Polonius's 'Safely stowed' corpse (4.2.1) and for Hamlet's despair in the transposed 'To be or not to be' soliloquy which he spoke just prior to his departure for England.

The puppetry with Polonius's corpse also brilliantly established a visual rhyme between the closet scene and the graveyard, the grave knave and the knaves in the grave. It was in Brook's graveyard scene that Polonius came back to life with a vengeance as he was reincarnated in the figure of the Gravedigger, Myers doubling the roles as Tim Weekes had done in Holloway's production. More uncannily still, Hamlet's puppetry with Yorick's cranium made both the king's jester and the king's courtier come back to life in the plastic property skull which the Gravedigger had impaled on a bamboo staff. In a production that used canes as swords, this consti-tuted a disconcerting replication of Polonius's death performed on the skull

---

[30] Cox, '*Titus Andronicus*', p. 188.

of his otherworldly double. Barbara Hodgdon describes how, handing the skull over to Hamlet,

the Gravedigger, ad libbing, says, 'Enjoy' – and Hamlet does. Turning the pole ever so slightly so that Yorick's head and body, as though responding to his questions, looks to Horatio, to the audience, and back to Hamlet, he's suddenly in a Charlie McCarthy world, inflected with a bit of Crab the dog: vaudeville and music hall crowding in as Yorick, Hamlet's opposite, double and mask, speaks for him. Carefully laying Yorick's 'body' down, Hamlet covers it with a purple cloth, shrouding the skull, now facing the audience, evoking John Donne's statue in St. Paul's.[31]

In the performance I witnessed, the scene provoked laughs from an audience who became very still when the scene turned to tragedy with the arrival of Ophelia's funeral. The visual rhymes that made one body morph into the next were continued here as Ophelia's corpse was simply represented by her scarf, a metonymy for the girl, evocation of the arras and simultaneously another shroud for Yorick's skull/Polonius's puppet corpse.

When, in the performance's concluding moments, Horatio 'topple[d] over Hamlet's still kneeling dead body with a single touch so that, replacing Yorick's, it too lay at the carpet's edge',[32] there was a sense of metonymic closure, all the dead bodies of the tragedy reunited in the figure of the dying Prince. But even here, the bodies did not remain quite dead. They refused to be simple stage properties and reclaimed the status of subjects. Echoing Holloway's production, Ophelia and the actor who had trebled as Rosencrantz, the Player Queen and the Priest quietly walked onto the acting area after Hamlet's death and lay down with the other corpses. As Horatio stood in their midst as the sole survivor, eerie music and a bright light announced a change of mood. Looking into the blinding light that streamed in from behind the audience, Horatio intoned 'But look, the morn in russet mantle clad / Walks o'er the dew of yon eastward hill' (1.1.171–2). As the dead rose, fixing their eyes onto the spot on which Horatio's were riveted, he asked 'Who's there?' (1.1.1). The wheel came full circle with an image that defied mortality while situating the living as always already within the realm of the dead. Hamlet's precocious declaration 'I am dead, Horatio' was not incongruous here but a statement that could be appropriate in the mouths of all the characters in the tragedy.

[31] Barbara Hodgdon, 'Re-Incarnations', in Pascale Aebischer, Edward J. Esche and Nigel Wheale (eds.), *Remaking Shakespeare: Performance across Media, Genres and Cultures* (Houndmills: Palgrave Macmillan, 2003), pp. 205–6.
[32] Hodgdon, 'Re-Incarnations', p. 206.

YORICK'S SKULL: *HAMLET*'S IMPROPER PROPERTY

As Adrian Lester's skilful skull-puppetry demonstrated, the most lively revenant in the tragedy is almost invariably Yorick's skull – the improper human property *par excellence*. Yorick not only refuses to be objectified, but in almost every incarnation on stage and screen he threatens to disrupt the theatrical framework, taking on a disturbing multiplicity of identities and meanings that epitomises both the semiotic disruption and the blurring of the boundaries between death and life that are at the core of the play's uncertainties. Far from being confined to a liveliness that is the consequence of his handling, this most incontestably dead human of all seems to have a will of his own regardless of his co-stars' and directors' intentions. If anyone is to misbehave on an all-important press night and upstage the wordy Hamlet, it is bound to be the silent Yorick. Reviewers of Warchus's production were only too delighted when Yorick obliged them by 'slip[ping] out of [the director's] control'. Robert Butler was one of several press-night reviewers who gleefully reported that 'Yorick's skull has a life of its own and rolls off the stage into the audience. Someone has to hand it back.'[33] It is difficult to imagine how Jennings's Hamlet went about recuperating the situation on this and on other nights, when the skull started to crack or was even '*shattered when lobbed through the air by Mr David*', the production's skull-bowling Gravedigger who eventually '*agreed to try a slightly lower curve on the lob*'.[34] When I saw the production, Yorick played up by deciding to behave. Jennings – possibly in gratitude – lovingly rubbed his forehead against the skull's, who allowed the scene to become one of the key images of mournful remembrance in the production.

At the best of times, Yorick can thus help Hamlet indulge in his grieving memory and convey the change of mood that characterises his encounter with the Gravedigger who started digging graves the day Hamlet was born (the time of birth meeting the place of death). At his most disruptive, on the other hand, the skull can play a very different memory game with his audience. In his memoirs, the mid-nineteenth-century Anglo-American actor and elocutionist George Vandenhoff includes a telling anecdote about a provincial performance of *Hamlet* at the Rochdale Theatre in Lancashire. Hamlet was played by a pretentious actor whom Vandenhoff identifies as Mr. C–, 'a most solemn and mysterious tragedian, of the cloak-and-dagger

---

[33] Butler, 'Warchus Puts His *Art* into His *Hamlet*'.
[34] Stage manager's reports 5 January and 5 March 1998. Shakespeare Centre, Stratford-upon-Avon.

school'.[35] The Gravedigger in the production, on the other hand, was played by Richard Hoskins, a 'low' comedian who thought the Hamlet in question ridiculous.

> The theatre was built on the site of an old dissenting chapel, which had formerly stood there, in which a preacher named Banks had held forth, and in the small grave-yard attached to which, the Doctor – for he was popularly dubbed doctor Banks – had been buried some twenty years ago; and his name was familiar yet. So, after answering Hamlet's question –
> 'How long will a man lie in the earth ere he rot?'
> Dick proceeded in due course to illustrate his answer by Yorick's skull; and taking it up, he said, in the words of the text –
> 'Now here's a skull that hath lain you in the earth three-and-twenty years. Whose do you think it was?'
> 'Nay, I know not', replied Hamlet, in his sepulchral, tragedy-tone.
> 'This skull sir', said Dick – pursuing the text thus far, and then making a sudden and most un-looked-for alteration –
> 'This was DOCTOR BANKS's skull!'
> And the word skull he pronounced like bull.
> Of course the house was in an uproar of laughter and confusion. The victimized tragedian stamped and fumed about the stage, as well he might, exclaiming, 'Yorick's, sir, Yorick's!'
> 'No', said Dick, coolly, when the tumult had subsided, taking up another skull, and resuming the text –
> '*This* is Yorick's skull, the king's jester; but' (going off again) 't'other's Doctor Banks's, as I *told* you.'[36]

Not surprisingly, Vandenhoff tells us, the performance ended in a fight in the grave between Hamlet and the Gravedigger rather than Hamlet and Laertes.

While Vandenhoff's anecdote may or may not be true, it does reveal the property skull's disturbing – and often hilarious – potential for excessive signification. In Vandenhoff's narrative, Yorick's skull, like the Ghost of Holloway's production, is both interchangeable and a polysemic theatrical sign which, unlike the Ghost, may reach beyond fiction to find its referents in real life. Andrew Sofer uses the visual arts concept of *anamorphosis* ('trick' perspective) to describe the skull's 'oscillation between subject and object', its capacity to be both a conventional, passive *memento mori* emblem and to take on a more active role in which its 'grinning silence . . . divest[s] Hamlet of his last defense against the inevitability of death: his incomparable way

[35] George Vandenhoff, *Leaves from an Actor's Note-Book; with Reminiscences and Chit-Chat of the Green-Room and the Stage, in England and America* (New York: D. Appleton and Company, 1860), p. 100.
[36] Vandenhoff, *Leaves*, pp. 100–1.

with words'.[37] The concept can be fruitfully applied to this anecdote, as well, for here the property skull slips from its identity as Yorick's (at least in the audience's and the pompous tragedian's expectations) to its identity as Dr Banks's without allowing its spectators to see it from both viewpoints at once. Because of its anonymity the skull, more than any actor, has the capacity to 'double' as both Yorick and any other fictional or real body, thus creating the type of 'flickering effect' I described in my opening discussion of the doubling of actors in Holloway's production. The effect need not be restricted to the audience: certainly, William Charles Macready was disturbed enough in his performance of Hamlet in Richmond (Virginia) on 20 December 1848 to mention in his diary that, for a performance that was unsuccessful with its audience by no apparent fault of his own, he had been given 'the skull, for Yorick's, of a negro who was hung [sic] two years ago for cutting down his overseer'.[38] At a time when mixed-race casting was a near-impossibility and the black American actor Ira Aldridge was not allowed to act on any of the major London stages, the levelling effects of death allowed the executed slave to come back to life and grinningly disconcert that epitome of white culture, the Prince of Denmark, as acted by one of the most prominent English tragedians of the age – a ghostly revenge of the slave on the symbolic centre of his oppressors' culture.

The extent of the skull's capacity for extrafictional reference and its concomitant potential to substantially influence the interpretation of the scene first became apparent to me when I began my research on Ron Daniels's second RSC production. In the middle of a stack of archival material about the production, I found a memorandum, dated 9 May 1989, that read: 'If André Tchaikovsky isn't actually playing Yorick this year, please can we have his skull back in the Collection for future reference, or whatever you do with skulls of dead pianists.' The story I managed to piece together from this point of departure is the following.[39]

In 1980, André Tchaikovsky, an Oxford-based classical musician, saw Michael Pennington's performance of the role of Hamlet in Stratford-upon-Avon. He was so taken by the macabre dialogue in the graveyard scene that on his way home he told his companion of his intention to bequeath his skull to the RSC so that he – or at least a part of him – might appear as

---

[37] Andrew Sofer, 'The Skull on the Renaissance Stage: Imagination and the Erotic Life of Props', *English Literary Renaissance* 28 (1998), 49, 55.
[38] *The Journal of William Charles Macready, 1832–1851*, ed. J. C. Trewin (London: Longmans, 1976), p. 257.
[39] My thanks to Roger Howells, the former production manager for the RSC, and to William Lockwood, the RSC's property department manager, for contributing anecdotal evidence.

Yorick in a future production of *Hamlet*. A few years later, the property department manager for the RSC, William Lockwood, received a call from an undertaker who asked whether the RSC might be interested in the cranium of a deceased client. Horrified, Mr Lockwood passed the question on to Terry Hands (at the time the RSC's artistic director), who promptly accepted the bequest. A mere ten days later, to Lockwood's discomfiture and the evident delight of the department's dog, Mr Lockwood received a cardboard parcel containing the freshly processed golden-toothed skull of André Tchaikovsky. After extensive airing, it found a provisional resting-place on a shelf in the property department.[40]

He briefly left the shelf for a photo-session with Roger Rees for the poster of Daniels's 1984 production, but was immediately sent back to rest, a fibre-glass cast of his cranium taking his place in the theatre. André Tchaikovsky's first genuine chance to star as Yorick came only in 1989, when Mark Rylance started to rehearse the title role of Hamlet in Daniels's production. A rehearsal note dated 13 February records: 'Mark Rylance has asked whether it would be possible to use the real skull that was donated to the RSC as Yorick's skull?' The property department complied, and Tchaikovsky appears to have spent one month in the rehearsal room preparing the role of Yorick. On 23 March, however, the first indication of trouble is casually mentioned in a rehearsal note: 'we will be using the real skull for Yorick but will need a stand by [sic] in case of accident'. What accident? Although Tchaikovsky must have been aware that playing Yorick would entail being 'knocked about the mazard with a sexton's spade' (5.1.85–6), Rylance's desire to grant Tchaikovsky's wish seems thus to have been paradoxically checked by a simultaneous desire to honour the dead. Eventually, squeamishness about the rough handling of real human remains seems to have triumphed. Claire van Kampen, the production's musical director and later Mark Rylance's wife, remembers that

As a company, we all felt most privileged to be able to work the gravedigger scene with a real skull . . . However, collectively as a group we agreed that as the real power of theatre lies in the complicity of illusion between actor and audience, it would be inappropriate to use a real skull during the performances, in the same way that we would not be using real blood, etc. It is possible that some of us felt a

---

[40] I am grateful to Claire Preston for bringing another version of this anecdote to my attention. Howard Marchitello's account is based on a United Press International report broadcast on 13 August 1982 (soon after Tchaikovsky's death). He reads Tchaikovsky's bequest (spelt in his account as 'Tchiakowsky' – I adopt the spelling of the RSC memo) as a fantastic dream 'founded upon a faith in some version of bodily immortality that aspires to nothing less than a recuperation of vitality, presence, and permanence from within a semiotics of death and absence'. *Narrative and Meaning in Early Modern England* (Cambridge: Cambridge University Press, 1997), p. 126.

certain primitive taboo about the skull, although the gravedigger, as I recall[,] was all for it![41]

On 7 April, a last rehearsal note records how Tchaikovsky was finally defeated in his quest for on-stage remembrance, although touchingly the understudy ordered to replace him was to be an exact look-alike: 'We are no longer using the real skull as Yorick but would like to use a cast of it (complete with teeth).'

In spite of his early retirement to the shelf in the property department, Tchaikovsky's presence in the rehearsal room left a deep mark on the production's interpretation of the tragedy's concluding moments. The graveyard scene opened with the gravedigger (played by Jimmy Gardner, the actor implicitly accused by van Kampen of having an inappropriate attitude towards Tchaikovsky's remains) using the skull as a pawn with which to illustrate the legal intricacies of Ophelia's inquest. Rylance's accusatory tone when his Hamlet commented that 'That skull had a tongue in it, and could sing once' (5.1.74), while ostensibly referring to the (at that point anonymous) fictional owner of the skull within the world of the play, was charged with an additional, reproachful meaning in its reference to the two actors' disagreement over the proper treatment of Tchaikovsky's head. When quizzing the gravedigger about the decomposition of bodies, Hamlet jumped into the grave to get a closer look at it all. It was thus in the grave that was shortly to be Ophelia's that he was handed Yorick's skull atop the Gravedigger's spade, where, as eleven years later in Lester's hands, it became a puppet that was mused over by a wistful Hamlet who strained to hear Yorick's silent answers to his questions, making the skull come back to life as his chopfallen interlocutor. The aimless existential despair of Rylance's Hamlet was here converted into focused, intense mourning and tenderness for the skull. Yorick seemed to have taken over the roles of the Ghost and Polonius as the old mole/perturbed spirit/foolish prating knave in the grave hovering on the brink between life and death, remembrance and oblivion.

Hamlet's composure in his confrontation with Laertes in the graveyard seemed to spring out of this encounter with death and memory in the shape of Yorick, whom he lovingly carried into the next scene, his cradling of the cranium mirroring Laertes's mournful rocking of Ophelia's body in the grave. Yorick was casually tucked under Hamlet's arm during his dialogue with Osric, deposited on the floor for Hamlet's handshake with Laertes and finally carefully set down on a mantelpiece, where Hamlet

---

[41] Letter, 19 August 1999. With thanks to Claire van Kampen for answering my questions on Mark Rylance's behalf.

Illustration 7: Hamlet (Mark Rylance) with custom-made replica skull in Ron Daniels's
1989 RSC production of *Hamlet*

'turn[ed] it so that its eyeless sockets faced the action, as a talisman during his duel with Laertes'.[42] How closely this performance choice was linked to Tchaikovsky's presence in the rehearsal room is clear from van Kampen's comment that 'Probably it was this very realness [of the skull] that fired Mark [Rylance]'s imagination to believe that the power of Hamlet's father's old jester was so great that, as a kind of talisman, or fetish, Hamlet takes him through Act V to his, Hamlet's own death.'[43]

The skull of Tchaikovsky and/or Yorick thus had the effect of doubling Hamlet's quest for revenge and confrontation with death with Mark Rylance's desire to honour the last will of Tchaikovsky, who became the company's own uncomfortable *memento mori* and its Ghost clamouring for posthumous remembrance. Because the property disturbingly kept its extrafictional and extratheatrical identity as the property (in the sense of ownership) of André Tchaikovsky the pianist, it resisted the company's attempts to appropriate it as an accessory. Instead, it became an 'improper property' that defied theatrical decorum. In a company such as the RSC that generally uses non-Grotowskian techniques, decorum dictates that theatrical signs which pertain to the human body (be they objects such as bones or blood or physical expressions such as pain or orgasm) should stay at a distance from their referent, a distance which, as Claire van Kampen put it, is bridged by 'the complicity of illusion between actor and audience'. Only when the real skull, with its real identity as André Tchaikovsky's head, was replaced by an identical-looking fake was the company able to adopt the property as an iconic sign that could stand primarily for Yorick rather than Tchaikovsky. Only once it had been fitted with a special hole in its base, custom-made to make it balance on the Gravedigger's spike,[44] could it be a decorous, 'proper' accessory that performed its work on stage as a means through which the audience might understand Hamlet's frame of mind. How easily such an appropriately distanced property can change its 'owner' and slip back into improper signification beyond the theatrical frame of reference is, however, apparent from the story of Dr Banks's skull. Even with a fake, the fact that the skull is a potentially polysemic signifier that is fairly indiscriminate in its signifieds (anything from a lawyer to Alexander the Great is possible) means that it can at any moment disrupt the fictional framework of the theatre and find a signified in reality. The skull as

[42] Stanley Wells, 'Shakespeare Production in England in 1989', *Shakespeare Survey* 43 (1990), 198. Rylance repeated this touch in his performance in the Globe Theatre in 2000, where Yorick watched the duel from a vantage-point on the floor (Tchaikovsky's ghost obviously still haunts the actor).
[43] Letter, 19 August 1999.
[44] Rehearsal note, 7 April 1989, Shakespeare Centre, Stratford-upon-Avon.

a property is thus particularly prone to producing what Martin Esslin dubs '"involuntary" semiosis' because, more than most other 'material objects on the stage or screen', a skull 'may contain signifiers that the originators of the performance (the designer, the director) did not intend to be perceived'.[45]

The theatrical anecdotes of Dr Banks, the executed slave and André Tchaikovsky all reveal Yorick's impropriety as a property and its extraordinary polysemic denotative and connotative richness as a theatrical sign. Even in its most straightforward reference to the dead jester, the skull is loaded with meaning, since the combination of death's head and jester's cap connotatively invokes the tradition of the dance of death. Thus in one of Hans Holbein's famous woodcuts, Death wearing a jester's cap grabs hold of the hand of the queen.[46] The skull as the 'antic death' – 'antic', in early modern English, being 'the usual epithet for Death and mean[ing] "grotesque", "ludicrous"' – thus links Hamlet's 'antic disposition' with his recognition of his own death.[47] It is obviously this concept that informs the cover-design of the documentary video-tape recording the rehearsals for Derek Jacobi's production of *Hamlet* with Kenneth Branagh in the lead, which is tellingly entitled *Discovering Hamlet*. In this image,[48] the parallel disposition of the skull and Branagh's face makes it clear that the discovery of Hamlet must happen through a contemplation of the relationship and similarity between hero and skull. The spine of the video cover is even blunter, with the emblematic picture for the 'discovery' of Hamlet reduced to the skull held up in Hamlet's hand. It is the task of the culturally knowledgeable consumer to work out the metonymy linking the skull to Hamlet's absent head and thus to the discovery of Hamlet's mystery. Thus already in its first, and most straightforward, meaning, the property manages to stand for Yorick as a fictional character, for iconographic Death in general and as such potentially for all the separate identities that Hamlet attributes to it (Cain, a politician, a courtier, a lawyer, a buyer of land, Alexander or Caesar) and for 'antic' Hamlet himself.

If on the spine of the *Discovering Hamlet* tape the skull stands for the absent Hamlet, it no less re-presents its *own* absence. Following its usurpation of Hamlet's place on the cover, the skull is elided in the documentary itself. All we see of Yorick is a four-second clip that is accompanied by a

---

[45] Martin Esslin, *The Field of Drama: How the Signs of Drama Create Meaning on Stage and Screen* (London: Methuen, 1987), p. 46.

[46] For Holbein's 'Dance of Death', see Francis Douce (ed.), *The Dance of Death: In a Series of Engravings on Wood from Designs Attributed to Hans Holbein* (London: G. Bell and Sons, 1902).

[47] Eleanor Prosser, *Hamlet and Revenge* (Stanford: Stanford University Press, 1967), p. 149.

[48] See the illustration in my 'Yorick's Skull: *Hamlet's* Improper Property,' *EnterText* 1:2 (2001), 210.

voice-over of Derek Jacobi talking about the production in general. Yorick's skull in fact signifies its own absence and lack: lack of the lips that Hamlet has 'kissed I know not how oft' (5.1.179–80), the absent presence of Yorick, young Hamlet's 'parental surrogate'.[49] Significantly, when referring to the identity of the skull, both Hamlet and the Gravedigger/Clown use the past tense: 'Whose *was* it?' Hamlet asks, and the reply is 'This same skull, sir, *was* Yorick's skull, the king's jester' (5.1.166, 171–2, emphases added). Past and present are collapsed in this object that both is and is not the jester who has been dead for twenty-three years, thus replaying the tragedy's earlier collapsing of past and present in the figure of the Ghost. Both the Ghost and the skull are theatrical signifiers whose presence points to an absence, whose present points to a past in a blurring of the boundary between life and death that is also exemplified by the Gravedigger's 'pocky corpses' that may be 'rotten before [they] die' (5.1.156).

If it remains unclear where Yorick is to be situated in time, the playtexts make it even more difficult to know *where* he belongs and what space belongs to him. We must assume that if the Gravedigger finds Yorick's remains as he is digging a fresh grave, the plot of the new grave is Yorick's old grave. But Yorick's is not the only skull that is found in the plot: he seems to have shared his grave with at least one other anonymous person. Ownership of the grave is further complicated by the Clown's assertion that the grave belongs to him and Hamlet's insistence that it must belong to the person the Clown is digging it *for*: Ophelia. The grave hence turns out to be 'common', another way in which death in the play is represented as a leveller who makes a 'King . . . go a progress through the guts of a beggar' and another way in which the graveyard scene problematises the distinction between 'the dead' and 'the quick' (4.3.30–1, 5.1.120) that has been haunting the play from the outset.

In its physical juxtaposition of Yorick's dirty remains – 'his fine pate full of fine dirt' is obviously smelly (5.1.101–2, 191) – and Ophelia's 'fair and unpolluted flesh' (5.1.229), the grave becomes the space where the cultural topos of Death and the Maiden is played out. In the visual arts, this motif reached its creative (and erotic) apex in central Europe in the first half of the sixteenth century. In Niklaus Manuel's *Berner Totentanz* (1516–19), for instance, Death was figured seizing a citizen's daughter from behind, his bony fingers plunging into her *décolletage*.[50] By the time of Hans Sebald

49 Martin W. Walsh, '"This Same Skull, Sir . . .": Layers of Meaning and Tradition in Shakespeare's Most Famous Prop', *Hamlet Studies* 9 (1987), 74.
50 Niklaus Manuel's original *Berner Totentanz* is lost, but copies of the frescoes are preserved in Albrecht Kauw's 1649 watercolour in the Historisches Museum in Bern.

Beham's portrayal of *Tod in Narrengestalt und Mädchen* (1541) – an engraving
that, with its combination of Death as a jester, a virtuous maiden associated
with the flowers in its background, and a motto reminding the viewer of the
transitory nature of beauty, is remarkably close to Shakespeare's graveyard
scene – the visual-arts motif had, however, lost its eroticism and much of
its iconographic power.[51] But what had become a cliché within the pictorial
tradition was revived and reinvigorated in music and literature, where the
topos transcended geographical and linguistic barriers, finding one of its
most memorable and erotically invested expressions in Romeo's question
to the seemingly dead Juliet 'Shall I believe / That unsubstantial death is
amorous, / And that the lean abhorrèd monster keeps / Thee here in dark to
be his paramour?' (*Rom* 5.3.102–5). In the graveyard scene, this poetic motif
inherited from the visual arts is picked up in Gertrude's reflection on the
substitution of the grave for Ophelia's bridal bed,[52] thus providing a verbal
gloss on the physical juxtaposition of Ophelia's body with Yorick's skull.
None of the early editions of *Hamlet* provides a stage direction indicating
what happens to Yorick's disinterred cranium, but theatrical and cinematic
expediency has often dictated its return into its grave alongside the body of
'One that was a woman' (5.1.128) – productions starring Mark Rylance are
the exception. Like the fashionable early modern tombs that superimposed
a sculpture of the living body over its decaying alter ego, Yorick's and
Ophelia's two stages of physical decay then provide a continuity with the
living bodies of the sparring Laertes and Hamlet who join them in their
grave (that is, if we accept the Q1 stage direction that stipulates that Hamlet
'*leaps in after Laertes*').

   Ophelia's corpse and Yorick's skull are, however, more than simply juxtaposed in the space of the grave. In a chapter devoted to describing how
'when Ophelia plays dead, she plays up', rising from the dead in her brother's
arms and 're-enter[ing] the field of play, her dead eyes gazing at the audience', Carol Rutter draws attention to the sense in which 'proleptically,
Yorick is Ophelia's double'.[53] In a move similar to the morphing, in some

[51] For a gloss on Beham's engraving, see William R. Levin, *Images of Love and Death in Late Medieval
    and Renaissance Art* (Michigan: University Publications, 1975), p. 71. In-depth discussions of the
    topos of Death and the Maiden in early modern Europe are provided by Jean Wirth, *La Jeune Fille
    et la mort: recherches sur les thèmes macabres dans l'art germanique de la Renaissance* (Geneva: Droz,
    1979) and Karl S. Guthke, 'Renaissance und Barock: Der Tod und das Mädchen – und der Mann',
    in his *Ist der Tod eine Frau? Geschlecht und Tod in Kunst und Literatur* (Munich: Verlag C. H. Beck,
    1997), pp. 94–143.
[52] For a discussion of 'the conceit of Death as usurping Bridegroom' see Michael Neill, *Issues of Death:
    Mortality and Identity in English Renaissance Tragedy* (Oxford: Clarendon Press, 1997), p. 58.
[53] Rutter, *Enter the Body*, pp. 41–2. Her discussion of the 'work' done by Ophelia's unruly corpse
    complements my own study of the play's unruly male not-yet-quite-dead bodies in performance.

performances, of the Ghost, Polonius, Yorick and sometimes, as I have shown, even Claudius and Hamlet, Yorick's skull here is both his own and Ophelia's: 'The skull makes the audience face up to death's horrors in a materially specific way that Hamlet's philosophizing has managed to avoid . . . Hamlet, holding the skull, thinks he holds the jester he loved; what he doesn't know is that, in this substitute, he holds Ophelia too. It is a bizarrely placed and displaced final love scene.'[54] Rylance's cradling of the skull that so poignantly anticipated the gesture with which John Ramm's Laertes took hold of his sister's corpse certainly did convey some of the transference of necrophilia from the property skull to Ophelia who, as Andrew Sofer points out, has herself 'been used as a prop throughout, by both Hamlet and her father; even her corpse gets shoved in the earth while God's back is turned, and the fact that she is upstaged at her own funeral is sadly appropriate'.[55] It is, in a way, not surprising that in its next early modern incarnation in *The Revenger's Tragedy* (an almost point-by-point reply to *Hamlet*), Middleton took the implications of this morphing of the death's head and his maiden to its logical conclusion, gendering the skull female so as to unequivocally turn it into the male revenger's necrophilic object of desire.

FILMING YORICK — CORPSES, CORPSING AND LEAVING THE CORPUS

If Yorick's skull is disturbingly polysemous on the page and the stage, it can be equally promiscuous in its signification on screen, where its value as a shocking property that is all too 'close to the bone' is often exploited through close-ups. In Laurence Olivier's 1948 film of *Hamlet*, the 'father' of *Hamlet* and Yorick on screen, the editing of playtexts and film takes the viewer straight from Ophelia's graceful Millais-inspired death to the gloomily comic scene of the Clown's digging of her grave. Eileen Herlie's voice-over describing Ophelia's 'muddy death' (4.7.158) thus links the poetic beauty of Gertrude's speech and of Olivier's/Jean Simmons's cinematic portrayal of 'the most beautified Ophelia' (2.2.109–10) to the earthy reality of the grave, from which the Clown retrieves Yorick's skull. While the Death-and-the-Maiden nexus is suggested through montage, *mise en scène* jolts the audience into a recognition of Hamlet's own connection with the skull when, a few seconds later, Hamlet's shadow enters the frame,

---

[54] Rutter, *Enter the Body*, p. 41.   [55] Sofer, 'The Skull', 55.

his head exactly covering Yorick's skull on the ground.[56] If in Hamlet's subsequent gentle musings over the remarkably sanitised skull and his final casual disposal of it in the grave there is little sense of disgust or of the potential difficulty involved in containing this property, this splendidly simple cinematic trope in which Hamlet's death is literally foreshadowed is a prime instance of the prop's extraordinary semantic power.

Whereas, to appropriate Horatio's phrase, the skull in Olivier's film is 'a property of easiness' (5.1.66), in Kenneth Branagh's films – both *In the Bleak Midwinter* (1995) and his marathon *Hamlet* (1996) – Yorick ceases to behave. The first indication that the Yorick of Branagh's 'completer than complete' film of *Hamlet* is up to more antics than he is normally allowed can be seen in the cover of the video-tape.[57] Surprisingly, in view of the iconographic tradition of production posters and video covers that dictates that Hamlet should be represented in some sort of interaction with the skull, Yorick is not featured on the front of the cover. Instead, the back of the cover includes a skull in one of the eight small inset photographs that frame the publicity blurb. There, instead of being engaged in its habitual deep mutual contemplation with the hero, the grinning skull is held by the grinning Gravedigger (played by Billy Crystal), both of them facing the viewer.[58] Upon closer examination it appears that, just as the Gravedigger has displaced Hamlet, Yorick, too, has been displaced from this emblematic picture by a rival skull. To a careful observer it furthermore becomes apparent that the still on the cover does not correspond to any moment represented in the film. The little picture on the cover, then, represents a triple displacement in which Gravedigger, skull and still all re-present without presenting the emblematic scene a viewer would expect on the evidence of most other *Hamlet* video covers and film posters.

Surely, with a director as aware of intertextuality as Branagh, such a teasing frustration of expectations is no coincidence. On his video cover both Hamlet, who turns his back on the viewer, and the skull are set up as elusive theatrical signifiers that point to a multiplicity of referents. Among many other references to previous performances and performers of Hamlet, Branagh's platinum-blond Hamlet with his duel involving a spectacular descent from a balcony clearly evokes Olivier's film performance,[59] in which

[56] Robert A. Duffy, 'Gade, Olivier, Richardson: Visual Strategy in *Hamlet* Adaptation', *Literature/Film Quarterly* 4:2 (1976), 148.
[57] Geoffrey O'Brien, 'The Ghost at the Feast', *New York Review of Books* 44:2 (1997), 15.
[58] See the enlarged inset image in my 'Yorick's Skull', 217.
[59] While Olivier claimed that he dyed his hair 'so as to avoid the possibility of Hamlet later being identified with [him]', it is more likely that Olivier was in fact 'quoting' Henry Irving who, in 1864,

the star's fifteen-foot head-first leap from the gallery onto the defenceless Claudius nearly killed the hapless stuntman who was knocked unconscious and lost two teeth – 'corpsing' in the transitive sense of nearly turning a living stuntman into a corpse.[60] The august collection of former and future Hamlets in Branagh's cast-list in fact presents the viewer with a whole selection of Danish Princes, so that any claim made by Branagh to being the sole iconic sign for Hamlet in the film is undermined by the proliferation of Princes in this celluloid Denmark.

Similarly, skulls also emerge as simultaneously specific and general signifiers in this film. In an early scene, Branagh's Hamlet scares Polonius by putting on a crude skull mask, so that 'antic Death' literally becomes one of the masks Hamlet puts on as part of his 'antic disposition'. As a mask, the face of death on a living head lends emphasis to the tragedy's repeated questioning of the boundaries between life and death at the same time as its potential to hide different heads behind its front implies the promiscuity of death. This implication is strengthened in the film's graveyard scene, where the five dirty skulls unearthed by the Gravedigger make death seem particularly 'common'. In Branagh's screenplay Hamlet's wry thought that 'if there were any more of these bloody things [the Gravedigger] could set up a skull shop' stresses this point.[61] Nevertheless it is amidst this proliferation of skulls that one skull becomes specific enough to disrupt the spatial and temporal setting of the scene, the fictional framework of the film and even the continuity of the screenplay. Yorick is set apart from his fellow expersons, to use Branagh's term,[62] in terms of both space and physiognomy. Yorick's skull is left behind after all the other skulls have been packed up, and his buckteeth make his identity all too apparent to Hamlet. Two brief

had worn a fair wig in homage to Charles Fechter's innovation of 1861. See Laurence Olivier, 'An Essay in Hamlet', in Brenda Cross (ed.), *The Film Hamlet: A Record of Its Production* (London: The Saturn Press, 1948), p. 15, and Austin Brereton, *The Life of Henry Irving*, 2 vols. (London: Longmans, Green and Co., 1908), vol. I, p. 57.

60 The anecdote is told very differently by Olivier's biographer John Cottrell, who reports Basil Sidney's (Claudius's) refusal to be Olivier's leap-victim and gives details of the stuntman's injuries, and by Olivier in his autobiography, who stresses his selfless (and remarkably self-centred) heroism: 'The dangers involved ... presented themselves to me in the light of the following five possibilities: I could kill myself; damage myself for life; I could hurt myself badly enough to make recovery a lengthy business; I could hurt myself only slightly; or I could get away with it without harm ... I felt so strongly then that this film was by far the most important work of my life that I regarded the first of the five possibilities with an unworried steadiness that gave me a mild feeling of surprise.' John Cottrell, *Laurence Olivier* (Sevenoaks: Hodder and Stoughton, 1977), p. 237, and Laurence Olivier, *Confessions of an Actor: An Autobiography* (New York: Simon and Schuster, 1982), pp. 152–4.

61 Kenneth Branagh, Hamlet *by William Shakespeare: Screenplay, Introduction and Film Diary* (New York and London: W. W. Norton and Company, 1996), p. 145.

62 Branagh, Hamlet, p. 148.

flashbacks underline the hero's recognition of the skull, taking the viewer to the living Yorick, impersonated by the notoriously bucktoothed stand-up comedian Ken Dodd, playing with the boy Hamlet and amusing the royal family.

In harmony with the play, these filmic analepses help blur the distinction between the dead and the living, the past and the present, and strengthen Yorick's role as a father-figure for Hamlet. At the same time, however, the flashbacks are dangerously disruptive. On the one hand, the skull's identification with Dodd's grinning face creates a semantic problem when Hamlet orders it to 'get . . . to my lady's chamber and tell her, let her paint an inch thick, to this favour she must come' (5.1.183–5). In the film's juxtaposition of the live Yorick's heavily made-up face with these lines, the point of Hamlet's misogynistic injunction that links this scene to his condemnation of women's 'paintings' (3.1.143) in the nunnery scene is blunted. On the other hand, while the flashbacks are long enough for the audience to recognise Ken Dodd as the model for the property's buckteeth, they are too brief for the viewer to move beyond that recognition into an involvement with Hamlet's nostalgic memory. In the figure of Ken Dodd, the flashbacks violently introduce an extrafictional referent into the scene in a way reminiscent of Richard Hoskins's evocation of Dr Banks. However disruptive, in the light of early modern examples of dignitaries who commissioned tomb sculptures of their own decomposing bodies years before their actual deaths,[63] there is something peculiarly 'authentic' in the fact that the skull was modelled on Dodd and given to him at the end of the shoot as a souvenir of the production and personal *memento mori*.[64]

The fact that in this case the extrafictional referent for Yorick's skull is very much alive is a key instance of the 'life-in-death' theme that haunts this film more than any other. Old Hamlet's scripted appearances as a Ghost are complemented by several cinematic flashbacks that present him alive or in the process of dying. A brief inset representing Hamlet's bloody imagination during Claudius's prayer scene shows Claudius being stabbed in the ear by Hamlet's dagger. Ophelia's burial is furthermore modelled on the vampire film,[65] a genre in which corpses are disruptively alive. Even Russell Jackson's film diary seems singularly preoccupied with the coming

---

[63] Roland Mushat Frye, *The Renaissance* Hamlet: *Issues and Responses in 1600* (Princeton: Princeton University Press, 1984), p. 232.

[64] Russell Jackson's film diary records the care taken to make the skull match its model ('A close-up of Doddy with teeth displayed to match our shots of skull') and the gift of the skull ('Has photos taken of his name on a chair-back (which tickles him pink) and Yorick's skull – which he is given as a memento'). 'The Film Diary', in Branagh, Hamlet, p. 201.

[65] Rutter, *Enter the Body*, pp. 51–2.

alive of dead bodies. The entry for 23 February reads: 'The morning starts
with Hamlet lying in state. Billy Crystal (First Gravedigger) has arrived for
make-up consultations, and comes on set while Ken [Branagh] is in the
coffin: Billy gets up the stepladder beside the catafalque and the corpse sits
up to chat.'[66] On 1 March, Kate Winslet is performing dead Ophelia when
a 'runner from the production office comes with a telephone message from
L.A. for Kate, but we don't know where she is, so messenger departs – then
we remember she's in the grave'.[67] The following day, the diary records
a different incident in the graveyard in which the actors 'corpse' in the
theatrical sense of the word:

The last day in the graveyard – general fatigue, because we've been in here too long.
The funeral has become a series of bits and pieces, close-ups, different p.o.v.'s on
and around Laertes who has to sustain and repeat the feelings again and again. The
tension breaks when Horatio goes to separate Hamlet from his adversary: Laertes
and the officers restraining him fall over in a heap, laughing, disappearing from
view in the monitor.[68]

Whether metaphorically or almost literally, corpses, heralded by Ken
Dodd's lively Yorick, are disturbingly alive in Branagh's production. Not
even in the screenplay does Yorick behave properly and 'play dead'. As if
it had not been up to enough mischief in the film itself, the skull does an
additional little comic turn in its script, where it refuses to stay put once
it has been disposed of. At least, this has to be inferred from the fact that
although Hamlet apparently '*throws the skull down*' in disgust at its smell,
a few lines down Yorick seems to have popped back into his hands, for,
as Ophelia's funeral approaches, Hamlet once more '*throws the skull to the*
FIRST GRAVEDIGGER'.[69]

In view of Yorick's improper behaviour in Branagh's 'serious' *Hamlet*, it
is hardly surprising that he is similarly vivacious in *In the Bleak Midwinter*
(or *A Midwinter's Tale*), Branagh's comedy about the making of an amateur
Hamlet. Kathy Howlett describes the black-and-white low-budget film as
both a 'parody of Laurence Olivier's *Hamlet* (1948) as the standard to which
all *Hamlet*s are held' and a 'showcasing of many of the same actors who
comically rehearse *Hamlet* for roles in Branagh's film *Hamlet* (1996)'.[70] Like
the Ghost's ambiguous suspension between death and life and its gesturing
to both past murder and future revenge, Branagh's parody points both
backwards and forwards, acting as the spectral corpse that heralds Branagh's

[66] Branagh, Hamlet, p. 192.   [67] Branagh, Hamlet, p. 195.
[68] Branagh, Hamlet, p. 196.   [69] Branagh, Hamlet, pp. 149–50.
[70] Kathy M. Howlett, *Framing Shakespeare on Film* (Athens: Ohio University Press, 2000), p. 17.

Illustration 8: Video-still of a ventriloquist auditioning for a role in *Hamlet* in Branagh's
1995 film *In the Bleak Midwinter*

Illustration 9: Video-still of the audience of *Hamlet* in Branagh's 1995 film *In the Bleak
Midwinter*

'revenge' on the memory of Olivier in his 1996 film. With the graveyard
scene not part of the film *per se* – a significant omission considering how
easily the macabre dialogue and unruly property would lend themselves to
a spoof – Yorick nevertheless manages to negotiate a central position on the
video cover of *In the Bleak Midwinter*. There, in a black-and-white group
photograph of the cast, his pink bony head conspicuously sticks out. If he
fears no more the heat of the sun, this is mainly because he is equipped
with sunglasses that irrepressibly gesture towards life. In fact, Yorick has
rarely been livelier than in his two brief appearances in the margins of
this film: the first when an auditioning ventriloquist performs 'Alas, poor

Yorick. I knew him, Horatio' (5.1.175–6) with a dummy Hamlet and skull, while another skull is perched on the director's pencils; the second when Yorick the jester appears as one of Fadge's (the designer's) painted audience members to watch the performance of *Hamlet*. Pastiche seems the only way to deal with the irrepressible Yorick within the framework of a comedy.

Yorick, in fact, has become such a well-known icon that his representation on stage and screen is by now no less clichéd and vexed than Hamlet's 'To be or not to be' soliloquy. Both elements of the play are immensely quotable and therefore also immensely removable: even if omitted from a performance, they are nevertheless always already there in what Barbara Hodgdon calls the audience's 'expectational text', the text that consists of the individual spectators' 'private notions about the play and about performed Shakespeare'.[71] Just as Hamlet's soliloquy can be removed from the corpus of *Hamlet* and grafted into Arnold Schwarzenegger's *Last Action Hero*,[72] Yorick, too, is instantly recognisable, as can be seen from his appropriation in *Shakespeare in Love*. When Joseph Fiennes's Shakespeare enters the back-stage space at Whitehall, there is a very brief moment in which Will Kempe is shown holding a skull before throwing it into a prop-box. The screenplay glosses this moment as 'he looks at the skull . . . in other words he reminds us of Hamlet'.[73] What the gloss omits is the skull's habitual semantic excess, for Yorick doubles here as both the skull and the clown/jester in full costume and make-up who is looking at him. The skull's later, and unscripted, reappearance in the film as a weapon with which Burbage – historically the future Hamlet – is knocked unconscious is yet another instance of the property's semantic richness and potential unruliness.

The property's combination of cliché and openness to pastiche might well be the rationale behind Michael Almereyda's decision to excise Yorick from the body of the play in the most recent screen *Hamlet*. If Branagh's film tries to stage as much of the corpus of *Hamlet* as it can, in the process reviving the corpses of old Hamlet, Priam, Hecuba, Rosencrantz and Guildenstern in a series of flashbacks while paradoxically almost entirely burying the First Quarto text, Almereyda's has been described by Samuel Crowl 'as the anti-Branagh *Hamlet* in its relentless slashing and repositioning of the text and in its radically imaginative film style'.[74] In a

[71] Barbara Hodgdon, 'Two *King Lears*: Uncovering the Filmtext', *Literature/Film Quarterly* 11:3 (1983), 143.

[72] For a brief account of the scene, see Deborah Cartmell, *Interpreting Shakespeare on Screen* (London: Macmillan, 2000), p. 4.

[73] Marc Norman and Tom Stoppard, *Shakespeare in Love* (London: Faber and Faber, 1999), p. 13.

[74] Samuel Crowl, '*Hamlet*', *Shakespeare Bulletin* (2000), 39.

film that consistently seeks to frustrate expectations and defy clichés, the tragedy's unruly property is relegated to the margins. Even in the screenplay, which, unlike the edited film, does contain a substantial part of the grave-yard scene, Yorick is conspicuous through his re-presented absence. The skull is, presumably, the 'something' referred to in the stage direction that immediately precedes the Gravedigger's 'Here's a skull that hath lien you in the earth' and that reads '*he* [the Gravedigger] *returns to the grave, pokes at something with his toe*'.[75] But instead of picking up the skull in order to enter into a profound contemplation of mortality, the screenplay's Hamlet '*kneels a moment, then stands up into frame wearing a rubber Halloween skull mask*'[76] – both a displacement of Yorick's skull onto commercial Halloween skeletons typical of the film and an intertextual reference to Branagh's sim-ilar use of a skull mask in the 1996 film. Although this scene was filmed as scripted, Yorick's near-appearance in the graveyard scene was eventu-ally edited out along with most of the graveyard scene. In his 'Director's Notes', Almereyda records that, although during filming 'the scene seemed to fly',

in the editing room it became clear that I'd failed to get it right. The tone and timing were off, and the whole episode seemed to sidetrack Hamlet's response to Ophelia's death. The movie worked better with the prized scene cut out. But we kept a vestige of Jeffrey's [Jeffrey Wright playing the Clown] performance, a chorus from the Dylan song, as a wistful souvenir.[77]

If the kicked-at 'something' and the rubber skull mask are in themselves oblique signifiers for the ever more absent Yorick, the song that recalls their erasure sets the deferral of meaning at yet another remove, becoming an enactment of post-structuralist *différance* at the same time as it encapsulates Hamlet's and *Hamlet's* search for elusive, unrepresentable, meaning, for 'that within which passeth show' (1.2.85).

Significantly, the only time within the final cut of Almereyda's film that Yorick appears as himself, the skull flickers across Hamlet's television screen, profoundly contemplated by Sir John Gielgud's uncredited appear-ance as Hamlet in a clip from Humphrey Jennings's 1945 documentary *Diary for Timothy*, a meditation on the future of a child born during the last days of the war.[78] The extract thus looks both forward to Almereyda's yet unbegotten and unborn *Hamlet* and backward, in the shape of Gielgud's

[75] Michael Almereyda, *William Shakespeare's* Hamlet: *A Screenplay Adaptation by Michael Almereyda* (London: Faber and Faber, 2000), p. 108.
[76] Almereyda, Hamlet, p. 108.   [77] Almereyda, Hamlet, p. 140.
[78] My thanks to Peter Donaldson, who helped me identify the clip, rectifying my earlier identifica-tion of it as Forbes-Robertson's *Hamlet* in 'Yorick's Skull'. A similar point can be made about both

artistic and biographical ancestry, to late-Victorian stage traditions. It is
yet another instance of the absent presence that surrounds appearances of
Yorick that Almereyda's screenplay does not identify the extract but simply
(and misleadingly) refers to 'snippets from a silent film "Hamlet"'.[79]
Furthermore, although Almereyda dedicates a whole appendix to the subject of 'An Inventory of Ghosts (*Hamlet* on Film)', he does not list this film
in his account of cinematic predecessors. Almereyda thus subjects both
Yorick and Gielgud's Hamlet to a simultaneous re-presentation and erasure
that are symptomatic of his film's attitude towards all its (re)sources,
whether textual, cinematic or material. Yorick's present absence, in this
latest, self-consciously postmodern, turn-of-the-millennium appearance,
evokes the end of the Victorian stage tradition, the beginning of *Hamlet*'s
and Yorick's appropriation by the film industry, and Yorick's own problematic status as a theatrical property. Almereyda's is a Yorick in quotation
marks at two removes (a quotation of a quotation, uncredited allusion to
an uncredited allusion), a Yorick who is and is not there, a sign of a sign
of a fictional referent that collapses not Hamlet's but *Hamlet*'s past with its
present. It is the epitome of the semiotically unstable, not-yet-quite-dead
corpses that lie at the heart of the indeterminacies of the play and that aptly
trope the textual instability of its corpus.

Forbes-Robertson and Gielgud, as both actors were deeply rooted in late-Victorian theatrical traditions, bridging the gap between Victorian theatre and the new medium of film.
[79] Almereyda, Hamlet, p. 51.

CHAPTER THREE

Murderous male moors: gazing at race in
Titus Andronicus *and* Othello

ALDRIDGE'S HANDS: THE PERFORMANCE OF RACE

at this end of this century it is just not ON for a white man to black-up . . . Foregoing the part, as Michael Gambon did a few years ago, is now the only route.

– Janet Suzman[1]

If one has to look like a subject to teach or study it, this is mysticism not scholarship. If anyone said I couldn't teach Milton or Shakespeare, that would be interpreted as racist.

– Henry Louis Gates Jr[2]

In his travel narrative *Voyage en Russie* (1866), the French novelist and travel writer Théophile Gautier includes a chapter dedicated to the theatres of St Petersburg. In it, there is the following extraordinary account of a performance of King Lear by Ira Aldridge (or 'Aldrigge', in Gautier's spelling), the prominent black actor who performed Shakespeare's major tragic roles, including those of Aaron and Othello, across Europe between 1824 and 1867:

Le répertoire d'un acteur nègre semble devoir se borner à des pièces de couleur; mais, quand on y réfléchit, si un comédien blanc se barbouille de bistre pour jouer un rôle noir, pourquoi un comédien noir ne s'enfarinerait-il pas de céruse pour jouer un rôle blanc? – C'est ce qui arriva. Ira Aldrigge joua, la semaine suivante, le roi Lear de manière à produire toute l'illusion désirable. Un crâne de carton couleur chair, d'où pendaient quelques mèches argentées, couvrait sa chevelure laineuse et lui descendait jusqu'aux sourcils comme un casque; un rajouté en cire comblait la courbure de son nez épaté. Un fard épais enduisait ses joues noires, et une grande barbe blanche enveloppant le reste de sa figure, descendait jusque sur la poitrine. La transformation était complète; Cordelia n'aurait pu se douter qu'elle avait pour père un nègre. – Jamais l'art du maquillage ne fut poussé plus

---

[1] Letter to the author, 19 November 1998.
[2] Eamonn McCabe, interview with Henry Louis Gates Jr, 'Henry the First', *Guardian Review*, 6 July 2002, 22.

loin. Par une sorte de coquetterie bien concevable, Ira Aldrigge n'avait pas blanchi ses mains, et elles apparaissaient, au bout des manches de sa tunique, brunes come des pattes de singe. Nous le trouvâmes supérieur dans le rôle du vieux roi persécuté par ses méchantes filles à ce qu'il était dans celui du More de Venise. Là, il jouait; dans Othello il était lui-même.

[The repertoire of a Negro actor would seem to have to confine itself to plays of colour; but, if one thinks about it, if a white actor covers himself with bister [brown pigment prepared from common soot] to act a black role, why should a black actor not powder himself with ceruse [white lead] to play a white role? – This is what happened. The following week, Ira Aldrigge acted King Lear in such a way as to produce all the illusion that was to be desired. A flesh-coloured cardboard skull, from which hung some silvery locks, covered his woolly hair and came down to his eyebrows like a helmet; a fill-in of wax filled out the curve of his flat nose. A thick layer of make-up coated his black cheeks, and a big white beard that covered the rest of his face went down onto his chest. The transformation was complete; Cordelia could not have suspected that she had a Negro for a father. – Never had the art of make-up been pushed further. Out of a kind of consciousness of his own appearance [*une coquetterie*] that can be easily imagined, Ira Aldrigge had not whitened his hands, and they appeared at the end of the sleeves of his tunic, brown like monkeys' paws. We found him better in the role of the old king persecuted by his wicked daughters than in that of the Moor of Venice. There, he acted; in Othello, he was himself.][3]

Gautier's account raises important questions about the performance of race, whether on stage or page.[4] In a move typical of much (white) liberal criticism of race in Shakespeare's drama, Gautier's endorsement of Aldridge's

[3] Théophile Gautier, *Voyage en Russie*, ed. P. Laubriet (Paris and Geneva: Ressources, 1979), pp. 155–6, my translation. The passage is also quoted in an English translation that takes greater liberties (and loses some of the precision in the racial vocabulary) in Herbert Marshall and Mildred Stock, *Ira Aldridge: The Negro Tragedian* (London: Camelot Press, 1958), p. 230.

[4] I am using the term 'race' loosely as, in the terms of a certain definition, 'an effective means of establishing the simplest model of human variation – colour difference'. This use of the term is combined with an awareness that 'race is a cultural rather than a biological phenomenon, the product of historical processes not of genetically determined differences'. Bill Ashcroft, Gareth Griffiths and Helen Tiffin, *Post-Colonial Studies: The Key Concepts* (London: Routledge, 2000), pp. 200, 205. It is useful to keep in mind Peggy Phelan's caveat that 'The same physical features of a person's body may be read as "black" in England, "white" in Haiti, "colored" in South Africa, and "mulatto" in Brazil. More than indicating that racial markings are read differently cross-culturally, these variations underline the psychic, political and philosophical impoverishment of linking the color of the physical body with the ideology of race.' *Unmarked: The Politics of Performance* (London: Routledge, 1993), p. 8. However, as Aldridge's white-face and Olivier's black-face just as much as the recent mainstream casting decisions for Othello and Aaron and critical responses show, on Western stages skin colour has for a long time been, and is still, the principal way of 'Othering' and 'reading' these characters. Ultimately, my use of 'race' comes close to the 'notorious indeterminacy' of early modern racial terminology, where the word 'Moor' was used as a blanket term to cover just about any deviation from the norm of (white) 'Englishness'. See Michael Neill, '"Mulattos", "Blacks", and "Indian Moors": Othello and Early Modern Constructions of Human Difference', *Shakespeare Quarterly* 49 (1998), 364, *passim*.

choice to whiten-up for the part of Lear is couched in language that is ultimately racist. This is most evident from his comparison of Aldridge's 'brown' hands with 'monkeys' paws' – an animalisation of the black man that can be found again and again, not only in Iago's characterisation of Othello as 'an old black ram' (1.1.87), but also in literary criticism and, yet more frequently, in theatre reviews and academic descriptions of performances of *Othello* across the centuries. A crass example is the hand-written comment, in the rehearsal copy of *Othello* marked-up for Marcus Moriarty and Edwin Booth in 1876, that Othello is 'an untamed animal – grandly majestic, fearful – with Africa's blood flowing in his veins'.[5] Black skin, in such descriptions, seems to make a man not quite human, as is also apparent in Gautier's slip when he assumes that the colour of human flesh ('*couleur de chair*') is necessarily white. Implicit in Gautier's choice of words is the notion that, in French (as in English), white skin is the standard attribute of the human species and that any darker shade constitutes a deviation from that norm.

One of the remarkable aspects of the traces left by Aldridge's long career is the way the accounts of his productions of *King Lear* and *Othello* suggest that, for this actor, both race and gender were identities that could be self-consciously performed and foregrounded as performances. His visibly unwhitened hands as King Lear went counter to his white colleagues' custom of covering their hands with dark gloves when playing Othello. They thus helped '[emphasize] the limits of role-playing and [assert] his own personhood'.[6] Conversely, the fact that he did need to 'put his arms into chocolate-coloured knitwear sleeves' as Othello also drew attention to his hands.[7] The reviewer of a performance in 1858 paid particular attention to this 'small peculiarity' of 'remarkable significance': 'We have before us an Othello with his hands ungloved, and the fingernails expressively apparent. We begin to perceive the play and action of the hand, and the remarkable assistance which its variety of gestures may give to the meaning.'[8] Aldridge's awareness of the visibility of his black hands is apparent in his customary stage business as Othello, recorded by his sometime Desdemona Dame Madge Kendal, of 'opening his hand and making you place yours in it; and the audience used to see the contrast'. The disparity was made greater

[5] Folger Prompt Othello 40, pp. 18–19.
[6] Sujata Iyengar, 'White Faces, Blackface: The Production of "Race" in *Othello*', in Philip C. Kolin (ed.), Othello: *Critical Essays* (New York and London: Routledge, 2002), p. 109.
[7] Gautier, *Voyage en Russie*, p. 154.
[8] *Athenaeum*, 31 July 1858, quoted in Owen Mortimer, *Speak of Me as I Am: The Story of Ira Aldridge* (Wangaratta: Owen Mortimer, 1995), p. 64.

by the fact that he 'always picked out the fairest woman he could to play Desdemona with him, not because she was capable of acting the part, but because she had a fair head'.[9]

It appears that Aldridge looked for the natural attributes that would enhance the racial difference between the two lovers as much as possible, using skin colour as one would use a costume as a means of making a theatrical point. Indeed, his casting choices may be seen as equivalent to the costume choices recommended by William Winter in Edwin Booth's promptbook:

Othello – First dress: A long gown of cashmere, wrought with gold and various colours. This is looped up to the hip, on the left side, with jewels. A Moorish burnoose, striped with purple and gold. Purple velvet shoes, embroidered with gold and pearl. A sash of green and gold. A jewelled chain. *Second dress*: Steel-plate armour. A white burnoose, made of African goat's hair. *Third dress*: a long, white gown, Moorish, with hood, and with scarlet trimmings. A white sash, made of goat's hair. Scarlet velvet shoes. Pearl earrings . . .

A costume for Desdemona is as follows: *First dress*: White satin train, trimmed with illusion and pearls. High, pointed corsage, with ruff. Long, puffed sleeves: pearls between puffs. Stomacher, elaborately embroidered with pearls. Girdle of the same. Diamond earrings, cross and pin. Mary Stuart cap, made of white satin and pearls.[10]

Just as Othello's 'dresses', according to Winter, 'although conformable to Christian ideas, are devised with a view to express the gorgeous barbaric taste of the Moor',[11] Desdemona's virginally white costume with its concealing neckline (the ruff) and simultaneous emphasis of the female form (the pointed corsage) not only expresses both her chastity and sexual attractiveness, but even more so marks her as white and European (no African goat's hair for her). Diamond cross and Mary Stuart cap further signal her status as a Christian sacrificial victim, while the pearls that adorn her and Othello alike establish a 'costume rhyming' between the two otherwise deliberately contrasted lovers.[12] Aldridge's casting of the fairest woman available in this context seems not to be an expression of his sexual interest in fair women, as Madge Kendal insinuates. Rather, it is a theatrically canny choice that facilitated the actors' performance of race which, in Booth's production, was primarily down to costume ('since to make Othello a Negro is to unpoetize the character, and to deepen whatever grossness may already

[9] [Dame Madge] Kendal, *Dramatic Opinions* (Boston: Little, Brown, and Company, 1890), pp. 29, 28.
[10] Folger Prompt Othello 3, p. 120.   [11] Folger Prompt Othello 3, p. 120.
[12] Lynda E. Boose and Richard Burt (eds.), Introduction, in *Shakespeare, the Movie: Popularizing the Plays on Film, TV, and Video* (London: Routledge, 1997), p. 5.

subsist in the subject of the tragedy', Booth's Othello was, in fact, no darker than 'a pale cinnamon colour').[13]

In what almost constitutes a return to the performance of femininity by early modern boy-actors, Aldridge's insistence that his Desdemonas 'wear sandals and toed stockings to produce the effect of being undressed' furthermore brought to the fore his conception that naked femininity, no less than race, was something to be performed.[14] Even if the requirement for toed stockings was an effect of Victorian prudery rather than of a postmodern awareness of the subversive potential of the performance of gender, the distance between the female lead's 'white' skin and her white stockings, like that between Aldridge's 'black' hands and white face, suggested that neither gender nor race need be fixed, unperformable identities. Aldridge's theatrical practice highlights the fact that, in a play concerned with the race and sexuality of its protagonist, the race, gender and sexuality of the characters who surround him are also in the spotlight.

In spite of the racist charge of Gautier's description of Aldridge, the account itself and the questions Gautier poses put into question the normative nature of whiteness and the unperformable innateness of race and gender. Gautier does not see Aldridge's Lear as usurping the white actor's privilege or as a racist parody of whiteness, nor does he take offence at the stereotyping of the white old man as having silvery locks, a high forehead and an angular nose (or whatever non-curvy shape the wax fill-in managed to produce). Instead, Gautier accepts Aldridge's creation of 'all the illusion that was to be desired' as the precondition for the success of the performance: well over one hundred years before 'colour-blind' casting was introduced as a theatrical convention,[15] it would have been unthinkable for Aldridge to perform Lear without grease-paint and have Cordelia know that 'she had a Negro for a father'. Gautier's account is remarkably innocent both in its assumption that the performance of race can be devoid of political implications or the charge of racism and in its acceptance of the easy reciprocity between the blackened-up white actor and the whitened-up black actor. A century before Jude Kelly's 'photonegative' production of *Othello* in which white actor Patrick Stewart, using no darkening make-up, acted Othello opposite a cast of predominantly African American actors playing the Venetians, Aldridge's performance of Lear suggested that 'race – not simply Othello's race, but all racial identity – can be seen as a performance, a series of discursive positions potentially available to all

---

[13] Folger Prompt Othello 3, p. 121.   [14] Kendal, *Dramatic Opinions*, p. 29.
[15] For a discussion of the politics of 'colour-blind' casting, see Richard Schechner, 'Race Free, Gender Free, Body-Type Free, Age Free Casting,' *Drama Review* 33:1 (1989), 4–12.

regardless of birth, rather as gender theorists have already claimed about femininity and masculinity'.[16]

Aldridge's whitening-up and the surprising equanimity of Gautier's response to it invite questions about whether Gautier is right in seeing no fundamental difference between a white actor blacking-up to play Aaron or Othello and the black tragedian's whitening-up to play Lear. Arguably, both types of racial impersonation can be seen simply as means of allowing an actor to play the part of a character of a different racial type and are, therefore, equivalent. The argument falls apart, however, when we take into consideration the roles that require such a performance of race. A black actor claiming the right to act one of Shakespeare's most powerful tragic roles within a white culture implicitly lays claim to being recognised as no less cultured and capable of tragic feeling than his white colleagues. Lear is an unselfconsciously white part, concerned not with the protagonist's race but with the suffering caused by his warped relationship with his daughters. Aaron and Othello, on the other hand, are roles that are subject to racial and racist stereotyping within the plays and whose fates and actions are intricately bound up with their racial alterity. In both roles, Jacquelyn McLendon identifies 'a *pattern* of inscribing blacks as devilish, suggesting that Shakespeare himself could not move beyond racial clichés'.[17] A white actor blacking-up to play these roles, as a result, is almost inevitably racist in his performance of racial Otherness and in his suggestion that these characters' race, rather than the racist attitudes of Romans or Venetians towards them, is the reason for their savage outbreaks of violence. Charles Fechter's 1861 acting edition of *Othello* includes stage directions that suggest that Othello's unnameable 'cause' for the murder of Desdemona is his realisation that he is black: the soliloquy and murder seem prompted by Othello '*accidentally touch*[ing] *the glass* [a mirror dropped by the sleeping Desdemona] *in which he sees his bronzed face*'.[18] Aldridge whitening-up for Lear is getting ready to act an old king who happens to be white. Fechter blacking-up for Othello is getting ready to act a man who kills his wife *because* he is black (or rather, 'bronzed'). No marvel that, in response to the most famous blacked-up Othello of the twentieth century, that of Laurence Olivier, black actor Hugh Quarshie remembers 'being nudged by classmates

[16] Denise Albanese, 'Black and White, and Dread All Over: The Shakespeare Theater's "Photonegative" *Othello* and the Body of Desdemona', in Dympna Callaghan (ed.), *A Feminist Companion to Shakespeare* (Oxford: Blackwell, 2000), p. 227.

[17] Jacquelyn Y. McLendon, '"A Round Unvarnished Tale": (Mis)Reading *Othello* or African American Strategies of Dissent', in Mythili Kaul (ed.), *Othello: New Essays by Black Writers* (Washington DC: Howard University Press, 1997), p. 129 (her emphasis).

[18] *Charles Fechter's Acting Edition: Othello* (London: W. J. Golbourn, 1861). Folger Prompt Othello 6.

when he first appeared, in much the same way as they had nudged [him] when, on a trip to the zoo, the class had stopped by the monkey cage'.[19]

Invoked again and again in discussions of Othello's race, Olivier's performance of 1964–5 on stage and screen is the infamous key example of extreme racial stereotyping in a white actor blacking-up to play Othello. Prompted by T. S. Eliot's and F. R. Leavis's reading of a fundamentally flawed Othello to look for defects in the character, and encouraged by director John Dexter to look at Othello 'objectively' and see him as 'a pompous, word-spinning, arrogant black general',[20] Olivier not only carefully coloured his whole body black but also 'Othered' most aspects of his characterisation. Olivier's admiring biographer described the actor's approach to the role as follows:

he resolved to . . . draw not a romantic, dark-brown Arab but an uninhibited jet-black Moor, negroid in every movement and gesture and physical detail. He developed the easy, swinging lope of the African and such general looseness of the limbs that it seemed as though he had altered the very assembly of his joints. His make-up was shaped with the same meticulous care. Beginning with the feet, he covered himself from toe to head with a first coat of liquid stain, then a layer of make-up containing some grease which he polished all over with a chiffon cloth to give a fleshy sheen. The palms and soles and thickened lips were incarnadined, the fingernails varnished a pale blue transparent, and a black moustache and crinkly wig completed a self-transformation that took him two and a half hours before each performance and an additional forty-five minutes for the undoing.[21]

The huge cross around his neck which he tore off on vowing revenge created a clear symbolism of superficial civilised Christianity and civilisation underlain by savagery, while his inclination to sensuality was epitomised in the rose he carried with him for his first entrance. It is ironic and barely believable that Olivier later claimed that his choice to black-up as much as he did was meant to counteract the 'shocking case of pure snobbery' he saw in actors and directors who felt that 'the Moor could not be thought a truly *noble* Moor if he was too black and in too great a contrast to the noble whites'.[22] The film of the production bears witness to how severely the nobility of Olivier's Moor was circumscribed by his pride. A near-contemporary commentator, praising the 'realism' of Olivier's impersonation, described this 'African lion' as 'not only a black man, but a

[19] Hugh Quarshie, *Second Thoughts about* Othello, International Shakespeare Association Occasional Paper 7 (Chipping Campden: Cloud Hill Printers, 1999), p. 4.
[20] Kenneth Tynan, 'Olivier: The Actor and the Moor', in Kenneth Tynan (ed.), Othello: *The National Theatre Production* (New York: Stein and Day, 1967), p. 4. Note the way the adjective 'black' has slipped into this string of negative characterisations as the final defining insult.
[21] Cottrell, *Laurence Olivier*, p. 354.   [22] Olivier, *Confessions*, p. 252.

proud black man' full of 'animal pride'; a 'childlike', 'exotic and alien presence'.[23] Alan Seymour, who saw Olivier's Othello as 'a cheeky nigger who has sauntered in from Westbourne Park Road', admitted that this characterisation might appal some viewers, but concluded that it was 'made legitimate by a triumphant performance which has the courage of its director's and star's convictions' – as if a good performance could legitimise racism.[24] By way of contrast, black critic S. E. Ogude remained unimpressed by Olivier's alleged 'realism', referring to this performance as 'simply [a study] in monstrosity'.[25]

Should Othello therefore be played by a black man? Hugh Quarshie's paper for the International Shakespeare Association in 1999 is one of the most carefully thought through deliberations on the subject. The danger Quarshie senses in the role – and he could equally have spoken about Aaron, whom he played in the 1985 BBC Time-Life video of *Titus Andronicus* – is that 'if a black actor plays Othello . . . he . . . risk[s] making racial stereotypes seem legitimate and even true'.[26] This is certainly the effect Aldridge's performance (or the perceived lack of it) had on Gautier, who felt Aldridge was 'better in the role of the old king persecuted by his wicked daughters than in that of the Moor of Venice. There, he acted; in Othello, he was himself.' Whereas Gautier apparently had no difficulties accepting that a black man could play the role of a white man perfectly, he felt that 'no European can imitate' the 'nonchalant oriental attitude and this casualness of the Negro'.[27] Other witnesses of Aldridge's performances insisted on the apparent 'naturalness' of his ferocity. According to a Russian critic, the cries of Aldridge's Othello

emerged terribly, naturally savage; the howls and moans of a beast, feeling that he is wounded like a man, were genuine, leonine, animal cries . . . Not the Moscow Maly Theatre, but the African jungle should have been filled and resounded with voices at the cries of this black, powerful, howling flesh. But by the very fact that that flesh is so powerful – that it is genuinely black, so naturally *un–white* does it howl – that savage flesh did its fleshly work. It murdered and crushed the spirit . . . in place of the highest enjoyment, this blatant flesh introduced into art, this *natural* black Othello, pardon me, causes only . . . revulsion.[28]

[23] James E. Fisher, 'Olivier and the Realistic *Othello*', *Literature/Film Quarterly* 1 (1973), 325–7.

[24] Alan Seymour, 'A View from the Stalls', in Tynan (ed.), *Othello*, p. 13.

[25] S. E. Ogude, 'Literature and Racism: The Example of *Othello*', in Kaul (ed.), *Othello*, p. 163.

[26] Quarshie, *Second Thoughts*, p. 5. See also the reflections of Hugh Macrae Richmond, 'The Audience's Role in *Othello*', in Kolin (ed.), *Othello*, p. 96.

[27] Gautier, *Voyage en Russie*, pp. 156, 155; my translation.

[28] Letter to the editor, *Dyen*, 29 September 1862, quoted in Marshall and Stock, *Ira Aldridge*, pp. 265–6, emphases in the original.

It is because of this perceived 'natural' savagery of the black actor's performance and the spectators' unwillingness to dissociate actor from role,
skin colour from natural disposition towards violence, that stories began
to circulate and cartoons to be published suggesting that Aldridge was
prone to killing his Desdemonas. Some Russian female leads seem to have
paid credence to the rumours: the St Petersburg correspondent of *Le Nord*
reports that one 'poor Desdemona was seized with such a fright on seeing
the terrible expression on the face of the Moor that she jumped out of
bed and ran away screaming with real terror',[29] and another is said to have
been 'frightened to such a degree in the murder scene that the actor had to
whisper reassurance to her in Russian'.[30]

Whereas in textual reproductions of the play, whether in editions or
critical readings, the construction of race in *Othello* and *Titus* can be explained as a feature of their origin in an England engaged in early colonial
enterprises,[31] in performance, where commentary is commonly restricted
to the textual component of the programme, the black actor's physical presence runs the risk of naturalising violence as black. Speaking of *Othello*,
Paromita Chakravarti observes that 'While a white actor can be thought
able to represent Othello's blackness, a black or Asiatic actor is considered
capable only of demonstrating his own negritude, unable to go beyond
what is held to be the undeniable "reality" of his colour'.[32] Performance
runs the risk of locking the black actor into his skin colour through the
text's racism.

It is as a consequence of such a naturalisation of racial stereotyping that
Ogude argues that 'it is a travesty of Shakespeare for a "veritable negro" to
play the role of Othello. A black Othello is an obscenity. The element of
the grotesque is best achieved when a white man plays the role.'[33] Hugh
Quarshie, on the other hand, nevertheless concludes that 'black actors
should continue to play the role; the racist conventions have persisted for so
long precisely because not enough of us have played the role and challenged
the conventions'.[34] Quarshie suggests that these conventions can only be
challenged if we recognise *Othello* as a 'seriously flawed play' in terms of
its representation of blackness, a play that requires some 'judicious cutting
and textual emendation' in order to produce 'a version . . . which shifts

[29] *Le Nord*, 23 November 1858, quoted in Marshall and Stock, *Ira Aldridge*, p. 227.
[30] M. I. Belizary, *The Path of a Provincial Actress* (1938), quoted in Mortimer, *Speak of Me*, p. 71.
[31] See, for instance, Virginia Mason Vaughan's excellent contextualisation of *Titus* in 'The Construction
of Barbarism in *Titus Andronicus*', in Joyce Green MacDonald (ed.), *Race, Ethnicity and Power in
the Renaissance* (London: Associated University Presses, 1997), pp. 165–80.
[32] Paromita Chakravarti, 'Modernity, Post-Coloniality and *Othello*: The Case of *Saptapadi*', in Pascale
Aebischer, Edward J. Esche and Nigel Wheale (eds.), *Remaking Shakespeare*, p. 49.
[33] Ogude, 'Literature and Racism', p. 163.   [34] Quarshie, *Second Thoughts*, p. 20.

the focus away from race and onto character'. The protagonist would, as a consequence, be shown to '[behave] as he does because he is a black man responding to racism, not giving a pretext for it'.[35] The result would be a play that speaks to modern audiences about modern social structures, a play that would dissociate itself from its historical origins and engage with racial tensions in today's world. Such a play would, as Quarshie acknowledges, perhaps no longer be Shakespeare's, but it would take account of the fact that performance is an immediate medium that speaks about the past in the present tense. Adaptations and full-scale updatings of *Othello*, in fact, already have an established screen history, going from Basil Dearden's jazz-milieu *All Night Long* (1961) to the recent controversial American high-school drama *O* that tackles race in the context of drug abuse and youth violence (2001), and, in Britain, Andrew Davies's reworking of the plot to reflect post-Stephen Lawrence attitudes towards racial equality in the Metropolitan Police (*Othello*, 2001). However, the ideal which I believe Quarshie is striving for is a play in which race no longer matters because it is performed in a world in which racial slurs have become as obsolete as the jokes about cuckoldry that are routinely cut from productions without provoking any major outcries. The aim of such a strategy is that the name 'Othello' be no longer automatically associated with the murder of a white woman by a black man, regardless of the circumstances (as happened with the O. J. Simpson case).[36] The day 'Othello' is no longer associated with blackness, one hopes, neither will it be coupled with male violence. Like Victorian crime historian Luke Owen Pike's extraordinary invocation of the character in his narrative of a 'female Othello' who, as her husband 'lay one night asleep in his bed, . . . took him by the neck and strangled him',[37] we may all one day apply the name to anyone smothering her/his partner in bed, regardless of race or gender.

MOTIVELESS MALIGNITY IN BLACK, WHITE OR BLUE: SEVEN AARONS, EIGHT PRODUCTIONS, 1857–1999

Meanwhile, in a world still marked by what Denise Albanese calls the 'intransigent asymmetry of overtly raced positions',[38] productions of both

---

[35] Quarshie, *Second Thoughts*, pp. 18–21.

[36] For discussions of the perceived relationship between O. J. Simpson's alleged murder of Nicole Brown Simpson and *Othello*, see, for instance, Barbara Hodgdon, 'Race-ing *Othello*, Re-Engendering White-Out', in Boose and Burt (eds.), *Shakespeare, the Movie*, pp. 23–44, Edward Pechter, Othello *and Interpretive Traditions* (Iowa City: University of Iowa Press, 1999), pp. 1–2, and Cartmell, *Interpreting Shakespeare on Screen*, p. 76.

[37] Luke Owen Pike, *A History of Crime in England* (London: Smith Elder, 1876), vol. I, p. 256.

[38] Albanese, 'Black and White', p. 227.

Othello and *Titus Andronicus* are politically charged in ways that make of racial casting choices as well as performance choices and textual interventions crucial indicators of the wider cultural climate. But whereas the problem of the staging of race in productions of *Othello* (to which I will return later in this chapter) has received extensive critical attention, modern productions of *Titus Andronicus* have been discussed mainly in relation to their representation of the 'horrors', leaving the uncomfortable question of race aside.[39] *Titus*, however, may well be the better case study for the representation of race: because of the play's multiplicity of racial positions – its 'Othering' not only of the Moor but also of the Nordic Goths – the play allows for a wider spectrum of subject positions to be expressed than does *Othello*. Furthermore, the play's very stigmatisation as 'Shakespeare's worst', as, in T. S. Eliot's notoriously harsh words, 'one of the stupidest and most uninspired plays ever written',[40] has freed it more than most other Shakespearean dramas from the insistence, by textual purists, that it remain unemended in performance. When Peter Brook's 1955 production included a number of lines written by the director, not a single reviewer seems to have noticed the non-Shakespearean material, though many commended the 'judicious' textual cuts which, in any other play, would have been declared a butchery. This textual flexibility, compounded with the unfamiliarity of the play to many audience members and the multiplicity of racial positions available, makes *Titus Andronicus* an ideal site for productions that engage critically with the Shakespearean original, using it as a means of exploring race relations in the wider culture.

Once again, it is Ira Aldridge who provides a convenient starting-point with his (unfortunately lost) startling *tour-de-force* rewriting of the play. Rather than reflect the cultural climate he lived in, Aldridge's rewriting seems to have set the play in an ideal post-Abolition society that tolerates mixed marriages and acknowledges the potential nobility of black subjects. As the reviewer for the *Era*, in the best surviving account of the production, reported in 1857:

Aaron is elevated into a noble and lofty character. Tamora, the Queen of Scythia, is a chaste though decidedly strong-minded female, and her connection with the Moor appears to be of legitimate description; her sons Chiron and Demetrius are

---

[39] Notable – and noticeably recent – exceptions are the unpublished article by Edward J. Esche and Nigel Wheale, 'An Aaron for the Times' and Virginia Mason Vaughan's 'Looking at the "Other" in Julie Taymor's *Titus*', *Shakespeare Bulletin* 21 (2003), 71–80.

[40] Jeremy Kingston, 'Curtains for Shakespeare's Worst', *The Times*, 22 May 1997; T. S. Eliot, *Elizabethan Dramatists: Essays by T. S. Eliot* (London: Faber, 1968), p. 31.

dutiful children, obeying the behests of their mother and – what shall we call him? – their 'father-in-law'. Old Titus himself is a model of virtue and the only person whose sanguinary character is not toned down much is Saturninus the Emperor, who retains the impurity of the original throughout.[41]

The mind boggles. The adaptation hardly seems to represent the mid-Victorian attitude towards black men (he was unable to perform either in America or on the main London stages, though he did marry a white Englishwoman). Nonetheless, Edward Esche and Nigel Wheale propose that Aldridge's effective reinvention of Aaron as a vehicle for his self-representation as a respectable citizen does, to an extent, 'address the concerns of the actor playing the role at that time: the rewritten Aaron is a response to 1) the rise of the black minstrels, 2) Aldridge's private life and 3) anti-slavery and abolition in the United Kingdom and Europe'.[42] The first post-Enlightenment Aaron is thus a character who poses a political challenge to the status quo of race relations. In this recasting of his first tragedy, Shakespeare is invoked as a legitimising figurehead at the same time as his text undergoes radical revision.

For interpreters more reluctant than Aldridge to proceed to a wholesale rewriting of the play, the racial casting of Aaron and the performance's attitude towards the character are fraught with difficulties, as each decision carries heavy ideological implications. More than most other productions, Gregory Doran's 1995 staging of *Titus Andronicus* in South Africa deliberately raised expectations of a critical engagement with the immediate cultural surroundings of the production and especially with attitudes towards race, claiming that the production was 'localising the play by highlighting its themes of racial tension and cycles of violence'.[43] With hindsight, Doran's decision to put on this intrinsically racist play in post-Apartheid Johannesburg with black South African actor Sello Maake ka Ncube in the role of Aaron can be seen as a risky choice if it was to avoid an identification between hate-filled violence, sexual transgression and blackness in a culture that was only beginning to learn to dissociate an individual's personality and predisposition towards crime from her or his race. When, in 1970, Dieter Reible had directed *Titus Andronicus* at the Hofmeyr theatre (Cape Town) as a challenge to the Apartheid government's racial politics, he had significantly cast a white Afrikaans actor as Aaron, allowing for a reading of the part as a projection of racist stereotypes onto the black 'Other'. In 1970, Reible's critically acclaimed staging had thus apparently managed

---

[41] *Era*, 26 April 1857. Quoted by Marshall and Stock, *Ira Aldridge*, p. 172.
[42] Esche and Wheale, 'An Aaron'.   [43] Doran and Sher, *Woza Shakespeare!*, p. 179.

to 'interrogat[e] racist ideology and [confront] white audiences with the institutionalized violence which underpinned the apartheid system'.[44] In 1995, by way of contrast, seeking an explanation for 'why the South Africans stayed away in droves' from Doran's Johannesburg run, Charles Spencer observed that 'You would have to search long and hard to find a less appropriate play with which to celebrate the transformation of South Africa'.[45] In accordance with Quarshie's suggestions for a non-racist production of *Othello* with a black actor in the lead, the director might, for instance, have cut the racist insults along with Aaron's more offensive lines. Doran, however, chose the opposite tactic, retaining the racist abuse and giving his Aaron more lines. He also readjusted the final scene to give Aaron's defiance of Lucius greater prominence, so that Aaron's were almost the last words spoken in the production, his defiance being followed only by Marcus' transposed speech on the rehabilitation of the Roman body politic (5.3.66–71). Leaving no scope for reconciliation, Ncube's performance emphasised the intensity of Aaron's hatred. His Aaron refused to enter into Tamora's love-games in the wood and reserved his only moments of tenderness for his baby son.

Ultimately, if Aaron's evil was attenuated, this was not due to his characterisation as much as to the fact that no other character in this production could provoke much sympathy. Antony Sher's Titus, played as a self-aggrandising, fair-haired Afrikaner general, and Jennifer Woodburne's strikingly blonde, arrogant, upper-class Lavinia (modelled, as in Taymor's film, on the inaccessible icon of Grace Kelly) only seemed to acquire humanity once they had been maimed. The lengths dark-haired Sher and Woodburne had to go to in order to bleach their hair for their roles speak volumes about the perceived need to distance them from the unsympathetic characters they were portraying. Saturninus and Bassianus came across as equally undesirable power-hungry and emotionally unstable would-be fascist leaders. In the end, the only character with some engaging qualities was Tamora, played by the dark-haired white South African actor Dorothy Ann Gould, who seemed vulnerable at first and who was genuinely upset by the sacrifice of her eldest son.

If, in Tamora, the production briefly found a perpetrator of violence who was neither bleached nor blackened into an 'Other' – taking Sher in his natural colour and accent as the point of departure for the projection of

---

[44] Rohan Quince, *Shakespeare in South Africa: Stage Productions during the Apartheid Era*, Studies in Shakespeare 9 (New York: Peter Lang, 2000), pp. 34, 37.
[45] Charles Spencer, 'This Is so Bad, It Isn't Even Scary', *Daily Telegraph*, 14 July 1995.

evil onto 'Others'[46] – she, too, was progressively 'Othered' by the production. This was partly an effect of the directorial decision that Goths and Romans alike should speak with what one offended local reviewer termed 'offensively exaggerated South Effrican accents',[47] so that in this world of universal depravity, evil and violence were consistently associated with one of the cultural groups hosting the production. Mixed-race ('coloured') actors Oscar Petersen and Charlton George, 'compellingly repulsive as [Tamora's] vile and giggling sons',[48] played Chiron and Demetrius as mentally retarded vicious savages whose unalloyed evil reflected back on their mother. Remarkably, Doran's casting seems to have been prompted by his desire for 'precision':

> The play deals with issues of race and therefore we do need to be precise about the colour of actors we choose. Aaron has to be isolated in his blackness. Saturninus and Tamora have to be white, otherwise there would be no scandal when Tamora produces a black child (with Aaron). Nevertheless, since we know Tamora has a penchant for black men, her three other sons don't need to be white as well.[49]

It was Tamora's repeated choice of black sexual partners that gave a first indication of how deeply 'African' she was at heart, so that when she played Revenge as 'a muscular, erotic tiger, a sensational apparition in African tribal headdress',[50] Revenge was less a woman than an African, projecting her aggression onto racial 'Otherness' in a 'blackening' of violence that complemented what I earlier described as its 'masculinisation' in Lavinia's rejection of revenge. It is hardly surprising in view of these racially charged directorial choices that the production became popular only once it was transferred to Britain, where Doran and Sher could count on Sher's status as a prominent South African expatriate to make their interpretation accepted, 'in political terms, as a mirror of South Africa'.[51]

Doran's visual association of Tamora's fierceness with Aaron's blackness was, in fact, based on the playtext's association of these two alien creatures, who are both described as 'ravenous tiger[s]' (5.3.5, 194). If, as I have argued,

---

[46] How much Sher, in spite of his South African origins, had come to see his compatriots as 'Other' is evident from his description of the cast, in which he distances himself and Doran from their responses to violence: 'the South Africans are curiously unmoved . . . Having grown up with violence, they view it in a more cynical, less sentimental way than Greg and I.' This distancing is fully acknowledged towards the end of the book in Sher's diary entry: 'The country which I'm now thinking of as *mine*, and which I'm re-saluting with "tears of true joy" – and with this production – is England.' Doran and Sher, *Woza Shakespeare!*, pp. 91, 254.
[47] Digbi Ricci, 'Titus Topples into the "Relevant" Pit', *Mail & Guardian*, SA, 31 March 1995.
[48] Charles Spencer, 'This Is so Bad, It Isn't Even Scary'.
[49] Doran and Sher, *Woza Shakespeare!*, p. 42.
[50] Lynda Murdin, '*Titus Andronicus*', *Yorkshire Post*, 14 July 1995.
[51] Michael Billington, 'A Brutal Sort of Interrogation', *Guardian*, 14 July 1995.

the play's gendering of violence is female, its repeated racist tags associate it no less with racial difference.[52] The effect is a triangle of dangerous alterity that, in spite of the overt opposition of Romans and 'barbarians', links Lavinia to Tamora and Aaron. It is certainly telling that the playtext portrays all three characters as capable of dangerous or transgressive speech that must be stopped violently – both Tamora's and Aaron's punishments are, after all, oddly oral. Insofar as, in their association with unruly speech and the female gendering and black racialisation of violence, evil, social disorder and aggression are displaced from the 'norm' of Roman masculinity with its ritualised violence of warfare and sacrifices, this projection of evil stigmatises these gendered and racial 'Others'. But whereas the subversion of standard genderings of violence and victimisation can represent a welcome empowerment of female characters, the association of evil and aggression with blackness, rather than subverting stereotypes, only works to reinforce them. Female and black subjects, though linked in their common scapegoating, ought to be considered separately if we are to heed Jyotsna Singh's warning that 'contemporary, Western feminist engagements with race . . . in trying to chart the complexities of the relation between race and gender oppressions, implicitly *collapse* the categories of difference by assuming a common history of marginalisation'.[53]

Nevertheless, the twentieth-century performance history of *Titus*, like the playtext itself, quite consistently links Aaron to Tamora through their exotic costumes. What is particularly interesting about Peter Brook's treatment of the character of Aaron in 1955 is the unselfconsciousness of the production's approach and critical reception. Production photographs show Anthony Quayle with blacked-up face and hands, wearing a lavish orientalised costume (including huge earrings) that effectively distinguishes him from the more soberly clad Romans while linking him with Maxine Audley's bejewelled exotic Tamora.[54] This link seems to have been sustained

---

[52] See, for instance, Emily C. Bartels, 'Making More of the Moor: Aaron, Othello, and Renaissance Refashionings of Race', *Shakespeare Quarterly* 41 (1990), 433–54, Eldred Jones, 'Aaron', in Kolin (ed.), *Titus Andronicus*, pp. 147–56, and Francesca T. Royster, 'White-Limed Walls: Whiteness and Gothic Extremism in Shakespeare's *Titus Andronicus*', *Shakespeare Quarterly* 51 (2000), 433–55.
[53] Jyotsna Singh, 'Othello's Identity, Postcolonial Theory, and Contemporary African Rewritings of *Othello*', in Margo Hendricks and Patricia Parker (eds.), *Women, 'Race', and Writing in the Early Modern Period* (London and New York: Routledge, 1994), p. 291. The issue of white feminists' improper appropriation of the discussion of race and the danger of glossing over white women's historical oppression of black men and women has been raised by a number of authors. See, for instance, Jane Gaines, 'White Privilege and Looking Relations – Race and Gender in Feminist Film Theory', *Screen* 29:4 (1988), 12–27, and Alile Sharon Larkin, 'Black Women Film-Makers Defining Ourselves: Feminism in Our Own Voice', in Pribram (ed.), *Female Spectators*, pp. 157–73.
[54] See the illustrations in Jonathan Bate (ed.), *Titus Andronicus*, pp. 57 and 64; p. 57 for Aldridge's Aaron.

throughout, with Aaron's early speeches remaining uncut and the prompt-book indicating a fair amount of physical contact between the two characters, who could be seen clasping, embracing, kissing and clutching each other. The cut of Aaron's long boasting monologue about villainies unrelated to the Andronici (5.1.124–44) was, I suspect, due more to Brook's sense of economy than to a desire to reduce Aaron's guilt. This is apparent from the concluding moments of the play, where Brook cut all of Lucius' recapitulation of the preceding events and even edited out his farewell from his father. What remained were Marcus' speech promising a restoration of the body politic and Lucius' condemnation of Aaron and Tamora, putting the blame for the preceding violence squarely on their shoulders.

By 1985, when Jane Howell taped the play for television and a future classroom audience, the most elegant solution seems to have been to use a black actor for the part of Aaron and to upstage him with an extravagant portrayal of feminine evil in Eileen Atkins's more convincingly wicked Tamora. With her outrageous make-up, a scaly costume and asides hissed directly into the camera in close-ups, Atkins's Tamora is more alien than Hugh Quarshie's jovial Moor. It is hard to imagine how any Aaron could have been used as the main scapegoat for violence beside this 'punk queen in a shock of unruly red and orange hair with small ghouls braided into it . . . Her make-up is overdone . . . and she appears in a gown cinched with a corselet made of what looks like fish scales – a creature who has no doubt oozed from the slime. All of these details contribute to the savage, animalistic effects desired.'[55] Significantly, in this emphasis on the female gendering of violence in Tamora, the violent woman is turned into a classical monster, part-woman, part-animal, who cannot ultimately threaten Howell's representation of Lavinia as a passive victim. Howell's conceit of taping the whole film from young Lucius' point of view, seeing the plot as the boy's nightmare (a distancing device that was later to be adopted by directors Silviu Pucarete and Julie Taymor), allowed her to de-emphasise Aaron's villainy and stress the Andronici's own capacity for violence. Her choice to have Aaron's baby killed for the final scene is obviously designed to provoke audience pity (since it disturbs young Lucius as the on-screen representative of the audience) and unmask Lucius Andronicus' cruel hypocrisy. Violence in this video is consistently obscured by elliptic cutting and camera-work and portrayed as endemic to Roman culture no less than to the culture of

[55] Mary Z. Maher, 'Production Design in the BBC's *Titus Andronicus*', in J. C. Bulman and H. R. Coursen (eds.), *Shakespeare on Television: An Anthology of Essays and Reviews* (Hanover: University Press of New England, 1988), p. 147.

the barbarian Goths,[56] with Aaron somehow left out of the equation as a case apart.

Howell's take on Aaron probably provoked no comment because she had managed to sideline Aaron while casting a black actor. In this she took account of the widespread feeling that black actors should be cast in the few non-white parts in the Shakespeare canon – a feeling which, at the time, was not yet supported by the type of thoughtful evaluation of the appropriateness of such casting that Quarshie himself was to engage in for his 1999 lecture on *Othello*. It is surprising, at a time when black actors were increasingly fighting to be cast in mainstream plays on mainstream stages, that Deborah Warner's solution to the problem of Aaron did not provoke a greater controversy. Her casting of Peter Polycarpou, a white actor of Mediterranean type who was not wearing any darkening make-up, as the 'coal-black Moor' was incongruous in an otherwise meticulously thought-through production. It is probably due precisely to the touchiness of the issue of race in *Titus Andronicus* that reviewers did not pick up on the actor's incongruous skin colour, choosing instead to comment on his 'cheerfully bloodthirsty manner which takes some of the sting out of the mutilations and dismemberings'.[57] It remained up to the director herself to observe in retrospect 'that Aaron should have been "a black, black, black man"'.[58]

As it was, the unedited racist insults made little sense, and it was up to Estelle Kohler as Tamora to introduce an atmosphere of the exotic and bar-barous in Rome – Michael Billington described her as 'some indolently sexy necrophile greeting pleas for compassion with amoral bewilderment'.[59] It is noteworthy that whereas Polycarpou's Aaron seems to have remained very much the same throughout the run, Tamora and her sons grew stronger as the production moved from Stratford to London. For the Pit season (1988), Tamora's usurpation of the male gender role was marked in her cos-tume: whereas in the Swan (1987) she had worn a skirt, in London she was wearing bloomers which gave her more freedom of movement and allowed her to adopt an even more (sexually) assertive stance. In her dialogue with Aaron in the wood, his talk of vengeance and blood seemed to arouse her, making her more involved in the subsequent run-up to the rape of Lavinia.

[56] I cover Howell's attenuation of violence in detail in 'Cutting/Framing Violence: The BBC/Howell *Titus Andronicus* (1985)', in José Ramón Díaz Fernández and Sofía Muñoz (eds.), *Shakespeare on Screen: The Centenary Essays* (forthcoming).
[57] Irving Wardle, 'Shakespearian Horrors Transformed into Farce', *The Times*, 14 May 1987.
[58] Goy-Blanquet, 'Titus Resartus', p. 43.
[59] Michael Billington, 'Horror and Humanity', *Guardian*, 14 May 1987.

Nevertheless, the fact that there was no obvious racial difference between Romans, Goths and Moors, and that such a difference was not even marked through differences in costume, obscured Shakespeare's opposition of Romans and barbarians, providing no scapegoat (however much under-mined by the playtext's portrayal of violence as endemic to Rome itself) apart from Tamora on whom to blame the 'horrors' of the play.

Such a sidelining of Aaron may be elegant, but it also refuses to genuinely tackle the play's racist language and its exploration of the scapegoating of 'Others' for the violence that is common to Roman, Goth and Moor alike. This cannot be said of Silviu Pucarete's highly stylised take on the tragedy, in which the use of Romanian decidedly worked in the director's favour when the production toured Britain in 1997. With all the references to Aaron's blackness incomprehensible to the English audience, the use of a half-naked corpulent white actor (Ilie Gheorghe) with a face painted in blue and a head covered in a red swimming cap did not seem inappropriate. Blue face, nudity and fat came to replace black skin as signs of Otherness, removing all implications of racism from the production while retaining a clear sense of opposition between Rome and its enemies. Chiron and Demetrius, too, were half-naked and obese, 'played like identical, axe-wielding Sumo wrestlers, blubbery pony-tailed boors who pad about the stage in unison, farcically malevolent'.[60]

In this production that heavily cut the speaking part of Lavinia's role, the dangerousness of speech was associated mainly with Aaron, giving him yet greater prominence as the central figure of transgression that needed to be exterminated so as to enable a restoration of order in the state of Rome. Aaron's disruptive speech was stressed by the conclusion of the performance, which (like Warner's staging) sought to render the audi-ence complicit in the violence of the play. During the curtain call, Ilie Gheorghe was absent, replaced by the image of his face on a television screen. The reason for this became clear to the spectators only once they were leaving the auditorium: in the foyer Aaron, buried up to his neck under a brown plastic sheet, was jabbering in Romanian at the bewildered patrons, who carefully stayed as far away from him as they could. There was a deeply unsettling quality about having to walk past this talking head with-out being able to understand his words or pay attention to his meaning. The spectators were thus forcibly made to collude in Aaron's punishment, the staging doing them the violence of coercing them into contributing to this

---

[60] Jeremy Kingston, 'Curtains for Shakespeare's Worst'. Arguably, this production replaced racism with 'fattism', but in doing so it also revealed the arbitrariness of the stereotyping of 'Others'.

act of passive aggression. While Pucarete's strikingly imaginative solution to the problem of representing Aaron on the modern stage was possible only because of the language barrier (and even there, the English surtitles that spelt out the abuse of blackness blurred the effect), it was the closest any twentieth-century production in Britain had come to representing Aaron as unequivocally evil while avoiding the implication of racism and retaining a clear sense of cultural opposition and scapegoating of 'Otherness'.

In America, meanwhile, Julie Taymor's 1994 stage production had tackled the issue of the racial stereotyping from within a culture where casting a white actor in black- or blue-face would have struck audiences as racist discrimination against black actors. Her casting of African American actor Harry Lennix, on the other hand, brought with it the old danger of negative racial stereotyping and the naturalisation of personal evil as a racial characteristic – what Charles Lamb, speaking of *Othello*, called 'sink[ing] Othello's mind in his colour'.[61] Rather than evade the problematic implications of Aaron's portrayal within the playtext, Taymor and Lennix seem to have chosen to give full rein to Aaron's villainy, prompting one reviewer to declare that 'the absolute pinnacle of wickedness is occupied by Harry Lennix, as Aaron the Moor, which may be the most politically incorrect role in English literature. Aaron is an African-Italian Iago, who glories in declaring that Black is Bad.'[62] The key to the paradoxical success of this strategy – a success which is made obvious by Lennix's stunningly charismatic performance in the film that arose from this production – is to be found in Taymor's and Lennix's linking of Aaron's villainy not to his race, but to his Iago-esque 'motiveless malignity'. This allowed him to get out of the trap of skin colour and perform Aaron's evil with gusto as if he were acting Iago instead. Lennix explains in his DVD commentary to the film version:

> I think this is the first time in Western theatrical literature that a Moor appears . . . but he is extremely Machiavellian, so he [Shakespeare] doesn't make him stupid and evil, he just, he makes him extremely intelligent and evil, which is a great deal of fun. He's the first great Shakespearean villain, it just so happens that he is black as well.

As a result, Lennix's Aaron in Taymor's film is a mesmerising *performance* of evil, the intelligent choice of an individual aware of the depravity of the world he lives in. As Lennix puts it, 'the question isn't so much why does he

---

[61] Quoted and discussed in Ruth Cowhig, 'Actors, Black and Tawny, in the Role of Othello, – and Their Critics', *Theatre Research International* 4:2 (1978), 138.
[62] Thomas M. Disch, 'Late-Winter Night of Tragicomedy', *Daily News*, 14 March 1994.

do what he does but why not'. It is also, thanks to the 'Othering' strategies of the film's design, a *performance* of race that, combined with the 'very fervor of the self explanation of [Aaron's] villainous morbidity', makes 'the supposed reality of his ordained evil double back as pronounced make-believe, pretense or acting'.[63] Aaron's ritual facial scarification, half-shaved head and the peculiarly oriental cut of his suit could be seen as displaced, orientalist forms of racist stereotyping. Within the design world of Taymor's Rome, however, in which everybody is making 'fashion statements', these features can be read as a choice, on the part of the character, to indulge in ethnic 'chic'. In the end, Lennix's portrayal of the character's dignity and intelligence succeeds in resisting the Romans' attempts, in their racist comments, to collapse black skin and moral evil, highlighting Aaron's choice of evil – 'Aaron *will* have his soul black like his face' (3.1.205, emphasis added) – instead.

One of the most striking features of Taymor's conception of Aaron is the way his performance of villainy and Otherness is visually related to Jessica Lange's blonde Tamora (this is, to my knowledge, the only production in which the Mediterranean Romans are darker than the Nordic Goths).[64] In an expression of ethnic 'chic' similar to Aaron's, Lange's body is covered in snake-like tattoos, and her costumes, golden breastplate apart, are erotically charged crossovers between smart Italian tailoring and looser, more exotic elements. There is no sense, in this film, of any endeavour to cancel out either Aaron's villainy or female evil as personified by Tamora. Instead, Aaron is represented as an independent, mercilessly clever manipulator of both Romans and Goths, whose fates he views with utter detachment. Meanwhile, the camera-work, picking up on Shakespeare's attribution of almost all soliloquies and direct addresses to the audience to his Vice-figure, privileges Lennix's Aaron as it fetishises his muscular body and repeatedly grants him close-up direct addresses to the camera in which he can indulge in his sadistic but wickedly appealing sense of humour.[65]

In the film's portrayal of his relationship to his son, on the other hand, he emerges as a deeply human, sympathetic figure. Significantly, the father's address to his baby is not a display for the camera but a private address in

---

[63] Imtaz Habib, *Shakespeare and Race: Postcolonial Praxis in the Early Modern Period* (Lanham: University Press of America, 2000), p. 98.

[64] In a personal interview on 28 August 2001, Julie Taymor confirmed that her racial opposition of blond Goths versus dark-haired, southern European Romans was a deliberate choice. In this, she is the only director to have taken into account the fact that moral evil and 'Otherness' in *Titus Andronicus* are identified both with what Francesca T. Royster ('White-Limed Walls', *passim*) calls Aaron's 'ultrablack' and Tamora's 'ultrawhite' skins.

[65] Esche and Wheale, 'An Aaron'.

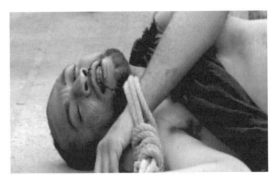

Illustration 10: Video-still of a close-up of Aaron (Harry Lennix) with bleeding
mouth in Julie Taymor's 1999 film *Titus*

which Aaron takes no account of his audience. The film, then, effects a turn-
around in the audience's sympathies: whereas, in the first half, Aaron's cold-
blooded planning of Lavinia's rape and dismemberment and his mutilation
of Titus' hand are fascinatingly repulsive, in the second half of the film his
victimisation at the hands of both Romans and Goths in Lucius' camp
transforms him into a sacrificial figure who is oddly reminiscent of Lavinia.
In fact, this film emphasises both characters' will to speak in the face of
danger, and links them through the visual rhyme of their bleeding mouths
when the infuriated Lucius finally strikes the bound and kneeling Aaron
across the face. 'In contradistinction to the grotesque racial impersonation
experienced by Shakespeare's original audience', Virginia Vaughan agrees
with me in seeing Lennix's Aaron as 'succeed[ing] in making the film's
audience identify with his point of view . . . Aaron is not the "other" he
was in Shakespeare's original, and the text's oppositions between good and
evil, civil and uncivil, moral and barbaric, which, to be sure, are to some
extent inverted in the play, are entirely imploded in the film.'[66] By the
end of the film, the iconic image of crucifixion portrays Aaron, and not
Lavinia or any of the Andronici, as the sacrificial victim over whose dead
body the commonweal can be restored: in the middle of the Coliseum,
the archetypal theatre of cruelty and ritual punishment, Aaron, with his
arms stretched out and tied to a beam, is slowly lowered into a hole in
the ground. At this crucial moment, Taymor explains, the spectators in the
Coliseum are 'Watching. They are silent. They are we.'[67] The audience's
silent endorsement of Lavinia's and Titus' revenges on the Goths is, at
the very end of Taymor's film, exposed as excessive when it includes the

[66] Vaughan, 'Looking at the "Other"'.   [67] Taymor, *Titus*, p. 185.

sacrificial starvation of the newly sympathetic Aaron. It is Aaron, and not Lavinia, who provides us with the film's last spectacle of obscenity – an obscenity not in Ogude's sense of a black man performing a grotesque portrait of his race, but in Lynda Nead's sense of an excessive image that assaults its viewers, disturbs them and motivates them into taking action.

THE SEMIOTICS OF RACE IN *OTHELLO*: LOOKING AT OR LOOKING TO?

By comparison with *Titus Andronicus'* crude racial stereotyping of Aaron, *Othello's* relatively sympathetic portrayal of its black hero has prompted a great deal of debate not only about his racial origins, but also about whether the tragedy is inescapably racist in its production of 'the black man as a violent "other"' or is 'court[ing] a racist impulse . . . only to explode any such response'.[68] Because Aaron is clearly a grotesque caricature, the association between skin colour and hate-filled violence in *Titus* can be shrugged off. This is the attitude evinced by Harry Lennix when he insists that Aaron's motivation has nothing to do with race and that his evil is a matter of choice. On the other hand, both he and Hugh Quarshie, as black Aaron-veterans, admit to having difficulties with the role of Othello. The problem lies in the fact that Othello's heroic status is increasingly undermined by the suggestion that there is no escape, for the black general, from the implications of his skin colour: in the end, Quarshie states, Othello 'behaves as he does because he's black'.[69] In his DVD commentary on Taymor's *Titus*, Lennix, who resents what he sees as Othello's stupidity, reports that during the filming he and Anthony Hopkins, who loves the part, ended up debating the (de)merits of the role for five hours.

Anthony Hopkins's attachment to the role of Othello may well have something to do with his performance of it in Jonathan Miller's BBC/Time-Life production of the tragedy in 1981. In accordance with the cultural context of the 1980s that was to result in Jane Howell's casting of Quarshie as Aaron in 1985, Miller initially cast African American actor James Earl Jones as Othello.[70] When British Equity barred this choice on account of Jones's nationality, Miller radically changed his attitude towards the play as a whole, arguing that 'the issue of colour has always struck [him] as

---

[68] Singh, 'Othello's Identity', p. 291, and Martin Orkin, 'Othello and the "Plain Face" of Racism', *Shakespeare Quarterly* 38 (1987), 176.

[69] Quarshie, *Second Thoughts*, p. 21.

[70] Mythili Kaul, 'Background: Black or Tawny? Stage Representations of Othello from 1604 to the Present', in Kaul (ed.), *Othello*, p. 19.

Illustration 11: Video-still of Othello (Anthony Hopkins), the codpiece, Othello's wife
(Penelope Wilton) and her servant (Rosemary Leach) in Jonathan Miller's 1981 BBC
video of *Othello*. Note the fact that Othello's face is as white as Desdemona's

an incidental feature of a play that sets envy against jealousy'. As a consequence, the video was focussed on 'restor[ing] the balance' between Iago
and Othello, with a strong Bob Hoskins as Iago opposite the Othello of
Anthony Hopkins, whom Miller saw as 'embody[ing] the exotic magnif-
icence of a foreign warrior, a Mediterranean magnifico who comes from
elsewhere'. Miller was to claim subsequently that he 'allowed the make-up
people to do too much' to Hopkins and that in a future production he
'would like to shave away the last remaining differences' between the Moor
and the Venetians.[71] I do wonder how much less work the make-up department could have done: Hopkins's Othello was a blue-eyed white man
with a bad need for a haircut and a suntan so slight that he was lighter-
skinned than Iago. Although the video retained many racist insults, race,
as in Warner's casting of Polycarpou for Aaron, was effectively sidelined.
It was so unimportant in the characterisation of Othello that there was no
ideological or racial obstacle in the way of Hopkins's impersonation of, and
emotional investment in, the doltish extravagant stranger who is duped
into killing his wife.

    As portrayed by Hopkins, Othello's violence is not a result of his racial
origin but rather of his violent phallic sexuality. His 'phallic sadism' is
symbolised by the lower part of his costume, aptly described by Lynda
Boose as an 'extraordinary pair of black trousers decorated with metallic
silver stripes that wind sinuously up his legs towards a huge silver codpiece

71 Jonathan Miller, *Subsequent Performances* (London and Boston: Faber and Faber, 1986), pp. 159, 147,
    159.

complete with leather thongs tipped with metal points'.[72] A walking erection, Othello is also characterised by his voyeurism, with the eavesdropping scene taped mainly from his point of view as he tries to see Iago and Cassio discussing Bianca at an angle and hear their barely audible conversation. In her thought-provoking analysis of the camera-work for this video, Boose concludes that Miller translates the play's 'strategy of withholding . . . into a film technique'. His camera, she argues, 'essentially situates its audience as Othello while it plays Iago, inviting and exacerbating voyeuristic desire by the deployment of designs meant to frustrate it'.[73] In the process, the viewer thus identified with Othello's subject position sees Desdemona as the elusive object of the camera's aggressively voyeuristic gaze. Her death, in keeping with this technique, is visible only as a reflection in a mirror, so that the video's implication of the viewer in the hero's voyeurism has the metaphorical and literal effect of diminishing Desdemona's stature at the end of the tragedy.

While Miller's approach to *Othello* can be interpreted as a 'cop-out' because it evades the play's investigation of racial tensions, the video's focus on intrusive gazing touches upon a feature that is crucial to the tragedy's representation of Othello's race. For Othello, like Aaron, is defined not only by the actor's real or fake skin colour (whatever its shade), but also by his own conception of his racial difference and by what the Venetians choose to see in his face. In Shakespeare's play race, rather than being intrinsic, is dependent on the gazes of the people who look at Othello. In the Duke's declaration that Brabantio's 'son-in-law is far more fair than black' (1.3.291), the signifier 'fair' is dislodged from the referent of Othello's skin – Othello can be as 'fair' as his wife, just as Desdemona's slandered name has the potential to be as 'begrimed and black / As [Othello's] own face' (3.3.390–1). Whereas throughout *Titus Andronicus* the semiotics of race are straightforward in their racist association of generic blackness with evil, in *Othello* the correspondence between skin colour and character is temporarily challenged. It is only in the second half of the play that Iago's racist and racialising view of Othello is shared by the protagonist, who consequently 'reverts to type: to wit, the speed with which his passion overrules his reason, the public assault on his white wife, the decision to assassinate his white best friend and murder his white wife with his bare black hands'.[74]

[72] Lynda E. Boose, 'Grossly Gaping Viewers and Jonathan Miller's *Othello*', in Boose and Burt (eds.), *Shakespeare, the Movie*, p. 190.
[73] Boose, 'Grossly Gaping Viewers', p. 195.   [74] Quarshie, *Second Thoughts*, p. 10.

The intrusive, suspicious, aggressive gaze that, in Miller's film, is linked
to Othello's phallic violence (his codpiece conceals the blade with which he
eventually stabs himself) and leads to the death of the lovers is also central to
Sergei Yutkevich's Russian film of *Othello*. Filmed in 1955, the year that saw
Anthony Quayle's exotic blacked-up Aaron in Britain, Yutkevich's Othello
is played just as unselfconsciously by blacked-up Sergei Bondarchuk. Even
more than Miller's video, this film is remarkable for its attention to the
fetishising, racialising and/or voyeuristic gazes of the characters. Following
a dumb show of Othello's courtship at Brabantio's house, the opening sequence shows Desdemona running to the window to watch her lover go
away, establishing her gaze as a look of love. She leaves the window and
walks to the globe Othello touched earlier, prompting a flashback sequence
in which we see, through her romanticising eyes, Othello's hardships,
enslavement and voyages as outlined in his narrative to the Senate. It could
not be made any clearer that this is the 'mind' Desdemona is in love with.
The final image of the flashback sequence, in which Othello stands proudly
in white robes at the helm of a ship, blends back into Desdemona's dreamy
gaze at the globe which now metonymically stands in for the journeying
Othello. Her loving gaze stands in contrast not only to the stern and disap-
proving looks of the senators in the subsequent confrontation (the camera
moves from one grim face to the next, ending up once again on Desdemona's gentle look at Othello), but also to the curious and malevolent
stares of the Venetians who fill the windows and assemble on the stairs
of Brabantio's house to enjoy his public disgrace. In another contrast to
Desdemona's gentle gaze, Iago's look at her is defined as voyeuristic and
sadistic in a powerful filmic metaphor of looking as a weapon when he
watches her conversation with Cassio in the reflection on his sword –
a piece of business powerful enough to have been 'quoted' by Kenneth
Branagh's Iago in Oliver Parker's 1995 film of *Othello*.

While Iago's spying, intrusive gaze is thus associated with sadistic cutting and the fragmentation of the object of contemplation, gazing is also
portrayed as potentially masochistic, as is evident in two parallel episodes.
In the first, Iago delivers his 'And what's he then that says I play the villain?'
monologue in voice-over (2.3.331–57) while looking at his own reflection
in the water of a well. The camera focuses on the reflection, which Iago
destroys by stirring the water at the end of the monologue. Looking at
himself leads Iago to an act of symbolic self-destruction. Othello's surren-
der to Iago's temptation here coincides with the moment when he himself
kneels down beside the well to look at his reflection in the water. This gaze
is obviously harmful to Othello, for, in a variation of Fechter's business

with the looking-glass, it accompanies the lines 'Ay, I am black, / And have not . . .' (3.3.267ff.). In their slightly altered form (Shakespeare's text reads '*Haply for* I am black . . .'), these lines make of Othello's newly acquired inquisitive gaze an introverted gaze that is directed at his own perceived racial inferiority.[75] The film's looking patterns come to a climax when, in the murder scene, we are treated to a quick succession of reverse-angle shots which make us see the killing alternately from Desdemona's and Othello's points of view. As a result, the viewer is involved in the murder as at once the owner of the outstretched hands that approach Desdemona's terrified face and the victim looking at her killer.

Yutkevich's film thus highlights the contrast between a loving gaze that accepts its object at its face value and an investigative gaze that is sadomasochistic in its effect and that seeks to see beyond the surface of things to a suspected hidden truth. What Yutkevich picks up on in these sequences is the connection in the playtexts (and especially the Folio text) between different types of gaze and the questioning of the integrity of the linguistic and theatrical sign. In fact, Shakespeare's first act is entirely dedicated to questions of evidence, the difference between being and seeming – a questioning of the sign that is encapsulated in Iago's declaration 'I am not what I am' (1.1.64), with which he defines himself as an actor playing a role. In its reversal of God's 'I am what I am' (Exodus, 3.14), Iago's declaration of hypocrisy becomes the *Leitmotiv* for the devilish semiotic disruption he instigates throughout the play.

For critics who work with neat binary oppositions – the conflict between Desdemona's love and Iago's hate,[76] Desdemona's 'divine principle' versus Iago's 'spirit of denial',[77] Iago as the centre of the 'anarchic forces' seeking 'the destruction in some form of the life principle of which she is the major embodiment'[78] – there is something troubling in the fact that of all the other characters in the play, it is Desdemona who most seems to share Iago's propensity for dissembling. She finds no harm in hiding her love from her father until she has secured Othello in marriage. On the Cypriot shore, she openly acknowledges the distance between her feelings and her actions when she declares: 'I am not merry, but I do beguile / The thing I am by seeming otherwise' (2.1.122–3). Friendship, to her, is

[75] See Peter S. Donaldson, *Shakespearean Films / Shakespearean Directors* (Boston: Unwin Hyman, 1990), pp. 95–6.
[76] Robert B. Heilman, 'Wit and Witchcraft: Thematic Form in *Othello*', in Susan Snyder (ed.), Othello: *Critical Essays* (London: Garland, 1988), p. 196.
[77] G. Wilson Knight, *The Wheel of Fire: Interpretations of Shakespearian Tragedy with Three New Essays* (London: Methuen, 1949), p. 114.
[78] Alvin Kernan, 'Barbarism and the City', in Snyder (ed.), *Othello*, pp. 206, 203.

something to be performed (3.3.21). Her later lie about the handkerchief has made her iniquitous in the eyes of some critics (it is one of the actions which convinced John Quincy Adams that she 'has her deserts'),[79] while others have either anxiously explained it away or ignored it altogether. Yet the lie is merely a way of avoiding an unpleasant situation. Her desire to avoid unpleasantness is also apparent when, at the beginning of the willow scene, she reminds Emilia that they 'must not now displease [Othello]' (4.3.15), even if this means dismissing Emilia against both their wills. Rather than asking us simply to distinguish evil deceitfulness (Iago) from good straightforwardness (Desdemona), the playtexts demand that we differentiate between hypocrisy whose aim is the destruction of social relationships and polite pretence which aims at constructing or maintaining such relationships.

It is in this context that we must see Othello's skin colour with its racist potential to denote fundamental Otherness and intrinsic evil – a potential fully acknowledged in the play's racial slurs.[80] The part in the other characters that is hidden because it is 'Too hideous to be shown' is made visible for the character of Othello in his skin colour (3.3.111). The divergence between Othello's actions at the outset and his 'blackness' is accepted by everyone as a social grace. At the beginning of the tragedy, he is allowed to define himself not so much through the colour of his skin as through his exotic past, his 'services', his 'parts', 'title' and 'perfect soul' (1.2.18, 31) – the aspects of himself that are highlighted in the flashback at the beginning of Yutkevich's film and that are identified with Desdemona's gaze of love. The Venetians are glad to accept a 'seeming' which promotes social ease – a general who was not 'far more fair than black' would be of no use to them (1.3.291). I am suggesting that in the figure of Othello, the play reverses the normal relation between interior and exterior: Othello's 'mind' is what he presents himself to be in his social relations, and is therefore the surface or façade that hides his 'underlying' blackness.

Othello hence portrays the smooth functioning of society as contingent upon the acceptance of outward show and the respect of the privacy of

[79] As quoted in Marvin Rosenberg, *The Masks of Othello: The Search for the Identity of Othello, Iago, and Desdemona by Three Centuries of Actors and Critics* (Berkeley and Los Angeles: University of California Press, 1961), p. 208.
[80] See especially the discussions of Othello's race by G. K. Hunter, *Othello and Colour Prejudice* (London: Oxford University Press, 1967), Anthony Gerard Barthelemy, *Black Face Maligned Race: The Representation of Blacks in English Drama from Shakespeare to Southerne* (Baton Rouge: Louisiana State University Press, 1987), Karen Newman, '"And Wash the Ethiop White": Femininity and the Monstrous in *Othello*', in Jean E. Howard and Marion F. O'Connor (eds.), *Shakespeare Reproduced: The Text in History and Ideology* (London: Routledge, 1987), pp. 143–62, and Virginia Mason Vaughan, *Othello: A Contextual History* (Cambridge: Cambridge University Press, 1994), pp. 51–70.

innermost feelings and thoughts – a respect, Iago himself points out, which is commonly granted even to slaves (3.3.138). Iago's means of disrupting social relationships, accordingly, is to assert that 'Men should be what they seem' (3.3.129) and imply that divergence between being and seeming is necessarily a sign of evil, as it certainly is in him. His perverted 'honesty', therefore, consists in revealing his thoughts to Othello – thoughts which Othello rightly supposes to be a 'monster . . . Too hideous to be shown' (3.3.110–11). Iago, then, opens up to Othello what Michael Neill, invoking the emergence of anatomical investigations in the sixteenth century, calls a 'new discourse of interiority', a discourse which seeks for hidden/hideous meanings beyond surface appearance.[81]

Such a desire to see beyond the surface of things to their 'true' nature is legitimate if directed towards the 'general enemy Ottoman' and the first Senator is wholly justified in distrusting the Turks' 'false gaze' (1.3.50, 20). When directed at persons within the same society, however, the playtexts portray such inquisitive looking as disastrous. Iago's inquisitive gaze is necessarily catastrophic for Othello, in whom it focuses on the blackness of his skin and the association of racial inferiority, to the detriment of the fairness of his deeds and mind. Desdemona's loving look at Othello is precisely a gaze that refuses to look for his blackness and instead focuses on the actions he recounted to her in his narratives. In her speech to the Senate, the visage she sees in Othello's 'mind' is related to his 'quality', his 'honours' and his 'valiant parts' (1.3.252–4), hence his social behaviour. By way of contrast, Iago's inquisitive gazing at Othello, which provokes Othello's own inquisitive introspection, inevitably leads to an effacement of Othello's fair self-presentation in his social interactions to reveal his intrinsic 'blackness' (in the racist usage of the word). At the end of the play, it is his behaviour that is revealed as 'begrimed and black / As [his] own face' (3.3.390–1). Othello eventually comes to see his self as distinct from 'Othello, that [was] once so good' (5.2.288) when he answers Lodovico's summons with: 'That's he that was Othello? here I am' (5.2.281) and kills his 'black' self as the 'circumcised dog' of his suicide speech (5.2.353).[82]

---

[81] Michael Neill, *Issues of Death*, p. 159. In 'Unproper Beds: Race, Adultery, and the Hideous in *Othello*', *Shakespeare Quarterly* 40 (1989), 383–412, Neill explains that the 'wordplay here . . . amounts to a kind of desperate iteration: what is *hide*ous is what should be kept *hidden*, out of sight. "Hideous" in this sense is virtually an Anglo-Saxon equivalent for the Latinate "obscene"' (394).

[82] For readings of Othello's suicide as 'civilization's last victory over the Turk' (Vaughan, *Contextual History*, p. 34), see also Rowland Wymer, *Suicide and Despair in the Jacobean Drama* (New York: St Martin's Press, 1986), pp. 86–95, and Derek Cohen, *The Politics of Shakespeare* (New York: St Martin's Press, 1993), pp. 13–14.

The playtexts, then, like Yutkevich's film, present two alternative ways of looking. The way of looking associated with Desdemona, with Cassio and initially also with Othello is summed up in Iago's comment that Othello 'hath devoted and given up himself to the contemplation, mark and denotement of [Desdemona's] parts and graces' (2.3.311–13). It is a way of looking which is concordant with being bounteous to the mind and self-presentation of the person contemplated. To this 'looking *at*', the play, through the figures of Brabantio and Iago, opposes 'looking *to*'. In Brabantio's and Iago's injunctions to Othello to 'look to' Desdemona (1.3.294; 3.3.200), 'looking *to*' becomes synonymous with looking *for* the hidden defect which, it is presumed, is inevitably there, waiting to be uncovered. The verbs of seeing associated with this inquisitive gaze are Iago's verbs 'observe', 'scan', 'perceive', 'note' (3.3.200, 249, 253, 254), all of which seek to go beyond the surface of their object to find its latent meaning. It is these inquisitive eyes that Iago teaches Othello to 'wear' in order to destroy both him and Desdemona (3.3.201). For 'looking *to*', as illustrated by the sadomasochistic looking patterns in Yutkevich's film and as Othello comes to realise when he reflects 'I saw 't not, thought it not, it harmed not me' (3.3.342), is injurious not only to the object but also to the wielder of the gaze. 'Looking *to*' is the look of jealousy, the look of the 'green-eyed monster' which turns back on its wielder, thus 'mock[ing] / The meat it feeds on' (3.3.168–9).

'Looking *to*', as defined by Brabantio and horribly apparent in Othello's murder of Desdemona, presupposes an underlying guilt in its object and is punitive in its project. Brabantio, if he had other children, would look to them and, certain of their deceitfulness, would 'hang clogs on them' (1.3.199). The same notion, linking the bearer of this look to punitive authority, underlies Othello's injunction to Cassio to 'look to the guard' (2.3.1). Authoritative and punitive, 'looking *to*' is furthermore associated with a perverse kind of pleasure, linking, as the erection suggested by Hopkins's codpiece implies, the voyeuristic look to sexual arousal. For although Othello complains that seeing in this way harms him, he keeps asking for more 'ocular proof' so that he may be 'satisfied' (3.3.363, 393). And lest we forget that this last term can have both a martial and a sexual meaning, Iago picks up on the ambiguity in Othello's words to unmask the sexual satisfaction which is intrinsic in the punitive look: 'how satisfied, my lord? / Would you, the supervisor, grossly gape on? / Behold her topped?' (3.3.397–9).

The gaze of the voyeur, as defined by Laura Mulvey, 'has associations with sadism: pleasure lies in ascertaining guilt . . . , asserting control and subjugating the guilty person through punishment or forgiveness'.[83] In *Othello*, the voyeur's desire to see the unseen and unseeable is linked to the wish to listen for what is not said and cannot be said, both because Desdemona's supposed deed is as unnameable as is Lavinia's rape in *Titus Andronicus* (4.2.75–81, 163–4, 5.2.2) and because language is represented as profoundly unstable and unreliable. Whereas, as I suggested in the last chapter, *Titus Andronicus* and *Hamlet* portray Lavinia and the Ghost as incomplete signs, in *Othello* it is Iago who presents himself as an incomplete sign in need of interpretation. Or rather, to be more precise, in his quality of en*sign*, Iago 'is not only a bearer of signs by nominal profession, but himself a "sign" by titular designation'.[84] He becomes the embodiment of the free-floating signifiers which he makes use of so abundantly. As James Calderwood observes, Iago's insinuations, 'Unanchored either to referents or to signifieds, . . . float free',[85] forcing Othello to infer/invent signified and referent so as to stop the painfully endless stream of possible interpretations. Iago's unanchored speech is violent, a 'pestilence' poured into Othello's ear (2.3.351). And since Iago's skill lies as much in uttering detached signifiers as in making Othello believe that Desdemona herself is such a detached signifier, the only way Othello can achieve semiotic fixture is by killing Desdemona.

STRIVING DESDEMONA: SACRIFICE OR MURDER?

Othello's soliloquy as he enters the bedchamber describes Desdemona as a white, smooth, translucent surface which he is afraid to pierce. His reluctance to break through that surface and shed her blood is a sudden unwillingness to assume the full implications of his voyeuristic gaze, trying to fetishise Desdemona's body at the very moment at which he is punishing it. But the sadistic voyeurism of 'looking to' prevails in his assumption of the authoritatively punitive role of 'Justice' who determines that the 'fatal' woman 'must die, else she'll betray more men' (5.2.17, 20, 6). Her death, Othello seems to believe, will mean the end of betrayal and semiotic uncertainty – hence his insistence on the definitiveness of the act, which is a relief in its irreversibility. It is only once Desdemona is dead that he will be sure of her, only once she is dead that he will be able to exchange

---

[83] Mulvey, *Visual and Other Pleasures*, pp. 21–2.
[84] David Lucking, 'Putting out the Light: Semantic Indeterminacy and the Deconstitution of Self in *Othello*', *English Studies* 75 (1994), 113.
[85] Calderwood, *Shakespearean Metadrama*, p. 61.

'looking *to*' for fetishising, loving, 'looking *at*': 'Be thus when thou art dead and I will kill thee / And love thee after' (5.2.18–19).

But Desdemona awakes, and that awakening plunges Othello back into his nightmare world of concealed meanings. By being alive and speaking, she disrupts his necrophilic dream of semiotic fixture in which he could safely label her 'whore', thus justifying his 'sacrifice'. Desdemona refuses to give him this satisfaction and fights to redefine his 'sacrifice' as a 'murder' (5.2.64–5). To the predetermined meanings he has fixed onto all the signifiers (so that, whatever she says, she is a whore), Desdemona opposes vehement denials and a request for Cassio's testimony. She thus reasserts language as a system in which signifiers *can* have straightforward referents, valuing personal testimony over and above inference, 'looking *at*' over 'looking *to*'. Her last minutes are spent in an attempt to clarify Othello's meanings, to mend what Lawrence Danson has described as 'a split between rival semantic systems' and ensure that she and Othello are speaking the same language.[86]

The scene is most remarkable for Desdemona's sheer resilience and what some commentators have obviously found her exasperating will to speak out against all odds. Thomas Rymer is famous for declaring in 1693 that 'We may learn here that a Woman never loses her Tongue, even tho' after she is stifl'd'.[87] Even Henry Jackson's account of a production in 1610 (the first eyewitness-report of a performance to have survived) betrays the author's annoyance at Desdemona's pleading and his relief once she is unequivocally dead: 'But truly the celebrated Desdemona, slain in our presence by her husband, although she pleaded her case very effectively throughout, yet moved [us] more after she was dead, when, lying on her bed, she entreated the pity of the spectators by her very countenance'[88] – an uncanny echo of Othello's necrophilic promise to love Desdemona 'after'. Unlike Charlotte Vandenhoff's sacrificial Desdemona of 1851, who was described by a delighted reviewer as 'sad, fearful, yet gentle as a bruised dove' when she 'ben[t] meekly to the implacable jealousy of the swart Othello, and receive[d] her death, while kissing the hand which [gave] it',[89]

---

[86] Lawrence Danson, *Tragic Alphabet: Shakespeare's Drama of Language* (New Haven: Yale University Press, 1974), p. 117.

[87] Thomas Rymer, 'From *A Short View of Tragedy* (1693)', in John Wain (ed.), *Shakespeare: Othello: A Casebook* (London: Macmillan, 1994), p. 45.

[88] Translation quoted in Callaghan, *Woman and Gender*, p. 90.

[89] *Tallis's Dramatic Magazine*, April 1851, 168; quoted in Carol Jones Carlisle, *Shakespeare from the Greenroom: Actors' Criticisms of Four Major Tragedies* (Chapel Hill: University of North Carolina Press, 1969), p. 244.

the playtexts portray a Desdemona fighting for her life. Till the end she protests, interrupting Othello, pleading desperately. Whether he '*smothers*' or '*stifles*' her (SD Q versus SD F), what both terms connote is a silencing, a forceful suppression of utterance.

But Desdemona has insisted throughout on having the last word and does so again. She moves or makes a noise (there is no stage direction), or possibly Othello simply mistakes Emilia's voice for Desdemona's, his wife's 'O Lord! Lord! Lord!' blending into Emilia's 'My lord, my lord!' (5.2.83–4). Whatever Shakespeare meant to happen at this point, it is evident that Othello makes a second effort at killing her, in the belief that to do so is a sign of mercy (5.2.86). And again, the killing is left incomplete, for Desdemona revives once more twenty-two lines later and makes a last effort at imposing her own meaning on her death: 'O falsely, falsely murdered!' (5.2.115), 'A guiltless death I die' (5.2.21) – a denunciation of the murder by a victim suspended between life and death that is all too reminiscent of *Hamlet*'s Ghost, evoking the possibility that the last act of *Othello* may become the first act of a revenge tragedy. There is certainly no scope, in the scene as scripted in the Quarto and Folio texts, for readings like René Girard's, who believes the murder 'fulfills [Desdemona's] most secret expectation', Leslie Fiedler's conception that it plays on 'the female dream of patient suffering rewarded', or André Green's assertion that Desdemona 'finds pleasure in her husband's abuse'.[90]

Desdemona, in her death scene, is a greater threat to Othello's supreme control than Rymer's annoying woman who simply won't shut up and/or die, for in her very last words she assumes the traditional role of the male tragic hero in her request for Emilia's posthumous vindication, upstaging Othello with her own 'cause'. My privileging of her murder over Othello's suicide in the present discussion is a conscious move on my part to follow Desdemona's prompt and resist Othello's and his academic backers' attempt to define the murder as a sacrifice and excuse it as an act done 'all in honour' (5.2.292). Indeed, Desdemona's richly ambiguous and much dis- cussed last words 'Nobody. I myself. Farewell. / Commend me to my kind lord – O, farewell!' (5.2.122–3) in their ambiguity and contradiction ('nobody' is different from 'I myself') allow me to follow Christine Gledhill's invitation to engage in 'negotiated readings' and deliberately '[exploit]

---

[90] René Girard, *A Theater of Envy: William Shakespeare* (Oxford: Oxford University Press, 1991), p. 293, Leslie A. Fiedler, *The Stranger in Shakespeare* (St Albans: Paladin, 1974), p. 124, André Green, *The Tragic Effect: The Oedipus Complex in Tragedy*, trans. Alan Sheridan (Cambridge: Cambridge University Press, 1979), p. 107.

textual contradiction to put into circulation readings that draw the text into a female and/or feminist orbit'.[91] I want to suggest that the injunction to commend her to her kind lord could be glossed sarcastically as 'defend my cause before my husband by law', with readings of the words 'commend', 'kind' and 'lord' which were all available in early modern English (*OED*).[92] This interpretation, which runs counter to the more common interpretation which vindicates Othello rather than Desdemona, is made possible by Desdemona's earlier use of the same type of sarcastic language, when after her mistreatment in the 'brothel' scene she stated "'Tis meet I should be used so, very meet' (4.2.109). In death as in life, Desdemona can be seen as an equivocal sign, open to voyeuristic inquiry (putting the critic in the position of Iago and murderous Othello) at the very time at which she is advocating non-inquisitive 'looking *at*'.

FROM WELLES TO PARKER: HOW TO KILL DESDEMONA IN A POLITICALLY (IN)CORRECT WAY

As in the urban myth surrounding Ira Aldridge, who was shown in a Russian cartoon arguing that if he killed his Desdemona he should just be given 'another Desdemona better than this one',[93] Orson Welles, who filmed the tragedy between 1949 and 1952 on a shoestring budget, seems to have based his interpretation on the opposition of a static, monolithic Othello (Welles himself) and Desdemona as the 'fair paper . . . / Made to write "whore" upon' (4.2.72–3). Under his direction, Othello, in Welles's words, is 'monumentally male and his story is monumentally a male tragedy',[94] whereas Desdemona is a blank space that is filled with three different, apparently interchangeable actors.[95] True to Shakespeare's representation of her as an equivocal sign, Welles's Desdemona is subject to voyeuristic inquiry and sadistic erasure, her part radically cut to accommodate a magnified Othello who remains heroic to the very end. With Welles's status as both director and star unmistakably shaping the film's conception of the central characters, Othello cannot but be a light-skinned man whose murder of his wife must seem somewhat justified. 'Othello's blackness', Peter Donaldson

---

[91] Gledhill, 'Pleasurable Negotiations', p. 75.
[92] See also Julia Genster's suggestion that Desdemona's last words are 'not an act of submission but a challenge'. 'Lieutenancy, Standing in, and *Othello*', *English Literary History* 57 (1990), 804.
[93] Marshall and Stock, *Ira Aldridge*, pp. 232–3.
[94] Orson Welles, quoted in Howlett, *Framing Shakespeare*, p. 57.
[95] See Vaughan, *Contextual History*, pp. 204–6, where Vaughan gives an example of Welles's attempt to erase his Desdemona that complements the present analysis.

observes, 'does not count for much in Welles . . . He is played as very light-complexioned, not at all rude or exotic in speech or manner, and little emphasis is given to lines that evoke his strangeness or cultural alterity.'⁹⁶ Instead of acting the 'Other', the actor-director Welles seems to identify Othello's point of view with himself. The 'Other', here, is not the alien Moor but platinum-blonde Desdemona as the icon of treacherous, unapproachable femininity.

Just as Welles can be seen to overidentify himself with Othello, his Iago, Micheál MacLiammóir, in his published diary of the filming process, takes his role beyond the world of the play and does his best to tarnish the film's principal Desdemona, Suzanne Cloutier (nicknamed 'Schnucks') in the eyes of his readers. His hero Welles, on the other hand, is portrayed as a man stretched beyond his patience. Faced with 'Schnucks the Indestructible, the admirable, maddening, solemn-eyed, bilingual Schnucks, a terror among the Desdemonas of the world', MacLiammóir evinces no surprise that 'Orson is planning to save the strangling scene till the very last for, as he says, the public will undoubtedly want to see her all through the picture as Brabantio's daughter, and who knows, honey, he continues, rolling his ominously patient eyes over her small and exquisite throat, what may happen by the time the murder is due?'⁹⁷ The joke, in view of the apparent recurrent tensions on the set as Welles seems to have bullied Cloutier into tears, is not entirely funny. Nor is the fact that real-life violence, betrayal and erasure seem to have gone into the slapping scene, in which the camera adopts Othello's sadistic/voyeuristic point of view to literally wipe Desdemona out of the frame:

This planned by Orson with . . . Othello out of camera but long shot of Desdemona slowly approaching camera for the lines:

DES. Trust me, I am glad on't.
OTH. (*out of camera*). Indeed!
DES. My Lord?
OTH. (*still out of camera*). I am glad to see you mad.
DES. Why, sweet Othello!
OTH. (*still out*). Devil!

Des. by this time is in Big Head of Pola; black hand of Othello suddenly strikes her across the face. Cut.
Poor old Schnucks did it countless times, moving beautifully . . . towards the camera, but once Big Head of Pola obtained could not prevent herself flinching

⁹⁶ Donaldson, *Shakespearean Films*, p. 118.
⁹⁷ Micheál MacLiammóir, *Put Money in Thy Purse: The Making of* Othello (London: Virgin, 1994), p. 141.

before black hand of Othello appeared, thus ruining the shot. Her lovely face went slowly numb under this treatment and its constant repetitions, her make-up repaired and repaired again by Vasco. Hours wore by, we all wilted . . . Schnucks did it again. Flinched. Again. Flinched. And again and again. And at last Orson, his face (unmade-up) now pale green and hanging in festoons, his hand in its Renaissance sleeve blacker than ever, said 'O.K., Schnucks, you can't do it. So here's what's going to happen. You just do it once more and I'm not going to strike you, see, we're going to cut on your line on your last "Why, sweet Othello!" and we'll take the blow in the face in another shot and we'll make that to-morrow when you feel fresh . . .'

So off we went again, and Schnucks, reassured and radiant, sailed into her close-up, no sign of a flinch, and got the best puck in the face you ever saw and 'Cut!' says Orson, and it was all over. 'Perfect. Thank you, Schnucks.'[98]

Not only in this scene, but throughout the entire film, Welles's camera-work alternates between a fetishising look (the radiant, sailing Desdemona of MacLiammóir's diary entry) that transforms her into an icon, 'the object of the male gaze . . . characteristic of classical narrative cinema', and a sado-voyeuristic point of view that seeks to fragment, diminish or erase the female body.[99]

Voyeuristic inquisitiveness and punitive erasure of the female body come to a climax in the film's murder scene. The scene, with its 'racial scandal'[100] of a black man murdering a white woman and its sado-erotic 'revel[ling] in the sheer brutality of the killing of Desdemona, giving detailed attention to the abuse, the mental and physical suffering, and the rough, violent conclusion',[101] is a test-case for any production's attitude towards race, gender and violence. Although the playtexts are unequivocal in calling for the murder to happen in full view of the audience, from the Restoration up to the end of the nineteenth century the killing of Desdemona was almost invariably hidden behind the bed-curtains.[102] For centuries, in fact, the whole last act was the object of numerous revisions in both playtexts and

---

[98] MacLiammóir, *Making of* Othello, pp. 153–4.
[99] Barbara Hodgdon: 'Kiss Me Deadly; or, The Des/Demonized Spectacle', in Virginia Mason Vaughan and Kent Cartwright (eds.), Othello: *New Perspectives* (London and Toronto: Associated University Presses, 1991), p. 222. For an analysis of the voyeuristic gaze of Welles's camera, see Kathy M. Howlett's chapter 'The Voyeuristic Pleasures of Perversion: Orson Welles's *Othello*', in her *Framing Shakespeare*.
[100] Neill, 'Unproper Beds', 391. How great this 'racial scandal' is even today is evident in Julie Burchill's observations on the taboo, in mainstream Hollywood cinema, against the representation of sexual encounters between black men and white women. See Julie Burchill, 'Too Hot to Handle', *Guardian Weekend*, 6 July 2002.
[101] Derek Cohen, *Shakespeare's Culture of Violence* (New York: St Martin's Press, 1993), p. 124; see also Pechter's chapter 'Death without Transfiguration', in his *Othello*, pp. 141–67.
[102] Julie Hankey (ed.), *Othello*, by William Shakespeare, Plays in Performance (Bristol: Bristol Classical Press, 1987), p. 316.

stagings, the most notorious being Talma's temporary introduction of a happy ending, with Desdemona's father rushing in at the last minute to save his daughter.[103] These revisions all sought the same effects: a toning down of the eroticism and brutality of the murder and a carefully stage-managed upstaging of Desdemona by Othello. Both these goals are as much the result of the decorum demanded by the audiences as a side-effect of the theatre's star-system in which the actor-manager concentrated his efforts in the last scene at directing the gaze away from the spectacle of the dying/dead woman onto himself as the star, making Othello 'the suffering victim of necessity and his own noble nature'.[104] Ignoring Desdemona's vocal and physical objections, Edwin Booth is representative of most of his male colleagues in being firm in his priorities in the murder scene: 'it is of more importance that Othello's face should be seen than Desdemona's dead body'.[105]

Welles's endorsement of the theatrical tradition that seeks to exonerate Othello in the last scene and give him a heroic death on which the play ends is obvious from the fact that he makes his Desdemona guilty of one last damning falsehood: she is only pretending to be asleep when Othello comes in to kill her. The relationship between voyeuristic looking and killing is foregrounded at two points during the murder: the first when Othello opens the curtain to discover Desdemona's body, the second in the act of killing itself, where he pulls a gauze over her face, thus impeding her sight, while his own crazed eyes move closer to her face until he covers her mouth with his, kissing/suffocating her till she is dead. In her incisive analysis of the film, Barbara Hodgdon describes how Desdemona's 'body, increasingly fractured and dis-membered by montage . . . is finally reduced to metonymical representations'. This contrasts with Welles's conception of Othello, who 'is represented, first, only as a massive shadow, a sign of encroaching darkness which then resolves to a seemingly disembodied face and gradually gains three-dimensionality as he moves forward in the shot until, finally, just before the murder, he becomes a grotesque single eye'. The sequence, Hodgdon concludes, 'represents the murder itself as a violation of sight'.[106]

The slowness of the killing, its explicit eroticisation and Desdemona's panic-stricken collaboration in the last instants turn what began as a typical

---

[103] Rosenberg, *Masks of Othello*, p. 32.
[104] James R. Siemon, '"Nay, That's Not Next": *Othello*, v.ii in Performance, 1760–1900', *Shakespeare Quarterly* 37 (1986), 47.
[105] Quoted in Horace Howard Furness (ed.), *Othello*, by William Shakespeare, vol. vi of *A New Variorum Edition of Shakespeare*, 27 vols. (Philadelphia: J. B. Lippincott Company, 1886), p. 292.
[106] Hodgdon, 'Kiss Me Deadly', p. 226.

Illustration 12: Video-still of Desdemona's (Suzanne Cloutier's) eyes as the gauze is pulled over her face in a literal erasure of her eyesight in Orson Welles's 1949–52 film of *Othello*

horror-film scenario (with the camera taking the victim's point of view, showing the intrusion of the killer in the shape of Othello's shadow on the bed-curtains) into a sacrifice with a consenting victim.[107] Desdemona's last words are spoken gently, forgivingly, before she almost disappears from the film altogether to make room for Othello's tragic end, when he himself becomes the object of the voyeuristic gazes of Lodovico and Cassio looking down on him from a skylight. Significantly, Othello's face at his suicide is seen in close-up and appears light against a dark background. No trace of Desdemona can be seen although he is supposedly holding her in his arms. He commits suicide on 'threw a pearl away richer than all his tribe, / Set you down this'. By cutting and altering Othello's last few lines, the racist implications of the suicide, in which 'white' Venetian Othello kills his black 'Turkish' self, are avoided. Welles's light-skinned Othello dies a heroic 'honourable murderer' guilty only of 'lov[ing] . . . too well' (5.2.291, 342), with Desdemona's protest that 'That death's unnatural that kills for loving' (5.2.42) quite forgotten.

The recent stage histories of *Titus Andronicus* and *Othello* are notably similar in the fluctuating attitudes towards race that they illustrate. Following Welles, Olivier's blacked-up Othello was roughly parallel to Anthony Quayle's blacked-up Aaron, followed by the denial of racial difference in the Miller/Hopkins *Othello* that is broadly contemporary to Deborah Warner's casting of white, unmade-up Peter Polycarpou as Aaron in 1987. Janet Suzman's outstanding 1988 Johannesburg production with the black South

---

[107] Clover, *Men, Women, and Chain Saws*, p. 31.

African actor John Kani in the lead therefore demands to be read as a reaction against these negations of the centrality of race in the early 1980s. The production also explicitly refers to and distances itself from Olivier's portrayal through its quotation of Olivier's first entrance smelling a rose. 'By quoting Olivier's fetish-African as Kani's ghosted other', Barbara Hodgdon observes, 'the film marks the difference between "the real thing" and the painted-on identity of Othello's (colonial) theatrical history, calling attention to the situatedness of an actor who . . . experiences first-hand what it means to be black in a pervasively negrophobic society'.[108] In doing so, however, Suzman can be said to have been guilty of conflating 'two different kinds of marginality: the one which arises out of displacement and another in which black people and cultures were victimised but not literally isolated from each other'.[109] Even if this is true, the resulting stage production and video recording were a powerful theatrical intervention into contemporary South African race politics.

To drive home the political urgency of her project, Janet Suzman herself introduced the screening of the production in Britain (Channel 4, 27 December 1988) with a pep talk about the South African context of the production. Her statement that 'the play addresses the notion of Apartheid four hundred years before the epithet was coined – and rejects it' reflects a certain anxiety in the production to prevent misunderstanding and condition the audience into seeing the tragedy as a vindication of miscegenation and Othello as a character driven to murder by Iago's subtle manipulation of racist discourses. The same concern pervades Suzman's lectures about her *Othello* project in 1996. In response to a draft of this chapter, Suzman denied that 'there [was] "anxiety" on my part: I looked carefully at Iago's speech in (III.iii lines 232–37) and knew we had a tight case; the speech is as if straight from the mouth of a doctrinaire apartheidist. Iago was a militarist black-uniform-wearing right-winger, causing mayhem and spouting bigotry . . . I simplify.' In the same letter, she concedes that 'Having been born and brought up in apartheid SA, I fear I am quite unable to see Othello except through the pervasive prism of colour'.[110] The sheer effort the production displays throughout to get this particular reading across reveals that this interpretation, even though it works well in the instance, is somewhat forcing the play against its grain. As a consequence, I suspect that, even though black commentators are divided on 'the critical question whether *Othello*

---

[108] Hodgdon, 'Race-ing *Othello*', p. 27.
[109] Ania Loomba, *Colonialism / Postcolonialism* (London: Routledge, 1998), p. 15.
[110] Letter, 19 November 1998.

is a racist play or a play *about* racism',[111] the strain in Suzman's production supports Hugh Quarshie's claim that a non-racist staging is only possible at the price of textual emendation and/or radical directorial intervention. Suzman's is a resisting reading, an attempt to canvass Shakespeare's support for a political struggle of which the seeds were barely sown when he wrote his tragedy.

The anti-racist reading is emphasised throughout in the obvious erotic attraction to Othello of Joanna Weinberg's Desdemona. Her fetishistic gaze at Othello – a gaze 'that keys a white woman spectator into Kani's exoticism and the sexual bond between them' – is doubled by a similar gaze in Cassio, who is 'Desdemona's "twin" in his devotion to and worship of Othello'.[112] Othello himself is characterised by love and attention directed at Desdemona, Cassio and, most touchingly, also at the aged Brabantio. Iago's insinuations, then, disrupt a haven of 'colour-blind' mutual affection, his annihilation of beauty epitomised in his destruction of the daffodils Cassio has offered Desdemona. The fact that Iago, and not Othello, is the evil character in the play is never in doubt, and we are treated to many a wicked laugh as well as to a representation of Iago's own marriage as abusive.[113] The Emilia of Dorothy Ann Gould (who was to play Tamora for Doran seven years later) emerges as a strong double for Desdemona both in her innocence – when she says that she 'should' commit adultery it is beyond doubt that she means 'ought to' and not 'would' – and in her forceful denunciation of the crime which leads to her death at the hands of her husband. It is appropriate that her rage is eventually focused on Iago, whom she slaps on either cheek, and not on Othello, thus eventually endorsing Desdemona's exculpation of Othello.

The production's ideological project is most clearly evident in Othello's murder itself. His kiss wakes the sleeping Desdemona, who reaches up to him to pull him towards her. Throughout her protestations of innocence she strokes him, and later clings to him as he is straddling her. When he finally puts the pillow over her face to smother her, her hands stroke his arms until her strength abandons her and they sink back down lifelessly. Othello's grief at her death is immediate and devastating – in this portrayal, killing Desdemona is equivalent to killing a part of himself, the murder with Desdemona's consent becoming a sacrifice on the altar of racism.

---

[111] Mythili Kaul, 'Preface', in Kaul (ed.), *Othello*, p. x.
[112] Hodgdon, 'Race-ing *Othello*', pp. 28–9.
[113] Suzman recalls that 'Emilia always seemed like an abused wife . . . She's obviously scared of getting on the wrong side of [Iago], knowing full well what the usual outcome is – a beating'. Letter, 1 October 1998.

Illustration 13: Video-still of Desdemona (Joanna Weinberg) stroking and clinging to her aggrieved Othello (John Kani) in Janet Suzman's 1988 video of her Market Theatre production of *Othello*

But repulsive sexual violence does not disappear from the production altogether. Instead, it is displaced onto two earlier scenes. In the first of these, Othello, having rejected Desdemona's offered handkerchief, violently grabs her, kisses her and strokes her body passionately to her utter confusion. The murder in its gentleness and reluctance hence figures as a conscious rejection of such 'primitive' sexual violence. The promise of sexual violence the play so obviously contains is in this production realised not in the murder of Desdemona but just before it, in the gang-rape of Bianca. This is a harrowing scene, with Iago exposing Bianca to the voyeuristic gazes of the (white) soldiers, shaming her publicly as a whore – a humiliation which Bianca manages to bear with dignity, her declaration 'I am no strumpet' gaining particular weight (5.1.121). Iago then leaves Bianca to the soldiers, who overpower her, one of them picking her up, baring her breast which he kneads aggressively, while another soldier pushes himself between her legs, lifts her up and runs out with her, followed by his mates. From back-stage, a dreadful scream of pain can be heard as she is gang-raped – a scream which Iago hears with relish. What happens, then, is that since '*At that point in the play, a feeling of gross sexual anarchy [seems] a priority as an image*',[114] this production, which aims at representing Othello as a noble man and miscegenation as positive, projects its sexual violence onto a group of white men with a white victim. 'Whitening' Othello requires a 'blackening' of the white characters, especially of Iago. How completely sexual violence is here displaced from Othello onto Iago emerges in Othello's wounding of

[114] Letter, 1 October 1998, Suzman's emphasis.

Iago: it is represented as a castration, blaming the tragedy on *white* male sexuality in an amazing reversal of traditional racist anxieties.

Ultimately, however, it is in her own lectures about the production that Suzman begins to slip off the tightrope her production is treading on and is in danger of falling into the murky waters that we are familiar with from Gautier's comments about Ira Aldridge. Just as Gautier supposed that playing Othello did not require the black tragedian to act since he could be 'himself', Suzman assumes that John Kani has an advantage over Laurence Olivier because Kani is 'the real thing'. Unlike Olivier, who is a 'sophisticate through and through' and could therefore not 'convey fully the vulnerable innocence of a man who has been conned – conned unto death', Kani in her eyes has the requisite 'innocence. I don't mean naïve, and I certainly don't mean dim, but rather a man whose nature would respond to betrayal without self-consciousness.'[115] She is dangerously close to collapsing the distance between character and actor in these statements and to subscribing to the naturalisation, if not of violence, at least of gullibility as a racial characteristic of black men; however, she courts an even greater danger when talking about the reasons for casting Joanna Weinberg as Desdemona. What she was looking for, she says, was 'chemistry' – but she did not seek it in Weinberg, apparently supposing that the white woman would be able to *act* the requisite passion (as indeed she did). Instead, Suzman's identification between black actor and role led her to look for 'the real thing' in Kani, so that the 'decisive factor' in the selection of Joanna Weinberg 'was that John's one good eye (he'd lost the other years ago in a police raid) positively lit up when he read with her'.[116]

I do have to admit to a feeling of discomfort about picking holes in Suzman's approach when her production is so clearly a landmark in the play's recent history and one of the frankest and bravest attempts to take up the racial challenge of the play. Especially when compared to Gregory Doran's and Antony Sher's Market Theatre *Titus Andronicus* of 1995, Suzman's take on the tragedy emerges as remarkable for its sensitivity to race politics within both the play and South African culture at large. Certainly, her production paved the way for Trevor Nunn's elegant and supremely well-received staging of the tragedy for the RSC in the small studio space of The Other Place in 1989 (Nunn and Suzman had divorced the year before Suzman's *Othello*). What is impressive in both the stage production's promptbook and the video that was subsequently marketed by

---

[115] Janet Suzman, 'South Africa in *Othello*', *Tanner Lectures on Human Values* 17 (1996), 275–6.
[116] Suzman, 'South Africa', 283.

the RSC is the detailed attention to relationships, whether social, military or marital. This exploration of human interaction makes of Othello not the sole hero of the tragedy but rather a tragic character among others – a democratisation of tragic stature which helps deflect attention from Othello's race onto the workings of human evil as concentrated in the character of Iago. Race, in spite of the much-publicised casting of the black Jamaican actor and opera singer Willard White in the lead, is portrayed as one weapon among others at Iago's disposal, not least because the production's Bianca is also black, so that Othello is no longer isolated in his racial Otherness.[117] Just as the tensions between White and other members of the company were due to his outsider status as a singer among actors rather than as a black man among whites, the production deflected attention from race onto other types of social hierarchy.[118]

Two characters who emerge as unusually powerful in Nunn's staging are Desdemona (Imogen Stubbs) and Emilia (Zoë Wanamaker).[119] Although, as usual, Iago is played by an actor (Ian McKellen) who is far older than the 28 years referred to in the play, Emilia is only a few years older than Desdemona, so that their friendship, which culminates in Emilia's death for the sake of Desdemona, is particularly intense and moving. Wanamaker's Emilia is undoubtedly an abused wife and hence, like Dorothy Ann Gould in Suzman's staging, an effective double for Desdemona. The women are set up against the exclusively male world of the military camp, with the consequence that Othello's violence is represented as an effect of male peer-pressures and the sexual insecurity of an older man with a young bride. Desdemona is a painful intruder in the homosocial world of the army, in which male bonding takes precedence over heterosexual love.

Another feature which Nunn's direction brings into sharp focus, and which contributes to the threat represented by Desdemona, is her disregard of the borders separating private from public as well as her careless

---

[117] This is a very different effect from that achieved by the racial (and racist) doubling of Olivier's blacked-up Moor with a particularly idiotic clown who seems to have walked straight out of a minstrel show. Whereas Nunn's casting makes a statement about the playtext's connection between Othello and Bianca, who 'is racialized as black, assigned a set of negative sexual characteristics associated with Africa and Africans', Dexter's blacking-up of both half-wit and hero taints the hero with the mental deficiencies of his double. See Joyce Green MacDonald, 'Black Ram, White Ewe: Shakespeare, Race, and Women', in Callaghan (ed.), *Feminist Companion to Shakespeare*, p. 196.

[118] White talked about these tensions (especially with co-star Ian McKellen) in 'The Worrying of Willard! Conflict Mars Singer's TV Acting Debut', *Reading Post*, 22 June 1990. By contrast, White in another interview described Imogen Stubbs as 'very encouraging throughout the production' ('Willard Rises to His Othello Challenge', *Evening Post*, 23 June 1990), so that the relationships between the central cast members seem to have closely mirrored those between their characters.

[119] For gender-sensitive readings of this production, see Vaughan, *Contextual History*, pp. 217–32, Hodgdon, 'Race-ing *Othello*', pp. 31–40, and Rutter, *Enter the Body*, pp. 142–77.

usurpation of male privilege. When she takes a stand before the senators, Stubbs's emphasis 'So much I *challenge* . . .' in her very first speech already portrays her as an unruly albeit charming young woman (1.3.188; emphasis added). The Duke's awkward gallantry in yielding his own seat, so that Desdemona may comfortably voice her plea to follow her husband, shows that her presence and the fact that she speaks before the Senate are far from usual for a young Venetian lady. Furthermore, her excited cry 'Tonight, my lord?' (1.3.279), in its youthful exuberance at the thought of immediate departure, strikes a note of triviality which is inadequate for the military crisis in which the scene is set, but which rings true for the young girl who is looking forward to leaving her domestic seclusion in order to discover the world at the side of her husband.

Throughout the production, Desdemona is characterised by 'downright violence and scorn of fortunes' in her unguarded speech and playfulness in her dealings with her husband (1.3.250) – a reading that is firmly anchored in the playtexts. Not only is her love itself twice described as 'violent' (1.3.345, 2.1.220), but her hallmark throughout is her 'free speech' (3.4.130, see also 3.3.188), as evident in her desire to 'trumpet' her love 'to the world' (1.3.251) as well as in her ability to speak 'stoutly' and to 'talk [Othello] out of patience' (3.1.45, 3.3.23) in her plea for Cassio.[120] This plea is here portrayed as a physical intrusion of Desdemona into Othello's work sphere, as she comes up to his desk at which he is working with Iago and ends up sitting on Othello's lap. The fact that this happens before Iago's eyes justifies Othello's reluctance to yield to her demand – this Desdemona is obviously doing her best to 'corrupt and taint [Othello's] business' (1.3.272). His request here for her to 'leave [him] but a little to [him]self' (3.3.85), justified as it is within the context, is nevertheless the first instance of a pattern of silencing which is paralleled in Iago's cruder opposition to Emilia's speech. Both husbands feel that their wives need not actually talk for their speech to be a nuisance: whereas Iago complains that Emilia 'puts her tongue a little in her heart / And chides with thinking' (2.1.106–7), Othello is afraid to '*expostulate* with her, lest her *body* and her *beauty* unprovide [his] mind again' (4.1.202–3, emphases added), so that Desdemona's physical attributes are perceived as her counter-arguments to his expostulation. It is hardly surprising that, in order to silence those talking bodies, the bodies themselves will have to be destroyed eventually.

---

[120] For a comparison between the free speech and subsequent silencing of Desdemona and Lavinia, see my '"Yet I'll Speak": Silencing the Female Voice in *Titus Andronicus* and *Othello*', in Patricia Dorval (ed.), *Shakespeare et la voix* (Paris: Société Française Shakespeare, 1999), pp. 27–46.

Nunn's production emphasises the fact that all the acts of silencing and of violence towards the two women happen within a framework which the play marks as domestic. In the playtexts, we can see this from Cassio's casual remark on the Cyprus shore that Iago in his slander of women is 'speak[ing] home' in the senses of both touching a sensitive point and referring to his domestic situation (2.1.165). The later scenes of physical violence against the women either occur in an enclosed domestic space (the conjugal bedroom) or are explicitly marked as a marital action in a public domain. White's Othello publicly strikes Desdemona with a slap of such force that she is knocked to the ground with the impact. The scene is implicitly contrasted with Cassio's beating of Roderigo, which 'is treated as a public act, a crime that must, like any act of cognizable violence even today, be pursued and punished by the state'.[121] Othello's striking of Desdemona, by way of contrast, may be disapproved of, but is not seen as punishable. Lodovico's reaction 'What! strike his *wife*!' neatly contains the act of violence within the private marital relationship (4.1.272; emphasis added). This would be but a weak observation were it not for its conspicuous repetition in the killing of Emilia, which similarly is defined by both characters and stage direction as Iago killing 'his wife' (5.2.234, 236, SD Q). As in the striking of Desdemona, this act of violence is the result of the woman's attempt to speak for her cause in public. On both occasions the husband warns his wife at least once to be careful about her utterances before he resorts to physical violence, and in both cases the violence directed against the wife is protested against by the other characters, but not considered of great consequence. This is a point Nunn painfully brings home in his portrayal of the death of Emilia, who in his production dies alone on a chair, unheeded by anyone, linked only to Desdemona through her evocation of the willow song in her dying words. Here, as in most productions, her dying wish to be laid by Desdemona's side is ignored, as is her death itself. Striking and killing a wife, then, although in the case of Desdemona the murder is considered to be punishable by law and 'monstrous' (5.2.186), is thus circumscribed as a domestic, private act.

Predictably, the combination of Stubbs's assertive, intelligent Desdemona with Nunn's emphasis on gender relations and the disruption of marital relationships produces a very powerful murder scene. The mood for this is set early on in the willow scene, with a beautiful, gentle intimacy and harmony between Emilia and Desdemona that barely manages to cover

---

[121] Ruth Vanita, '"Proper" Men and "Fallen" Women: The Unprotectedness of Wives in *Othello*', *Studies in English Literature 1500–1900* 34 (1994), 348.

up both the women's distress at the breakdown of Desdemona's marriage. It thus sets up the ideological context within which the wife-killing demands to be read – a context that is notably free of racism and focuses on the issue of jealousy instead. Nunn's attention to the willow scene allows for a re-accentuation of the murder in favour of Desdemona, making it easy to see why male actor-managers routinely subjected the women's conversation to what early-nineteenth-century tragedian Sarah Siddons denounced as a 'barbarous mutilation'.[122] Significantly, Nunn also refrains from applying the routine cut of Othello's brief appearance in the street scene that follows. Instead, Othello's presence is emphasised when he straddles Cassio's body to deliver the lines in which he acknowledges Iago's teaching and the concomitant need to kill Desdemona. Peer-pressure thus makes its last appearance in the context of discordant public violence.

As a contrast, the sense of ritual and control at the beginning of the last scene is strongly conveyed when Othello enters wearing an exotic white robe and carrying a scimitar. This is the moment that the entire play has been preparing us for, the moment when Othello casts off his social self-definition as 'white' (as symbolised through his military uniform) and adopts his 'native', 'black' costume to commit the act that will prove to those in the audience who were looking *to* him rather than *at* him that they were correct in suspecting that he is far more black than fair.[123] White's change of costume for the murder is a risky directorial choice and is uncomfortably close to Olivier's tearing off his cross when vowing revenge. Suddenly, in a production which has consistently avoided the charge of racism by foregrounding marital violence in both mixed and white couples and by portraying a black Othello who is thoroughly 'white' in everything but his skin, the possibility is opened up for a racist reading of the murder. The change of costume is moreover contradictory in view of Othello's own perception that he is about to perform a sacrifice for the sake of 'white' male solidarity – rather than an emancipation from white male culture, Othello sees his act as what will seal his alliance to that culture. The only way, apart from its visual effectiveness, the change of costume can be justified is in exposing the voyeuristic audience's underlying desire to see him dressed as a racialised 'Other' for the murder.

Whatever the explanation for this disturbing directorial choice, the order and ritual which Othello is trying to impose on his act, and which is also

---

[122] Quoted in James Boaden, *Memoirs of Mrs. Siddons* (London: Gibbings and Company, 1893), p. 321.

[123] Vaughan sees this as a moment of emancipation, but does not take account of the audience's possible racist reading: 'It is as if, convinced of Desdemona's Venetian perfidy, he has rejected "passing" at last and chooses instead his native dress.' *Contextual History*, p. 231.

evident in his rigid impersonality when answering Desdemona's questions, break down under Desdemona's resistance. Stubbs's vigorous Desdemona shatters his control, forcing Othello to commit a disturbingly messy murder. She fights Othello with all her might, alternately crying and shouting at him, and even tries to escape, but finds that Othello has locked the door. Finally, he flings her on the bed and lowers himself onto her, his hand covering her mouth. A long time passes before she goes limp and he rolls off to lie beside her on his back. What we witness is more the climax of a rape-snuff film than a sacrifice. Later, when Emilia is in the room, Desdemona revives with a horrible croak. The camera's close-up on the face of the dying woman makes it clear who has won the struggle for the last word. Race or male heroism, in Nunn's production, do not overshadow the women's struggle, and gender relations – both heterosexual and homosocial – are shown to be the cause of the 'tragic loading of this bed' (5.2.361). Furthermore, although it is clear from Iago's cold-blooded stare at the dead bodies that *he* is the villain of the piece, no-one who has witnessed this particular murder will be able to excuse it glibly. Under Trevor Nunn's sensitive direction the murder is neither the result of race or racism, nor motivated by sadistic and voyeuristic male phallic sexuality gone awry. By allowing the company to explore the gender relations as scripted in Shakespeare's play, Nunn's staging shows that an emphasis on gender might be the solution to the problems of racism posed by the tragedy.

It is the more surprising and disappointing that only six years after Nunn's intelligent production, the pendulum seems to have swung back in Oliver Parker's feature-film adaptation of *Othello*. Parker's casting of African American actor Laurence Fishburne in the lead – the first black actor to play Othello on the big screen – superficially suggests an awareness of the tragedy's racial dimension and promises an interpretation on a par with Harry Lennix's extraordinary appropriation of Aaron under Taymor's direction. On a closer view, however, Parker's *Othello* appears to be ultimately more racist than its predecessors. Whereas, as John Ford argues, Olivier's racist impersonation of a stereotypical black man at least had the potential to 'betray [the production's intentions] by foregrounding the artificial dynamics of social and theatrical construction',[124] Parker more insidiously appropriates Fishburne's body to naturalise the film's racist interpretation. Not only does Fishburne carry the 'baggage' of his previous role as 'the emotionally needy, drug-addicted, wife-beating Ike Turner in *What's Love*

---

[124] John R. Ford. '"Words and Performances": Roderigo and the Mixed Dramaturgy of Race and Gender in *Othello*', in Kolin (ed.), *Othello*, p. 163.

Got To Do With It?' into this film,[125] but, as if his body were not black
enough, Parker uses jewellery and tattoos to mark his body as an eroticised,
exoticised, violently inscribed 'Other'. In Taymor's *Titus*, the multiplicity
of racial positions and the ethnic 'chic' available to all characters allowed
the marks on Lennix's body to be legible as a choice. By contrast, Fishburne's less articulate Moor (he commonly expresses himself with grunts
and glares) rather invites the viewer to see these markings as an expression
of his violent, primitive character.

Parker's desire to emphasise the 'passion and romance' of the relationship between Othello and Desdemona results in a representation of both
their bodies as fetishised objects of an eroticising gaze.[126] 'The audience',
writes Francesca Royster, 'is encouraged to enjoy . . . [Fishburne's] physical
Othello, to take pleasure in his body, in his rages and even in his murder
of the play's heroine. All this, conveniently, is accomplished by reducing
Othello's black identity to an appetizing and culturally acceptable icon:
the athletic black male body.'[127] An early flashback to Othello's courtship
of Desdemona shows her less enthralled by Othello's narrative than by
the tattoos on his hand and head. A later shot of Othello seen through
Desdemona's eyes focuses on his crotch as he is unfastening his belt, reducing his attraction to exotic sexuality in a way that, in its reinforcement of
racist stereotypes, stands in stark contrast to Suzman's portrayal of the couple's eroticism. Both lovers in Parker's film are, in fact, 'Othered' in a way
that poses serious questions about the policies governing the film's casting.
While the Franco-Swiss Irène Jacob's talent as an actor is not in doubt, her
accent at crucial moments becomes an insurmountable obstacle. This and
the drastic cuts of her lines (she hardly gets a chance to plead for Cassio)
undermine the very eloquence that, as Nunn showed, is a major reason
for Othello's suspicions and jealousy. The consequent focus on her body,
which is underlined by shots of her adultery with Cassio as fantasised by
Othello, debases both her and Othello, whose obsession with sex is thus
exposed while the audience has been given all the visual proof it needs to
condemn Desdemona.

With Desdemona thus 'bewhored', identified as 'Other' and silenced by
her accent, and Othello similarly fetishised and reduced to his sexuality,

[125] MacDonald, 'Black Ram', p. 190.
[126] Parker, as quoted by Hodgdon, *The Shakespeare Trade*, p. 67.
[127] Francesca T. Royster, 'The "End of Race" and the Future of Early Modern Cultural Studies',
Shakespeare Studies 26 (1998), 66. Royster's and my own reading of Fishburne's fetishised body run
counter to that of Philip Kolin, who sees his Othello as 'empowered because of his racial strengths'.
See Philip C. Kolin, 'Blackness Made Visible: A Survey of *Othello* in Criticism, on Stage, and on
Screen', in Kolin (ed.), *Othello*, p. 66.

Illustration 14: Video-still of Emilia (Anna Patrick), Desdemona (Irène Jacob), Othello (Laurence Fishburne) and Iago (Kenneth Branagh) in Oliver Parker's 1995 film of *Othello*

the audience is perversely invited to share Iago's point of view. As played by Kenneth Branagh, Iago is not only the bearer of the gaze and the controller of what the film spectator is allowed to see, but – as he is one of the film's few speakers of RP and Shakespearean verse – his words (along with those of his fellow-RSC veteran Michael Maloney as Roderigo) carry the greatest cultural authority. Whereas Ian McKellen's strong Iago in Nunn's production had resulted in an exposure of domestic violence and the strength of peer-pressure, Branagh's Iago spends most of the film in an ugly competition with Othello and Desdemona, a struggle from which he emerges as a winner in the final scene. There, Othello is racialised more than ever through his costume and the cleansing ritual he performs before the murder. While Desdemona's pleas are disabled by her increasingly thick accent, her vehement physical struggle against Fishburne's muscular and savagely violent Othello is doomed to be ineffectual from the start. He smothers her with a pillow, erasing both her face and her speech. It takes only one attempt to kill her, Desdemona's last lines are cut, and the camera focuses on Othello's face as Desdemona's fighting hand becomes loving, stroking his face in silent acceptance of her death.

As in Welles's film, where Desdemona is only pretending to be asleep, Parker first taints Jacob's Desdemona through her nude scenes with Cassio before erasing her almost entirely from the film. Unlike Welles's Othello who benefited from this erasure, however, Fishburne is not left at the centre of attention for long. In Parker's heavily cut script, both Othello and Emilia are quickly upstaged by Iago, who once more appropriates language and the camera that follows him in his escape from the room in which, to Parker's credit, the dying Emilia is sharing Desdemona's death-bed. When Iago is brought back to the bedchamber, the main focus is on him. Othello's gaze is locked in Iago's even while he is talking to Cassio. The camera neglects the women's bodies on the bed until Othello commits suicide and painfully pulls himself up to the hidden Desdemona for his final kiss. A reaction shot shows a flash of genuine emotion across the face of Iago who, at the end of the scene, crawls halfway up to Othello's body on the bed, resting his head on Othello's knee while triumphantly staring at the camera. When Cassio opens the window to let the sunlight in, the film's final shot of the bed emblematises its interpretation of the tragedy: in the foreground Iago is lying on the legs of the centrally positioned Othello, whose body is partly covering Desdemona on his left. Emilia is pushed to the margins of the intradiegetic frame created by the bed-curtains. Despite Fishburne's powerful performance, in the *Othello* of the nineties Iago is the hero and wielder of the racist and misogynist gaze that has reduced Othello and Desdemona to their physicality and disabling 'Otherness'. With its leads played by a real black man and a real white woman, Parker's film disturbingly naturalises racial and sexual inferiority by showing it as embodied, not performed.

CHAPTER FOUR

En-gendering violence and suffering in King Lear

King Lear at the Royal Shakespeare Theatre Stratford-upon-Avon, 1993: the actors enter to take their curtain calls. First the minor characters: soldiers, servants, nameless men. Then Lear's daughters enter with their husbands, retreating to make room for Gloucester, his sons and Oswald. The applause reaches a climax when the production's Lear (Robert Stephens) enters alone to take his bow. The hierarchy of the curtain call is simply and effectively choreographed to sum up the play as interpreted by Adrian Noble.[1] Welcomed with relief by at least one (male) reviewer as 'a sensible traditional reading of the play, resisting the misplaced revisionism that has disfigured other recent productions',[2] Noble's 'humanist-expressionist' staging is a prime example of the privileging of Lear and the violence this privileging is predicated upon.[3] Like Brian Cox's Lear on the cover of this book,[4] Noble and Robert Stephens's Lear push the other characters, and especially the female characters, out of the frame of the play. What is left behind is an empty space that is usurped by Lear's suffering.

Noble's reading of the play as a universal, 'great' tragedy was clear-cut, one-sided and 'virile'. The set was dominated by two obvious visual symbols of national and cosmic disorder: a huge paper map of Britain (without Northern Ireland) covering the stage that was gradually ripped up to reveal a blood-red floor underneath, and an equally oversized moon hanging over

---

[1] For a discussion of the productions by Noble (1993), Brook (1962–71) and Hytner (1990) that I am indebted to, see Carol Rutter's 'reading of not the play of the king but the play of the daughters' in 'Eel Pie and Ugly Sisters in *King Lear*', in James Ogden and Arthur H. Scouten (eds.), Lear *from Study to Stage: Essays in Criticism* (London: Associated University Presses, 1997), p. 174.

[2] John Gross, 'He Chips Away Here and There', *Sunday Telegraph*, 23 May 1993.

[3] Victoria Radin, 'Just the Man for the RSC', *Observer*, 27 June 1982.

[4] A typically partisan account of the rehearsal process and theatrical run of this production can be found in Brian Cox, *The Lear Diaries: The Story of the Royal National Theatre's Productions of Shakespeare's* Richard III *and* King Lear (London: Methuen, 1995).

the stage that burst apart to 'bleed' sand (as a rehearsal note put it rather melodramatically) after Gloucester's blinding.[5] Even though these 'large, clunking symbols' were condemned in the press as 'ploddingly obvious',[6] they were obviously important enough to the director to be retained for the length of the Stratford and London runs regardless of the fact that the bleeding moon often proved dysfunctional and that the torn paper floor was responsible for an extraordinarily high accident rate as actors tripped up or slipped on scraps of paper. (Thankfully, the idea to have limbs sticking out of the sublunary sand dune was abandoned during rehearsals.)

With this emphasis on the macrocosm, it was fairly predictable that the microcosm of family relationships would be accorded less importance. Rather than waste his audience's energies on working out for themselves which characters to condemn and whom to endorse, Noble helped them along with visual and aural aids, using all theatrical sign systems available to him to reduce the 'secondary' characters into simple plot-functions. He costumed Goneril in green, prefiguring the green-eyed monster of her later jealousy, and Regan in purple to reinforce her highly sexualised characterisation (in particular during the blinding of Gloucester and in her encounters with Edmund). Cordelia, by way of contrast, was costumed in 'true' blue, the same colour as that worn by France in a neat instance of 'costume rhyming'. To drive home the point of Goneril's usurpation of male rule, she was later dressed in jodhpurs while Regan, to emphasise her hyper-femininity and aggressive sexuality, reappeared in a strapless gown. Cordelia, on the other hand, continued to wear a modest dress even in the midst of her military campaign. Theme music further assisted the audience in associating the appropriate emotions with each character: gloomy, ominous tunes for the wicked sisters, Cornwall and Edmund, as opposed to gentle, sentimental music and soft blue light for Cordelia's reunion with Lear – enough to provoke a reviewer to quip that he 'half expected a large sign to descend reading, "Sad Bit"'.[7]

Noble's directorial signposting was so strong that it almost entirely obliterated the efforts of Janet Dale (Goneril) and Jenny Quayle (Regan) to represent their characters sympathetically. In fact, they had neither been able to explore in rehearsal many options that would have interested them nor been informed of the type of music that was to accompany their entrances and exits. In a revealingly frank interview with Jackie McGlone,

---

[5] Rehearsal note, 25 March 1993, Shakespeare Centre, Stratford-upon-Avon.
[6] Paul Taylor, 'More Sinn'd Against', *Independent*, 24 May 1993, and Charles Spencer, 'Back from the Abyss to Invest Madness with a Human Face', *Daily Telegraph*, 22 May 1993.
[7] Andrew Smith, 'Lear's Blood Lust', *Chase Post*, 27 May 1993.

the female performers talked about their treatment in the rehearsal room. Abigail McKern (Cordelia) in particular gave a sharp account of Noble's rehearsal practices: 'Very often I was the only woman in the rehearsal room and Adrian Noble is a bit of a boy's director. He loves all the fighting and so on, so it was like being in a boys' club. All lads together.'[8] That's but a trifle here, however, for the production was no more interested in the views of Goneril and Regan than its director was in those of the women in his cast. Certainly, Goneril's angry complaint about the unruliness of Lear's red-coated knights was rendered perverse by the staging, since those well-behaved cheerful gentlemen could hardly have caused a substantial upheaval in her household. Paul Taylor wondered 'how such spruce toy soldiers could be anything other than model guests'.[9] When the actor's attempt at humanising her character resulted in Goneril being close to tears at the end of her confrontation with Lear (1.4), the contrast with her costuming and theme tune merely made her breakdown smack of further hypocrisy. Regan, too, was portrayed as cool, and her deliberate cruelty was disturbingly sexualised, equating female sexuality with violence. Charles Spencer's review accordingly described Jenny Quayle as 'bring[ing] a chilling sexuality to Regan, experiencing an almost orgasmic pleasure in other people's suffering'.[10] As a result, all three sisters were immediately identifiable as stereotypes and plot-functions rather than 'real women': two 'pelican daughters' (F 3.4.71) and a third 'Who redeems nature from the general curse / Which twain have brought her to' (F 4.5.199–200).

   In his presentation of the daughters as types, Noble let himself be taken in and ruled by the dominant reactionary reading strategies of the conflated playtext he was working with. Both the Quarto and the Folio playtexts are structured so as to juxtapose the daughters' potentially subversive presences either with the charismatic narrative force of Edmund and his plot to disinherit his brother or, even more effectively, with Lear's towering rage, which obliterates their viewpoint through rhetorically amplified invective. Such is the weight of Lear's authority and his verbal if not merely temporal domination of the play (especially in the drawn-out storm scenes), that it is all too easily forgotten that his daughters never actually show him the door. It is Lear who walks out of his daughters' lives, he who banishes them to the margins of the play. The play, in turn, assists him by carefully providing intermediaries through whom the audience's empathy is directed towards the only truly 'appropriate' recipient of pity: Lear. The function that

---

[8] Jackie McGlone, 'Fair Dos for Daddy's Girls', *Theatre Records* 166 (11 March–30 May 1993), 94.
[9] Paul Taylor, 'More Sinn'd Against'.   [10] Charles Spencer, 'Back from the Abyss'.

Emilia fulfils in *Othello*, sympathising with Desdemona and denouncing her murder, so that she can be seen as an 'extension' of Desdemona, is here taken over predominantly by men (Kent, Gloucester, Fool, Edgar and Albany) who pity Lear and condemn his two elder daughters. Cordelia, the first character to be wronged and, if considered in the paradigm of *Titus Andronicus* and *Othello*, the potential principal recipient of sympathy from observers both on and off the stage, is here removed from the action. She only reappears when her ill-treatment at the hands of her father is sufficiently forgotten to allow her to become yet another intermediary who removes all guilt from Lear ('No cause, no cause' F 4.6.69) and stresses only the compassion that must be felt for him. As Janet Adelman argues, the Cordelia of act 4

is largely the Cordelia of Lear's fantasy ... Insofar as the Cordelia of 1.1 is silenced, insofar as we feel the Cordelia who returns more as an iconic presence answering Lear's terrible need than as a separate character with her own needs, Shakespeare is complicit in Lear's fantasy, rewarding him for his suffering by remaking for him the Cordelia he had wanted all along; Shakespeare too requires the sacrifice of her autonomy.[11]

Cordelia is instrumentalised by Shakespeare's plot to enhance Lear's suffering.

In fact, the playtexts' intradiegetic pointers appear almost clumsy in their insistence on Lear as the proper object of pity: Lear's knight thinks his master wronged even before Goneril has started to cross her father intentionally, Gloucester pities Lear from the moment Lear leaves the shelter of his house, and Cordelia and Kent both choose to 'forget and forgive' (F 4.6.77) almost as soon as they are banished and lend support to Lear's claim that it is he who is 'mightily abused' (F 4.6.64). Lear himself provides one of the most explicit pointers in his affirmation that he 'should ev'n die with pity / To see another thus' (F 4.6.47–8). He is only outdone by the excessively compassionate Edgar, a character whose main function seems to be to mediate between play and audience with his regular commentary and soliloquising. His hyperbolic declarations of compassion are strengthened yet further by the anonymous gentleman who seems to have walked onto the stage only to reinforce the point that the mad Lear is 'A sight most pitiful in the meanest wretch, / Past speaking of in a king' (F 4.5.197–8).

This persistent manipulation of audience sympathies culminates famously in the play's intense focus on Lear's alternating hope and despair in the

---

[11] Janet Adelman, *Suffocating Mothers: Fantasies of Maternal Origin in Shakespeare's Plays:* Hamlet *to* The Tempest (London: Routledge, 1992), pp. 124–5.

moments leading up to his death. There, dissident spectators who may have transferred their main focus of attention from Lear to the sexual intrigue, duel, murder and suicide of the secondary plot – after all, Lear is conspicuously absent from the first 210 lines of the final scene – are roughly reminded of their guilty neglect of the protagonist by Albany's exclamation 'Great thing of us forgot' (F 5.3.211). Albany's inclusive pronoun 'us' extends beyond the stage to embrace the equally oblivious audience, and, if Cordelia's death and the pain it causes her father are a direct result of Albany's forgetfulness, the audience also partakes in the responsibility for her death. A. C. Bradley's resonant question 'Why does Cordelia die?' may well find its answer here:[12] she dies because characters and spectators have dared take their eyes off Lear's tragedy. Because, for an instant, Edmund's death is more than 'but a trifle here' and anticipation of the arrival of Goneril's and Regan's bodies 'alive or dead' has eclipsed all other expectations (F 5.3.269, 205). She dies so as to make her father suffer, to once more concentrate all the empathy on Lear's torment on the rack of this tough world. Tellingly, Bradley never asked 'Why is Cordelia killed?' but instead chose to imply that dead Cordelia is deliberate, even cruel, in her refusal to respond to her father's supplication that she should 'stay a little' since her survival would 'redeem all sorrows' (F 5.3.245, 240). In a move familiar from the criticism of *Titus Andronicus* and *Othello*, the female victim is blamed for her violation. When I weep at the end of a performance of *King Lear*, I am never quite certain whether it is in empathy for the infinite sorrow of the dying king or in rage at letting myself be manipulated into sharing this sorrow.

If obvious, the manipulation that becomes so humiliatingly punitive in the final scene is also pervasive and hard to get rid of. What I find particularly grating is that it is so unashamedly gendered and that, whereas the racialisation of violence in *Othello* provokes strong responses, many still seem to accept the gender stereotypes and valorisation of aged masculinity in *King Lear* as unproblematic. Lear's fierce denunciations of his daughters insistently harp on their depraved femininity. Strikingly, there is no difference in the type of abuse reserved for Cordelia from that heaped on her sisters: Lear associates her, too, with torture (her ingratitude, Lear claims, 'like an engine wrenched [his] frame of nature / From the fixed place' F 1.4.238–9) as well as with images of cannibalism and barbarity. Whereas the worst insult Kent has to suffer when he has incurred Lear's displeasure is

[12] A. C. Bradley, *Shakespearean Tragedy: Lectures on* Hamlet, Othello, King Lear, Macbeth (London: Macmillan, 1983 [1905]), p. 100.

'recreant' (F 1.1.165), a term which is appropriate for the legal relationship that binds the two men, Lear experiences the perceived rebellion of his daughters as so unnatural that it threatens his physical and mental integrity if not the order of his world. Gloucester's reaction to Edgar's equivalent apparent betrayal is no worse than the string of invectives 'Abhorred villain, unnatural, detested, brutish villain – worse than brutish!' (F 1.2.72–3). Lear, in contrast, uses the imagery of disease corrupting the body natural and politic of the king that we are familiar with from the Ghost's account of his curdling blood in *Hamlet* when he describes Goneril as a

> disease that's in my flesh
> Which I must needs call mine. Thou art a boil,
> A plague-sore, or embossèd carbuncle
> In my corrupted blood.   (F 2.4.211–14)

When Lear curses the 'Degenerate bastard' and 'sea-monster' Goneril (F 1.4.223, 231), he produces a disturbing combination of abject images of feeding ('Detested kite' F 1.4.232) with breeding and the serpentine that is strongly reminiscent of the clusters of imagery associated with Tamora, *Titus*' female 'Other'. The images recur with obsessive frequency: Goneril is described as a vulture (F 2.4.124) and a serpent (F 2.4.150, F 5.3.289), while the sisters' cannibalistic ingratitude and ferocity are conveyed by Lear's question 'Is it not as this mouth should tear this hand / For lifting food to't?' (F 3.4.15–16), an idea summed up in his metaphor of the 'pelican daughters' (F 3.4.71). The opposition established in *Titus Andronicus* between Lavinia's empty orifice and Tamora's devouring mouth and obscenely fertile womb, both associated with the 'detested, dark, blood-drinking pit' (*Tit* 2.2.224), is replayed here in Lear's fixation on Cordelia's ultimately silent lips as contrasted with the devouring mouths and monstrous sexuality of his elder daughters: 'Beneath is all the fiend's: there's hell, there's darkness, / There's the sulphurous pit, burning, scalding, / Stench, consumption' (F 4.5.122–4). Albany, too, turns against his wife and Regan with insults that evoke the ghost of the 'barbarous' 'ravenous tiger, Tamora' (*Tit* 2.2.118, 5.3.194) when calling them 'Tigers, not daughters ... Most barbarous' (Q only 4.2.38–41). Whereas 'the actions of Cornwall and Edmund are primarily assessed according to judicial points of view, the female characters almost always entail judgements about the intangibility, danger, and uncontrollability of female nature'.[13] It is no wonder, then, that in Noble's uncritical production

---

[13] Doris Märtin, *Shakespeares 'Fiend-Like Queens': Charakterisierung, Kontext und dramatische Funktion der destruktiven Frauenfiguren in* Henry VI, Richard III, King Lear *und* Macbeth (Heidelberg: Carl Winter Universitätsverlag, 1992), p. 133; my translation.

the sisters' evil was so obviously identified by Jackie McGlone as 'feminine, irrational and self-destructive, a matter of arbitrary lusts, petty schemes, and sudden rages'.[14]

The flip-side of the invective with which Lear attacks his perceived tor-mentors is his appropriation of the vocabulary of physical torture. Although it is Edgar who emulates the beggars that 'Strike in their numbed and mor-tified arms / Pins, wooden pricks, nails, sprigs of rosemary' (2.3.15–16), and although Gloucester experiences the worst bodily torture, Lear alone is en-titled to lines such as 'To have a thousand with red burning spits / Come hissing in upon 'em!' (F 3.6.15–16) or 'I am bound / Upon a wheel of fire, that mine own tears / Do scald like molten lead' (F 4.6.40–2). A compari-son of these complaints with the simplicity of Gloucester's 'O, cruel! O you gods!' and 'All dark and comfortless' (F 3.7.67, 82) – his only exclamations expressing pain during his actual mutilation – shows the enormity of Lear's usurpation of the discourse of torment.

The effect of this is a strange transference of suffering whereby the pain experienced by 'secondary' characters seems in the playtexts to add to and emphasise Lear's own anguish. This technique of transference allows Shakespeare to amplify Lear's experience of distress without having to put his hero through excessive physical mutilation (a development away from the strategies used in *Titus Andronicus*). Thus when Lear gives away his power, his loss of status and vocal authority is almost immediately enacted by Kent, who 'diffuses' his speech and 'razes' his 'likeness' (F 1.4.2, 4). The decay of Lear's mental powers is similarly embodied first by Fool (as long as Lear still has some control) and later by Edgar/Tom, onto whom Lear projects his own plight: 'Didst thou give all to thy daughters, / And art thou come to this?' (F 3.4.47–8). Through the dispossessed Edgar/Tom's verbal echoing of Lear's dispossession of himself and Cordelia in the state-ment 'Edgar I nothing am' (F 2.3.31), Edgar/Tom is set up from the very beginning of his exile not so much as an independent character with a fate of his own but as a sounding-board who serves mainly to amplify Lear's mental breakdown and anguish. Edgar/Tom's physical abjection and the nonsensical and dislocated language he produces in particular can be read as an embodiment of Lear's own condition.

The same can be said of Gloucester, whose treatment at the hands of his sons is less a parallel to Lear's experience with his daughters than an augmentation of it. The crossover whereby Gloucester's eyes are put out by Lear's children rather than his own sons can be read as a hijacking of

---

[14] McGlone, 'Fair Dos', 94.

the Gloucester plot by Lear, making Gloucester the surrogate victim of the daughters' revenge on Lear for his curse on Goneril 'You nimble lightnings, dart your blinding flames / Into her scornful eyes' (F 2.4.154–5) – it is Goneril who initially professes Lear to be 'Dearer than eyesight' (F 1.1.55), and it is she who first has the idea to 'Pluck out' Gloucester's eyes (F 3.7.5). The revealing slip in the promptbook of Cicely Berry's production for the RSC in 1988, where a marginal note specifies that at the end of the blinding the 'Servant [crosses] to *Lear* [and] unties him' (emphasis added), shows just how successful the strategy of projecting Gloucester's physical torment onto Lear has been even with theatre professionals. Nicholas Hytner made a similar point when he reminisced that the subtext of the blinding scene in his 1990 RSC production was that Gloucester had become a father-substitute for Regan.[15] Within the playtexts, Lear's appropriation of the earl's blindness even becomes explicit in act 5 scene 4 (Folio), when he offers him his own eyes to cry with in a scene in which Gloucester's pain is no more than the plinth on which the towering monument of Lear's mad anguish is erected. The disproportion between Gloucester's eleven lines and Lear's ninety-five lines in their dialogue here leaves little doubt as to whose experience is privileged by the tragedy.

'THIS HORRID ACT': WATCHING THE BLINDING

The blinding of Gloucester in act 3 scene 7 of *King Lear* occupies the same strategic place as the killings of Mercutio and Polonius, marking the point of no return for their respective tragedies, and is used to the same effect as Lavinia's rape in *Titus Andronicus*. 'This horrid act' (F 3.7.84) constitutes the point of no return where psychological violence becomes physical – in Carol Rutter's words, whereas 'the violence before the blinding . . . is entirely rhetorical and theatrical . . . After the blinding, violence is discharged into the play. Thereafter, killing abounds: the atrocity works some kind of release.'[16] This scene of deliberate on-stage cruelty is in many ways central to the play and encapsulates the interrelated issues of the privileging of Lear, the reflection of his suffering in and its magnification through other characters, the demonisation of the elder daughters and the play's manipulative and punitive strategies.

The violence of the scene is so intense and unmitigated that many critics have questioned its function, its moral value and its very stageability. G. Wilson Knight, in a searching chapter entitled 'King Lear and the

---

[15] Conversation with Nicholas Hytner, 8 November 2000.   [16] Rutter, 'Eel Pie', p. 201.

Comedy of the Grotesque', pointed to the 'satanically comic' element of the scene and emphasised the interdependence of Gloucester's physical and Lear's mental agony when he argued that 'The gouging out of Gloucester's eyes . . . helps to provide an accompanying exaggeration of one element – that of cruelty – in the horror that makes Lear's madness'.[17] Most influentially, at the beginning of the last century, Bradley distinguished between the experiences of reading and of watching the play in performance. In the study, Bradley explained, 'the physical horror, though not lost, is so far deadened that it can do its duty as a stimulus to pity, and to that appalled dismay at the extremity of human cruelty which it is the essence of the tragedy to excite'. For the reader, the scene can thus lead to the experience of fear and pity that is at the basis of Aristotelian catharsis, the concept that underpins Bradley's analysis. But matters are different for the theatregoer because, according to Bradley, 'the mere physical horror of such a spectacle would in the theatre be a sensation so violent as to overpower the purely tragic emotions, and therefore the spectacle would seem revolting or shocking'.[18] There is, then, a sense of excess in the reinforcement of the narrative's violence through its physical enactment in the theatre. What is 'properly' tragic on the page is 'revolting' or 'shocking' on the stage because of the theatre's collapse of semantic and somatic violence. It is one thing to know that Gloucester is blinded, but quite another to listen to and, especially, to *watch* the mutilation, to use our own eyes to witness the removal of somebody else's eyes in a space (the theatre) that is so contained that the audience, if it does not intervene, is made to feel complicit in the violence perpetrated. The whole thing is made worse, of course, by the fact that the blinding is represented as a punishment for Gloucester's desire to *see*, that is, to do exactly what the audience is doing.

Even if Bradley's statements could be explained as the product of late nineteenth-/early twentieth-century sensibilities, the fact that today theatregoers still find the scene literally unwatchable confirms his intuition about the scene's excess in the theatre. In fact, most contemporary productions deliberately introduce the interval just after Gloucester's eyes are put out so as to cause minimal disruption when the faint-hearted leave the theatre.[19] Spectators who do not know the plot and are thus not prepared to run for the exit at the relevant moment sometimes find that their bodies protect them from the spectacle of the blinding. Thus, at a performance of Noble's 1993 production of the scene at the Barbican

[17] Knight, *Wheel of Fire*, p. 169.   [18] Bradley, *Shakespearean Tragedy*, p. 205.
[19] Peter Holland, *English Shakespeares: Shakespeare on the English Stage in the 1990s* (Cambridge: Cambridge University Press, 1997), p. 3.

Theatre in London, 'A PATRON FAINTED IN THE CIRCLE, AND RE-
COVERING, SHOUTED LOUDLY "WHAT ARE YOU DOING, WHAT
ARE YOU DOING?"'[20] This reaction shows both an instinctive refusal to
be subjected to the spectacle of excessive violence and the patron's obvious
feelings of involvement and co-responsibility for the on-stage blinding. The
patron would probably agree with Bradley's rejection of this spectacle of
violence as 'revolting or shocking'.

So would Nahum Tate, whose 1681 adaptation of the play effectively
supplanted Shakespeare's playtext(s) and held the stage well into the nineteenth century. Tate not only infamously changed the tragic ending to
make Cordelia survive, but he also seems to have found the blinding too
offensive to stage in its entirety. What we see in his version is the build-
up to the blinding but not the act of violence itself, which takes place
off-stage and is performed by Cornwall's servants. It is, in fact, only in
the mid-nineteenth century, and surprisingly as part of Samuel Phelps's
endeavour to attract a more middle-class audience to the unruly subur-
ban Sadler's Wells Theatre,[21] that an attempt was made to stage the whole
scene of the blinding. The promptbook for Phelps's 1845 production is
a fascinating document that bears witness to the actor-manager's selfless
preoccupation with staging a scene in which he himself (he played Lear)
does not appear.[22] Within a theatrical culture that did not lavish much
time on ensemble rehearsal, the obvious effort put into the rehearsing of
this scene is evidence of an extraordinary will to break away from Tate
and explore the horror of Shakespeare's central scene of torture in all its
implications for the representation of gender and violence. It is also evidence
of the extreme practical difficulties and cultural pressures that impinge
on the staging of this brutal scene as scripted in the Quarto and Folio
playtexts.

In a manner unusual for this particular promptbook, the blinding scene
is heavily marked-up in what represents a palimpsest of three different
acting texts, each cut more radically than its predecessor. In a first phase,
the text was cut for rehearsal by somebody sitting at a desk visualising the
scene. As with the many cuts and manuscript stage directions in the rest
of the promptbook, the hand is very legible and a ruler was used for the

[20] Stage manager's report, 26 May 1994, Barbican Theatre, London.
[21] Kerry Powell, *Women and Victorian Theatre* (Cambridge: Cambridge University Press, 1997), p. 47.
[22] Folger Prompt King Lear 19: Samuel Phelps, Sadler's Wells, 5 November 1845. George Taylor draws
    attention to Phelps's exceptional approach: his 'productions were remarkable for careful ensemble
    playing, a concentration on the clear delivery of the text, and the avoidance of complicated and
    gimmicky business'. *Players and Performances in the Victorian Theatre* (Manchester: Manchester
    University Press, 1989), p. 19.

neatly demarcated cuts. This first version of the scene retained Regan's and Goneril's statements 'Hang him instantly' and 'Pluck out his eyes', as well as the servant's intervention and death. The intention to carry out the blinding on-stage is not only apparent from the inclusive text, but also from a drawing of a chair with 'Gothic Backing'. The special chair, which is turned with its back towards the audience, seems designed not to crush Gloucester's arms when it is tilted backwards to allow Cornwall to '[*tread*] *out one of his eyes*', as the printed stage direction specifies. (How little the staging of the scene has changed in the intervening century and a half is evident from a rehearsal note for Deborah Warner's 1990 National Theatre production, which asks for the 'Chair for blinding' to have '"hand holds" cut into on back so when lowered to floor, fingers don't get trapped'.) But while Phelps's first cut retained the blinding, it also introduced a significant shift of emphasis away from Regan's involvement in the violence: it did away with both her demand for Gloucester's second eye to be blinded and her killing of the servant, which was attributed to Cornwall alone. Some of her lines were furthermore given to Cornwall in a clear attempt to re-gender the scene's violence as male.

Nevertheless, these alterations to the scene apparently proved insufficient to make this display of violence – and especially female violence – palatable for Phelps's audience. In the scene's second stage of theatrical revision, more lines were crossed out, this time by somebody presumably in the rehearsal room, since the writer did not use a ruler and the hand is shaky, as of someone not working on the hard surface of a desk or table. This rehearsal cut got rid of Goneril's and Regan's statements about hanging Gloucester and plucking out his eyes. It also eliminated Cornwall's graphic threat 'Upon these eyes of thine I'll set my foot' and shortened the conflict with the servant. Although the second revision drastically reduced the scene's verbal violence, the physical violence – which Phelps had striven so hard to retain – was finally found to be unstageable altogether. As a result, a third revision radically pared down the acting text to a very brief interrogation (the fight with the servant was entirely cut), followed by Regan's manuscript order 'Out with his eyes. Servants, unbind Gloster Then thrust him out at gates, and let him smell his way to Dover' – a line that attempts to recapture her original cruelty in a textual revision that had consistently sought to erase both her and her involvement in the scene's violence.

The battle that seems lost in the final version of Phelps's 1845 acting text, in which the blinding simply becomes one of the 'few inevitable omissions' mentioned in passing by the critic for the *Athenaeum* (who was otherwise greatly impressed with Phelps's faithfulness to 'both the genius and judgment of the poet'[23]) was, however, gradually won over the next few years. The final radical cut of 1845 was reversed in 1855, when a new hand marked the cross-out of the blinding and fight with the servant as 'Ret[ained] 1855'. Five years later, a new promptbook for Phelps's 1860–6 productions at Sadler's Wells and Drury Lane included nearly the whole scene, with the graphic stage directions '*Gloster is held down in his Chair, while Cornwall plucks out one of his Eyes, and sets his Foot on it*' and '*Tears out Gloster's Other Eye, and throws it on the Ground*'.[24] Regan's request for the blinding of the second eye was still cut and her insult 'How now, you dog' was still attributed to Cornwall, as was the killing of the servant, but most of her other lines were retained, rendering her complicit if not active in the performance of cruelty. If Phelps's lead was not generally followed over the next decades, so that it is likely that Bradley had never actually seen the scene staged when he wrote his *Shakespearean Tragedy* (it is cut in the promptbooks of his contemporaries Henry Irving and Edwin Forrest), Phelps's repeated attempts to stage the blinding are evidence of his realisation of the centrality of the scene and the importance of its graphic cruelty even (or perhaps especially) in a production that strongly organised both acting text and performances around the central figure of the suffering king.[25]

Certainly, from the mid-twentieth century onwards, and possibly as a consequence of a new ethical awareness of the importance of not averting one's eyes from human cruelty following the Holocaust, theatre practitioners have mostly concentrated on how to stage the blinding in such a way as to provoke precisely the type of reaction recorded in the stage manager's report for the Barbican Theatre. Revolt and shock, post-war performers seem to think, are emotions to be encouraged in an audience that is made complicit in the violence it is forced to watch. Bradley's quest for 'the essence of tragedy', which is predicated on a unified liberal-humanist subject as its audience and on performance conditions that separate the subject from the performance as an object of contemplation and edification, is vividly

---

[23] 'Music and the Drama', *Athenaeum*, 8 November 1845, 1084. The reviewer for the *Spectator* similarly notes that Phelps's staging showed 'the closest possible adherence to the text of Shakespeare', implying that staging the blinding in full was still *im*possible ('The Theatres', *Spectator*, 8 November 1845, 1065).

[24] Folger Prompt King Lear 20: Samuel Phelps, Sadler's Wells and Drury Lane, 1860–6.

[25] See Shirley S. Allen, *Samuel Phelps and Sadler's Wells Theatre* (Middletown CT: Wesleyan University Press, 1977), who notes that Phelps, unlike his rival Macready, 'emphasized the suffering of Lear, probing the depths of his agony in despair and degradation' (p. 173). This centrality of Lear in Phelps's staging is evident throughout the promptbook, in which the other parts are cruelly cut, and is emblematised in the hand-written stage direction for the last scene: 'Re-enter Edgar followed by Lear bearing Cordelia with the 5 Officers. Soldiers gather round when Lear lays Cordelia on his knees in Centre.'

opposed by Charles Marowitz, Peter Brook's assistant director for what is still considered the most important twentieth-century production of *King Lear*. In the programme of the 1964 revival of Brook's original 1962 RSC production, Marowitz blandly states that 'One of the problems with Lear is that like all great tragedies it produces a catharsis. The audience leaves the play shaken but reassured.' As a consequence, Marowitz writes,

> To remove the tint of sympathy usually found at the end of the blinding scene, Brook cut Cornwall's servants and their commiseration of Gloucester's fate. Once the second 'vile jelly' has been thumbed out of his head, Gloucester is covered with a tattered rag and shoved off in the direction of Dover. Servants clearing the stage collide with the confused blind man and rudely shove him aside. As he is groping about pathetically, the house-lights come up – the action continuing in full light for several seconds afterwards. If this works, it should jar the audience into a new kind of adjustment to Gloucester and his tragedy. The house-lights remove all possibility of aesthetic shelter, and the act of blinding is seen in a colder light than would be possible otherwise.

Brook's staging thus sought to remove precisely the aesthetic distance so cherished by Bradley, applying the Folio cut of the servants' commiseration and bathing the audience in the house-lights in a (possibly inadvertent) emulation of early modern performance conditions. Brook's theatre is still didactic, but under the influence of Brecht and Artaud it is a didacticism that seeks simultaneously to distance and involve the spectator and fracture any easy assumption of subjectivity. Cut and house-lights were copied by Adrian Noble in 1993, so that the model outrage of the Barbican patron was provoked by a staging of the scene similar to Brook's. Both Brook and Noble took great pains to portray the blinding itself as realistically and horribly as possible: Brook's Cornwall skewered Gloucester's first eye with one of his golden spurs, and a rehearsal note of Noble's production specifies that 'a request has been put in for the first eye to be squidgy (ie not a perfect eye) and the second eye to be able to pop and jelly to come out when Cornwall squashes it'.[26] The directors seem to have felt that a symbolic staging of the blinding along the lines of Brook's representation of the atrocities in his 1955 *Titus Andronicus* would have been inappropriate (all fifteen twentieth-century productions I have studied opted for a realistic representation of the blinding). I strongly suspect that what Brook and Noble were trying to achieve was a situation in which fiction and reality would become indistinguishable for the spectators for whom the cold light had effaced the barrier separating them from the stage. By making them share the same

---

[26] Rehearsal note, 19 April 1993, Shakespeare Centre, Stratford-upon-Avon.

fictional space, they made the off-stage witnesses share in the responsibility for the atrocities that happened within that space. The Barbican patron's outrage shows just the kind of purely empathic response that cancels the distinction between object and representation, where tragedy's supposed 'stimulus to pity' is no longer aesthetically distanced as Bradley wishes but morally and emotionally involving.

Such a moral and emotional involvement of the spectators, such an empathic mode of spectatorship, I want to suggest, is what Shakespeare might well partly have had in mind when he wrote this scene. Its fevered pace – half-lines in quick succession, repetitions of 'Wherefore to Dover' that drive the action to its climax – creates excitement mixed with horror, binding the audience in a spell that only allows them to react (if at all) when it is too late. There is a strong sense of inevitability about the scene's horrific climax that simultaneously ties the spectators into inaction while making them – me – guilty of passively condoning such violence and, at some sickening level, enjoying it too. (Which spectator familiar with the plot is not fascinated by how it is done? How far is this delight in the mimetic skills of the actors removed from delight in what they mime? And how many 'naïve' audience members ever react with the Barbican patron's exemplary outrage, destroying the barrier between stage and audience and pointing to the scene's dubious ethics in terms both of its content and of its violation of the audience?) Empathy can here be disturbingly mixed with aesthetic appreciation and, possibly, even sadistic pleasure. The scene thus performs its own violence on the audience, which is unsettled and torn between conflicting subject positions and which is perversely punished for not intervening when theatrical conventions as well as the pace and structure of the scene precisely work to prevent such intervention.

When Gloucester's eyes are put out, the violence comes as a release after a long build-up of tension. At the end of the sequence of storm scenes that has insistently invited the audience's empathy with the passive suffering of Lear, Gloucester's clumsy plotting and his desire to see Lear reunited with Cordelia and revenged on his ungrateful daughters has turned him into a figure of hope that promises to break the deadlock through the active, if covert, pursuit of vengeance. The play teases its readers and audience with the promise of a revenge plot analogous to that of *Titus Andronicus*, whose central section with the maddened protagonist's inaction is resolved by the Andronici's concerted revenge, which the audience is invited to endorse in accordance with the patterns of identification in rape-revenge narratives. In *King Lear*, by way of contrast, the audience is quickly punished for its identification with the 'good' characters' desire for retribution.[27] There is a clear change in attitude towards revenge between *Titus Andronicus* and *King Lear*. Here, either 'successful' revenge (Edgar's fights with Oswald and Edmund) is juxtaposed with scenes that upstage it with larger devastation (the loss of the war, Cordelia's and Lear's deaths), or attempts at revenge are frustrated. Gloucester's eyes are put out as a direct result of his assertion that he 'shall see / The wingèd vengeance overtake such children' (F 3.7.63). The same situation is replayed when the servant, an on-stage witness and surrogate for the off-stage audience,[28] comes to Gloucester's help only to be doubly punished by his own death and the removal of Gloucester's second eye. Edward Pechter draws attention to the fact that the servant, too, has called for vengeance ('My lord, you have one eye left / To see some mischief on him' F 3.7.78–9). This establishes a pattern from Kent's assault on Oswald, via Gloucester's plotting and the servant's defence of Gloucester, to Cordelia's military campaign, whereby the plot consistently punishes its characters and audience for the 'thrill of moral rectitude' that accompanies their desire for revenge.[29] Kent is stocked, Gloucester blinded, the servant killed and Cordelia defeated for the same refusal to passively accept the infliction of pain (mental or physical) that provoked the patron at the Barbican to shout 'What are you doing? What are you doing?'

Furthermore, the blinding is obviously a punishment for seeing, for witnessing the children's cruelty towards their father as the audience does ('See't shalt thou never' F 3.7.64). Stanley Cavell compellingly argues that 'the isolation and avoidance of eyes is what the obsessive sight imagery of the play underlines' and that Cornwall carries out the blinding 'to prevent Gloucester from seeing, and in particular to prevent him from seeing *him*'.[30] If in his stage production Peter Brook sought to implicate his audience as guilty witnesses by making them see the cruelty more clearly, in his 1970 film of *King Lear* he altered his technique to make the audience momentarily take Gloucester's place and see nothing. The film cuts from a shot of Cornwall's back as he is approaching Gloucester holding a heavy iron spoon to total blackness accompanied by a sound bridge of Gloucester's cries.

[27] See Edward Pechter, 'On the Blinding of Gloucester', *English Literary History* 45 (1978), 181–200.
[28] Harvey Rovine, *Silence in Shakespeare: Drama, Power and Gender* (Ann Arbor: UMI Research Press, 1987), pp. 80–4.
[29] Pechter, 'Blinding of Gloucester', 187.
[30] Stanley Cavell, 'The Avoidance of Love: A Reading of *King Lear* (1987)', in Frank Kermode (ed.), *Shakespeare:* King Lear: *A Casebook* (London: Macmillan, 1992), p. 222.

Then, as Gloucester apparently reopens his one good eye, we are sitting in his place looking up at Cornwall staring down at us. The film thus stages a direct assault on the viewer's sight in a shocking disempowerment that aligns the viewer with the victim. Film as a medium precludes the type of intervention by and interaction with its audience that Brook could invite in the theatre. But his handling of the scene in the film, where he delays the servant's intervention to leave Gloucester and viewer bound impotently to watch and wait for the second eye to be removed, is perfectly suited to this medium.

A theatrical rather than cinematic way of representing the blinding as a punishment for seeing rather than for vengefulness alone was explored by the 1974 RSC studio production at The Other Place. The director was Buzz Goodbody, co-founder of what was allegedly Britain's first feminist theatre company, member of the Communist Party and the first woman to direct the tragedy for the RSC.[31] From the start, Goodbody's production seemed designed to assault its spectators with unpleasant truths, upbraiding them for their inaction while making it difficult for them to find surrogate figures on-stage that would enable them to voice their protests vicariously. For the first few performances, the play proper was preceded by a prologue in which the actors of Lear (Tony Church) and Edgar (Mike Gwilym) declaimed recent government statistics showing the extent of unrelieved poverty in Great Britain. These they juxtaposed with excerpts from Elizabethan va- grancy laws, collapsing the time gap between the play's composition and its performance as well as the gap between representation and reality. The audience was thus invited to exercise critical aesthetic detachment in order to think about the issues of poverty and cruelty at the same time as moments of intense identification with characters made the viewers them- selves experience the represented evil and cruelty. David Suchet's Fool spoke the prophecy with the house-lights up, removing all aesthetic shelter in a move reminiscent of Brook's blinding.

Apparently, it was not only the audience that remained without the habitual distance separating them from the representation: in rehearsal, too, Goodbody's technique worked to break down boundaries and expose her actors to the cruelty of the play. Significantly, this exposure was gendered, turning the daughters into victims of their father's inappropriate sexual intrusion in a reversal of the play's foregrounding of the violence committed *against* Lear. Goodbody, Colin Chambers reports, took 'solo sessions with

---

[31] Colin Chambers, *Other Spaces: New Theatre and the RSC* (London: Eyre Methuen and TQ Publi- cations, 1980), pp. 11–12.

the daughters and Tony Church, who had to shut his eyes and explore their bodies with his hands, describing what he felt as their father Lear: they went as far as forcing Goneril's legs apart when Lear curses her womb, to drive the point home'.[32] In performance, Goodbody's reassessment of the playtexts' gender roles was evident not only from the elision of the roles of Cornwall and Albany, which had the effect of identifying power and violence with Regan and Goneril instead, but from other little touches like the fact that every night a randomly chosen female member of the audience would become the object of Edmund's leering attention when he stroked her face.

In the absence of Cornwall, the blinding was performed by a threateningly circling and spitting Regan (Lynette Davis) with a hairpin and the help of four thugs in steel helmets – the juxtaposition of the phallic (yet oddly feminine) object and the fetishised female hair strangely suggestive of the power of the feminine in this production. The promptbook records that the lights were dimmed to half for Gloucester's first eye and switched off altogether for the second. No servant intervened, just as earlier a textual cut had deprived the audience of self-righteous identification with Kent's assault on Oswald and a later cut removed Edgar's fight with Oswald. Gloucester's 'All dark and comfortless' was spoken in the total blackout enveloping both him and the viewers who were made to share in his blindness as they strained to hear 'the sound of a tearful snuffling as Gloucester smells his way to Dover'.[33]

At the very least since Samuel Phelps in 1845 wrote a new line for Regan in which she ordered Gloucester's blinding, and even more markedly since Peter Brook broke with theatrical tradition and 'dared to direct King Lear ... from a standpoint of moral neutrality',[34] the blinding of Gloucester has not only become the key scene for provoking the audience into futile protests and/or painful identification with the victim of cruelty, but it has also become a central scene in which the balance between the genders is negotiated around the perpetration of violence. The violence *en*gendered by Lear's actions in the opening scene is en*gendered* by his daughters' actions in the centre of the tragedy. Although Goneril is absent from the actual blinding, both playtexts (which, apart from Quarto's inclusion of the servants' dialogue at the end of the scene, are almost identical) implicate her in it through her initial suggestion of Gloucester's punishment. The three short lines

[32] Chambers, *Other Spaces*, p. 63.   [33] John Elsom, 'Family Crisis', *Listener*, 31 October 1974.
[34] Kenneth Tynan, 'The Triumph of Stratford's Lear', *Observer*, 11 November 1962.

REGAN   Hang him instantly.
GONERIL   Pluck out his eyes.
CORNWALL   Leave him to my displeasure.
                        (F 3.7.4–6)

at the opening of the scene set up the rivalry in evil that leads to the dreadful ensuing escalation of violence. Cornwall has the last word and remains clearly in control of wife, sister-in-law and Edmund, issuing short orders that are obeyed by everyone. Once Goneril and Edmund are gone, however, the playtexts show Regan increasingly challenging Cornwall's authority. As in her earlier scenes with her husband, where she interrupts him (F 2.1.118–19) and is obviously keen to outdo him in cruelty ('Till noon? Till night, my lord, and all night too' F 2.2.128), here Regan begins to interrupt Cornwall to insist on greater cruelty ('Hard, hard!' F 3.7.30). It is she who first lays hands on Gloucester by 'plucking' him by the beard, and it is to her that Gloucester addresses his protests against his and Lear's treatment. Although Cornwall tries to reassert his authority (F 3.7.49–50) and the playtexts make it obvious that he is physically responsible for the blinding, Gloucester's words fix our attention on Regan's hands as the instruments of cruelty: hers are 'robbers' hands' with 'cruel nails' that threaten Lear's 'poor old eyes' (F 3.7.38, 53–4). With her request 'One side will mock another; th'other too' (F 3.7.68) and her physical attack on the servant (Q '*She takes a sword and runs at him behind*' or F '*kills him*'),[35] the balance of violence definitively tips towards Regan. Physical violence is compounded by psychological cruelty in her nasty revelation of Edmund's complicity and in her brutal witticism 'let him smell / His way to Dover' (F 3.7.90–1). When the dying Cornwall asks for her assistance, the Folio '*Exeunt*' leaves it unclear whether his last command is obeyed – certainly, his three unanswered appeals 'Follow me, lady . . . Regan, I bleed apace . . . Give me your arm' suggest that she may well be hesitating or even refusing to comply (F 3.7.92–5). Quarto's singular '*Exit*' allows for a solitary departure for Regan, leaving the dying Cornwall behind to be disrespectfully discussed and eventually carried out by his servants. Whereas up to the blinding it is possible to anticipate a bloodless resolution to the play and to side with the daughters against the father, at the end of this scene it is difficult to dissociate Regan from the atrocity in which she has taken part. The blinding thus becomes the pivot of the play as well as the central point at which the play demands that the audience

---

[35] For a discussion of the Quarto stage direction, which she sees as emphasising Regan's underhandedness, see Margarete Munkelt, *Bühnenanweisung und Dramaturgie: Hinweise zu Interpretation und Inszenierung in Shakespeares* First Folio *und den Quartoversionen* (Amsterdam: Verlag B. R. Grüner, 1981), p. 201.

Illustration 15: Regan (Patience Collier) watching Cornwall (Tony Church) blind
Gloucester in Peter Brook's 1962–4 RSC production of *King Lear*

take sides – almost inevitably the side of the oppressed and violated old
men as opposed to the cruel younger women. Significantly, the scene also
sees the death of Cornwall, so that this male–female polarisation is yet more
clear-cut: the monsters of the second half of the play are a bastard and two
adulterous women.

Unfortunately, neither of the extant promptbooks of Peter Brook's 'morally neutral' production and revival reveal much about his handling of gender in this scene, though they do specify that Regan kills the servant and assists Cornwall with his exit. There is nevertheless enough evidence available to suggest that Brook's 'moral neutrality' was achieved thanks to an effort to dissociate the elder daughters from the cruelty of the blinding. Tellingly, the 1962 promptbook records that on receiving the news of the blinding 'Goneril move[s upstage centre] with a cry' – she, at any rate, does not condone this cruelty. This corresponds to the moment in Brook's film when a cut in the middle of the blinding takes the viewer from Gloucester's kitchen to the carriage in which Goneril, apparently sensing that some- thing terrible has just happened, flinches and buries her head in her hands while Edmund beside her remains impassive.[36] Brook's film never permits any doubt about Cornwall's absolute control: he does not need to raise his voice for Goneril and Regan to accept his authority when he silences them with 'Leave him to my displeasure', and the languid and dishevelled Regan, who seems to have come straight out of bed, does not interrupt him. There is a disturbing eroticism about her reclining figure that adds to the obscenity of the violence she lazily condones. A production photograph conveys the same message, showing Patience Collier's Regan listlessly watch- ing Cornwall gouge out Gloucester's second eye. At the same time, however, in both film and production photograph she seems oddly detached from the scene and dependent on Cornwall's initiative. Her request for a rougher treatment of Gloucester is cut in the film, and she does not even pluck him by the beard. Instead, she remains strangely calm until Cornwall is attacked by the servant. Then, all of a sudden, she grabs a machete and hacks away at the hapless servant in a murderous frenzy that reveals her despair at the potential loss of her husband. Her eyes fill with tears when she tells Glouces- ter of Edmund's betrayal. She rushes to Cornwall and clasps him in a strong embrace as soon as he asks for her help. Against all odds, and with the help of textual cuts, this Regan's eroticised cruelty is played as a result of her desperate dependence on her husband, while Irene Worth's Goneril, in spite of her forceful earlier confrontation with Albany, is portrayed here as altogether incapable of 'this horrid act' (F 3.7.84).

This re-accentuation of the blinding and the play as a whole in favour of the 'evil' sisters was carried in a different direction by Nicholas Hytner's 1990 RSC production in which he and his company deliberately set out to

---

[36] See Michael Mullin, 'Peter Brook's *King Lear*: Stage and Screen', *Literature/Film Quarterly* 11:3 (1983), 193, for an account of how the film may be used as 'a window through which we can look to see performances otherwise lost with the closing of the production'.

perform a 'feminist' reading of the play.[37] Like the Regan of Brook's film, Sally Dexter's Regan looked dishevelled, vulnerable and erotically charged, a large shawl covering her night-gown. But whereas Brook had done without the plucking of Gloucester's beard, in Hytner's staging Regan was all too willing to participate in the torture of the old man. (She pulled the hairs so viciously that on one night she managed to rip the entire fake beard off the actor's face – the stage manager's report dryly asks 'COMIC VALUE?')[38] In contrast to the awful slowness of the scene in Brook's film, here the pace was feverish, with Regan working herself into hysteria in her questioning of Gloucester. When Cornwall brusquely interrupted her, she looked at him in surprise but then complied. Gloucester's insults seemed to throw her off balance and she slowly backed away under their force before curling up on the floor, sobbing loudly. Cornwall's rush towards Gloucester to put out his first eye therefore appeared partly motivated by a desire to protect his wife, who, with a horrible scream, ran up to him to stare down at Gloucester's bleeding face.

Although she exacted the removal of the second eye with the tremor of terror in her voice, she lost all inhibition when her husband was attacked. Legs apart and fierce, holding the sword in both hands, she stabbed the servant in the back. Now that she had killed a man, nothing prevented her from throwing herself on Gloucester to assist her husband in putting out his second eye. The remaining servant turned away from the scene, refusing to witness the frantic attack on the old man. There was a ghastly cry as, the mutilation completed, the couple jointly raised Gloucester's chair back to its upright position. Regan, by now, had not so much gained the nasty self-assurance I normally associate with her order to 'Go thrust him out at gates, and let him smell / His way to Dover' (F 3.7.90–1) as lost all self-control. She laughed hysterically with tears in her voice and perversely hugged and stroked Gloucester's head while she revealed Edmund's betrayal to him, reminding the audience of the close relationship with Gloucester that had been evident in her behaviour in act 2 scene 1. While the wounded Cornwall collapsed downstage, she looked at her bloody hands in horror and maniacally started to try to wipe them, Lady Macbeth-like. 'How is't, my lord, how look you?' (F 3.7.91) was addressed at the exiting Gloucester, not at her dying husband. She ignored Cornwall's request for help, standing in a spotlight, her chin high and a bloody hand going through her hair. Unlike Brook's Regan, she had won the 'high-engendered battle' of violence

---

[37] Conversation with Nicholas Hytner, 8 November 2000.
[38] Stage manager's report, 24 November 1990, Shakespeare Centre, Stratford-upon-Avon.

Illustration 16: Regan (Sally Dexter) with bloodstained hands and blinded Gloucester
(Norman Rodway) in Nicholas Hytner's 1990 RSC production of *King Lear*

in this scene, but she had done so at the cost of her sanity. Along with
Estelle Kohler's increasingly unhinged Goneril, this portrayal of Regan in
the blinding scene earned the sisters Benedict Nightingale's verdict that
'Both of them seem badly in need of Valium, psychoanalysis, or both.
They are frustrated, exhausted, at the end of a tether which finally breaks,

liberating all that suppressed anger and barely contained madness.'[39] The dangerously unhinged Regan directed by Hytner was rendered sympathetic not through a distancing from the violence, but through its very excess, revealing the mental scars left by a traumatic childhood with John Wood's unpredictable Lear.

TRICKY NEGOTIATIONS: TAKING 'THE WOMAN'S PART' IN HYTNER, McLUSKIE AND EYRE

While Regan's mental scars were particularly painfully visible in the scene of Gloucester's blinding, Hytner's production as a whole repeatedly insisted on a reading of the tragedy as starting 'with a father who screws up his daughters. If, after that, you get a sniff of cosmic disorder then that's OK.'[40] Like Goodbody before him, he thus inverted the dominant reading on which Noble was to base his production in 1993 to reveal not so much the victimisation of the father as that of his daughters.

In seeking to 'open this play up for a contemporary audience',[41] Hytner based most of his production on the Folio text rather than on a conflated modern edition. For the last two decades, textual critics have persuasively argued that the Folio represents an authorial revision of the Quarto that substantially changes several emphases of the play.[42] Among these alter-ations, as Hytner was aware, Shakespeare seems to have been at pains to give his audience more freedom in deciding with whom to side, removing some (though by no means all) of the most obvious intradiegetic pointers for audience sympathy. The Folio text also features new pieces of dialogue that help to make more 'rounded' characters out of Goneril and Regan by giving them a stronger motivation for their actions that allows their actors to approach them using a more character-based, 'truthful' performance style than that current in Shakespeare's theatre.[43] Accordingly, though Hytner

---

[39] Benedict Nightingale, 'The Raw Power of Emotion', *The Times*, 12 July 1990.

[40] Nicholas Hytner as quoted by Michael Owen, 'A Lear to Remember', *Evening Standard*, 6 July 1990.

[41] Email, 14 November 2000.

[42] See especially Gary Taylor and Michael Warren (eds.), *The Division of the Kingdoms: Shakespeare's Two Versions of* King Lear (Oxford: Clarendon Press, 1983), and R. A. Foakes, 'The Texts of *King Lear*', in Jay L. Halio (ed.), *Critical Essays on Shakespeare's* King Lear (London: Prentice Hall International, 1996), p. 21.

[43] Defining contemporary mainstream acting styles is a headache, as actors and directors are trained at different institutions and use different approaches to their craft. Generally, however, even when the productions are eclectic in their setting and distancing in their approach, actors tend to attempt to create the illusion of a recognisably unified human being, glossing over discontinuities in the playtexts or finding elaborate 'biographical' explanations for them in order to achieve this illusion of

eventually retained the Quarto's mock trial with its insistence on Lear's mistreatment by his daughters, the 1990 production quickly gained fame for its sympathetic portrayal of the daughters. Jay Halio was one of several academic reviewers who picked up on the impact of the Folio text on the characterisation of the daughters, pointing out that Estelle Kohler's initially dignified Goneril 'quickly revealed cracks in her demeanor when Lear proves a danger as well as a burden in 1.3–4. Following the Folio text, which omits some important lines in those scenes while adding others, her role is less self-assured, less nasty, as Randall McLeod has shown, than in the quarto version, and Kohler played it accordingly.'[44] Although reviewers failed to comment extensively on Alex Kingston's interpretation of Cordelia, even she was accorded a more ambiguous treatment than is usual. In particular she appeared peculiarly contrary in her intentional provocation of her father's wrath after he had seemed quite satisfied with her declaration that she obeyed, loved and honoured him. She later gave the impression of being aware of her shared responsibility for her father's tragedy, making 'No cause, no cause' sound as much a demand for forgiveness on her own behalf as a negation of her father's guilt. Certainly, this must have contributed to Paul Lapworth's impression that 'What this fascinating production achieves above all is the denial of an easy identification with any one viewpoint – "change places, and handy-dandy" you are Goneril and Regan rather than Cordelia'.[45]

What strikes me as rather perverse about most stagings, including Hytner's, that take 'the woman's part' is that in order to explain and render sympathetic the elder sisters' appalling behaviour and repeated recourse to unrestrained verbal and physical violence, the productions (understandably) have had to reconstruct a family history in a move reminiscent of Mary Cowden Clarke's *The Girlhood of Shakespeare's Heroines* (1850–1). The diluted teachings of Stanislavsky and his successors, blended in an eclectic mixture with a pseudo-Freudian psychoanalysis of textual symptoms, inform the women actors' and their directors' discussion of those roles, confirming Penny Gay's assertion that 'any modern actress . . . sets about "creating a character" by finding an explanation for all her speeches and

a coherent person. Sarah Werner, in talking about Juliet Stevenson's conception of her art, suggests that part of 'mainstream theatre tradition' is 'the convention of naturalistic or truthful acting' (in her *Shakespeare and Feminist Performance*, p. 41). Thanks to Carol Rutter, Robert Shaughnessy and Mary Luckhurst for sharing their thoughts on this subject.

44 Jay Halio, 'Five Days, Three *King Lears*', *Shakespeare Bulletin* 9:1 (1991), 21.
45 Paul Lapworth, 'The Cubed Roots of Tragedy', *Stratford Herald*, 20 July 1990.

actions in terms of a consistent and comprehensible psychology'.[46] Thus Clare Higgins, the Regan of Deborah Warner's production at the National Theatre in 1990, declared that 'the violence she shows to Gloucester is really the violence she would like to direct towards her own father. It's very simple, really.'[47] Even in Adrian Noble's unsympathetic production, Jenny Quayle (Regan) felt that her character was an abused child: 'I think when she is watching the torturing of Gloucester, she simply wants to see someone hurt as she has been hurt. There are things which make you angry in every family. I can't say there was incest in our family exactly, but we all have memories which are sexual, involving men or women, and which make us very angry.'[48] Nicholas Hytner, in conversation, revealed a similar desire to uncover a 'Method' motivation for the characters' actions when he reminisced about the central 'discovery' that apparently motivated all the rest of the production, namely that Lear and his daughters love each other but always feel that they cannot get enough love to satisfy their needs. This, he said, lay behind Lear's contradictory cursing of Goneril that was immediately followed by a tight hug, and it was also the motivation for Regan's tenderness towards Gloucester as a father-substitute just after his blinding.[49] Goneril, too, is given additional psychological depth by her interpreters. Estelle Kohler, in many ways a wonderful Goneril in Hytner's staging, went beyond the textually justified grounds for her complaint against her father ('Basically my octogenarian old dad decides he is going to come and live with me, and he's just completely impossible. He turns the place inside out and I'm at the end of my tether'[50]) when she decided that Goneril is desperate for children and *therefore* reacts so strongly to Lear's curse. This move towards psychologisation of the part is the more remarkable because Kohler's previous work for the RSC includes the part of Tamora in Deborah Warner's 1987 production of *Titus Andronicus*, an interpretation that did not seek to provide its evil characters with a past history to motivate their deeds. As recent productions of *King Lear* show, however, the type of reading that in academia was discredited by L. C. Knights as long ago as 1933 (*How Many Children Had Lady Macbeth?*)

---

[46] Penny Gay, *As She Likes It: Shakespeare's Unruly Women* (London and New York: Routledge, 1994), p. 4.

[47] Clare Higgins, as quoted by Margaret Horsfield, 'To the King, Nine Daughters', *Guardian*, 12 July 1990.

[48] Jenny Quayle, as quoted by McGlone, 'Fair Dos', 94.

[49] Conversation with Nicholas Hytner, 8 November 2000.

[50] Horsfield, 'To the King, Nine Daughters'.

seems to thrive in today's mainstream theatre that generally seems to be centred on 'truthful' character rather than plot.

This would not be so deplorable if the projection of psychological depth onto Shakespeare's evil women could somehow undo their involvement in the blinding of Gloucester (as Brook's film nearly succeeded in doing) and edit the play in such a way as to decentralise Lear's suffering, remove the demonisation of the sisters and give more prominence to alternative points of view. While this was achieved in Jane Smiley's Pulitzer-prize winning *A Thousand Acres* (1991), it is noteworthy that the medium of the rewriting is not the theatre but the novel, a literary genre that allows for subtle shifts in point of view, detailed characterisation and narratorial insight into the psyches and pasts of the characters. The novel's attention to the individual and its adaptation of the plot allow Smiley to recast *King Lear* in a revisionist and resistant manner. Such a recasting can only be attempted but not effected by a psychologisation of characters by performers in the theatre that is not accompanied by a radical restructuring, if not rewriting, of the playtexts along the lines of the Women's Theatre Group's and Elaine Feinstein's *Lear's Daughters* (1987), which works as a 'prequel' to Shakespeare's play and excludes Lear from its list of characters.[51] In productions that make use of Shakespeare's playtexts, Kathleen McLuskie importantly warns that

A feminist reading of the text cannot simply assert the countervailing rights of Goneril and Regan, for to do so would simply reverse the emotional structures of the play, associating feminist ideology with atavistic selfishness and the monstrous assertion of individual wills. Feminism cannot simply take 'the woman's part' when that part has been so morally loaded and theatrically circumscribed.[52]

Performing a playtext as strongly gendered as *King Lear* 'against' its dominant misogynist ideology, even in the revised playtext of the Folio, is far more difficult than performing *Othello* against its dominant ideology, where the problem is rather one of race and Desdemona is a sufficiently appealing character with enough lines to build a strong case for a negotiated character-based reading. This, I have argued, is what Trevor Nunn

---

[51] The Women's Theatre Group and Elaine Feinstein, 'Lear's Daughters', in Daniel Fischlin and Mark Fortier (eds.), *Adaptations of Shakespeare: A Critical Anthology of Plays from the Seventeenth Century to the Present* (London: Routledge, 2000), pp. 217–32. As the Fool points out, this play consists of 'Three princesses . . . Two servants . . . One king offstage . . . One Queen dead' (p. 217 – note the lower case for 'king').

[52] Kathleen McLuskie, 'The Patriarchal Bard: Feminist Criticism and Shakespeare: *King Lear* and *Measure for Measure*', in Jonathan Dollimore and Alan Sinfield (eds.), *Political Shakespeare: Essays in Cultural Materialism* (Manchester: Manchester University Press, 1985), p. 102.

achieved in 1989 when he re-accentuated the play in favour of Desdemona and Emilia and exposed the cruelty of their murders without needing to rewrite their parts (though the re-accentuation did involve key directorial interventions). In *Othello*, Desdemona's virtue is unmistakable while not making her shallow (unlike two-dimensionally saintly Cordelia), Othello's sexual paranoia is blatantly unjustified and all his and Iago's misogynist attacks on their wives are therefore ultimately disqualified. In *King Lear*, on the other hand, Goneril and Regan are not only demonised by the male characters, but the whole play represents them as 'monstrous' women who are capable of 'unnatural' and strongly sexualised anarchic violence. This stands in stark contrast to the socially regulated and controlled types of violence associated with the men (war and duels), which are represented as necessary for the restoration of order and justice.

What Hytner's production achieved was a portrayal that explained the sisters' motivation, but the price it had to pay for humanising Goneril and Regan is that 'real' women rather than obvious cultural archetypes were shown to be neurotic monsters. Arguably, such a humanisation of the wicked sisters could be read as an empowering move on the part of the female performers and the production. As Penny Gay suggests,

women can choose, to a certain extent, how far their performance will embody – or perhaps more accurately, refuse to embody – their culture's idea of femininity . . . a determined actress (or actor) can disrupt such voyeurism [the cultural perception of women] by investing all the textualities of the production (speeches, costume, body language, how she inhabits the stage space and how she relates to the other performers) with her own individual energy; in a sense, by fighting for her role, as the embodiment of a *particular* woman enclosed in a narrative that pretends to be universal.[53]

While I do see and admire Gay's point, I can't help feeling that if the only way we can humanise Goneril and Regan is by showing them to be 'in need of Valium, psychoanalysis, or both', with the result that their 'particularised' fates can be read by a part of the audience as nevertheless representative of 'women's' susceptibility to overemotional unhinged responses to provocation, I had rather they, like Iago, remained inscrutable, motiveless monsters securely tied up in the framework of an obvious fiction. Similarly, Cordelia's 'excess of womanly virtue'[54] is easier to stomach if she can be read as an indisputable emblem with a symbolic function rather than as the representation of a 'real' woman whose ideal virtue women spectators are bound to fall short of – I find Cordelia almost more difficult

[53] Gay, *As She Likes It*, pp. 3–4.   [54] Horsfield, 'To the King, Nine Daughters'.

as a point of entry into the play than her sisters. Ultimately, however, this issue is as much open to debate as is that of whether to cast a black man or a white man as Othello or Aaron: casting a black man to 'inhabit' the part and make it believable as a 'person' demands that the actor somehow make sense of the play's stereotyping of the role – which, Quarshie suggested, could only be effected through textual emendation – whereas making a white man play Othello would, in Ogude's words, foreground the 'element of the grotesque' in the role.[55] Should we perhaps, in a return to early modern performance conditions, encourage men to play Lear's daughters in order to emphasise the element of projection in the writing of these parts?

If not a solution, then at least a compromise may have been proposed by Richard Eyre's production at the National Theatre (Cottesloe) in 1997 (the 1998 video, while reproducing much of the original blocking, is greatly reduced in length and power). Like Hytner's, Eyre's acting text was based on the Folio and conflated with some Quarto readings in rehearsal, taking full advantage of textual indeterminacy to shape a playtext specific to the production and its contexts.[56] The staging did not break with the traditions of character-based acting and mimetic realism, nor did director and actors shrink from recreating a history for their dysfunctional family that could motivate the daughters' rage against their father (the short documentary that preceded the screening of the video in 1998 revelled in psychological rhetoric). Nevertheless, the intimate acting space of the Cottesloe Theatre – the play was staged in a traverse with the audience sitting on either side – and the stylish and stylised colour schemes of the design already indicated that the play had to be read on both an illusionistic and an archetypal/emblematic level.

The production thus replicated to a certain extent the radical uncertainty of the early modern stage described by Catherine Belsey, who argues that between 1576 and 1642 'the [public] stage brought into conjunction and indeed into collision the emblematic mode and an emergent illusionism. The effect was a form of drama capable at any moment of disrupting the unity of the spectator.' As a consequence,

---

[55] See the subsection 'Aldridge's hands: the performance of race', in chapter 3 of this volume, pp. 103–11.
[56] Grace Ioppolo, 'The Performance of Text in the Royal National Theatre's 1997 Production of *King Lear*', in Grace Ioppolo (ed.), *Shakespeare Performed: Essays in Honor of R. A. Foakes* (London: Associated University Presses, 2000), p. 181. Ioppolo argues that 'Eyre's production of *King Lear* demonstrates that a conflated text becomes a more mediated text than an original text of the Quarto or Folio, and that mediated texts remain for modern reading and theatre audiences, who have become accustomed to them, the real, "original" Shakespearian texts' (p. 191).

the plays [were] able to move between two kinds of spectacle, one emblematic, implicating the spectator in its meanings, the signified, and the other illusionist, showing the transcendent spectator sense-data, referents which constitute the raw material of experience. The conjunction of the two, or indeed the superimposition of one on the other, is capable of generating a radical uncertainty precisely by withholding from the spectator the single position from which a single and unified meaning is produced.[57]

Accordingly, in Eyre's juxtaposition of illusionism and emblematic staging, it became significant that Edgar sat down in the chair previously occupied by Cordelia while Edmund chose to take possession of Lear's chair. Edmund was acted by Finbar Lynch as a charming Vice-figure dressed in a long black leather coat that visually opposed him to Edgar in his white shirt. He had no trouble establishing a relationship with the audience that allowed him to be both character and type, easily slipping from one representational mode to another without needing to make recourse to Noble's clunking symbols. The sisters, on the other hand, were not obviously distinguished through their costumes and appeared as individualised characters, not monsters. Strikingly, Anne-Marie Duff's Cordelia was so bitter and venomous in her farewell to her sisters that it was difficult not to feel sorry for them and disenchanted with the little sister's self-righteousness. The scales were weighted in the elder sisters' favour throughout the first part of the play. Lear's outrageously vicious invectives made Goneril (Barbara Flynn) break down in tears, putting her hands on her stomach as if to protect her womb from his curse, his knights having dumped their muddy saddles and hunting gear on her pristine white tablecloth – a shorthand for Lear's daily show of disrespect and a nod to Peter Brook's 'morally neutral' staging. Unlike the Regans of most other productions considered here, Amanda Redman's Regan was played as the strongest sister from the start, a smart blonde whose cajoling airs with her father could barely hide her steely determination to rule him. As such, she was easily identifiable for her audience as the 'archetypal psychotic blonde; a fine composite drawn from cinema's *Fatal Attraction, Basic Instinct, Body of Evidence* and *The Hand that Rocks the Cradle*'.[58] The large prominent scar on Redman's arm (visible in the production photograph reproduced on page 181 (illustration 17)), however, helped to mark her also as a victim of aggression who is trying to

[57] Catherine Belsey, *The Subject of Tragedy: Identity and Difference in Renaissance Drama* (London: Methuen, 1985), pp. 26, 28–9.

[58] Darren Kerr, '"This Horrid Act": Blinding Gloucester on Screen', Conference paper, Shakespeare: Authenticity and Adaptation, DeMontfort University, Leicester, 9 September 2000.

protect herself from such violence as Ian Holm's Lear constantly seemed to threaten with his riding whip.

With the storm the scales began to tip in favour of Lear. As the two large walls on either side of the traverse came crashing down on the stage with a reverberating bang, revealing the rain pouring down on the outer walls, a genuine chill invaded the theatre. Lear's desire to 'Expose [himself] to feel what wretches feel' (F 3.4.34) was as literal as the cold: he stripped off entirely, exposing his body to the elements and the embarrassed gazes of the audience sitting just a few feet away. There was as little aesthetic distance as there was physical distance between the spectators and the suffering protagonist. The storm scenes were brilliantly played, with Edgar/Tom (in a highly acclaimed performance by Paul Rhys) hugging the naked Lear in a gesture of male fellow-suffering that obliterated the memory of Lear's terrible domination of his daughters and worked to undo their early prominence. Unusually, the interval was placed at the end of the sequence of storm scenes, leaving the audience with their minds focussed on Lear's utter dispossession and anguish.

When the lights went up again for the second half of the play, the mood had changed, as had the point of view from which the action was viewed. Goneril and Regan were no longer simply women, but had become the larger-than-life monsters of Lear's imagination. Suddenly, their sexuality was played up. While Cornwall was addressing Goneril, Edmund ran his hand down Regan's back, visibly exciting her. Goneril then took hold of Edmund's hand with an inviting smile that left little doubt about her intentions. This business not only openly associated the sisters with the Vice-figure but also projected a strong sense of ferocious sexuality into Regan's behaviour during the blinding scene. She was cold and cruel from the start, fiercely competing with her husband for control, shouting the order to bind Gloucester (Timothy West) harder and plucking his beard with obvious relish. Once Cornwall had put out Gloucester's first eye, she roughly seized the victim's head from behind, eager in her request 'One side will mock another; th'other too' (F 3.7.68). She came into her own when she killed the servant who was being held by the wounded Cornwall, who then thumbed out the second eye while Regan held Gloucester's head. The blinding completed, Regan let go of their victim with a squeal of disgust. In the lull that followed, she took control of the situation as she revealed Edmund's treachery with deliberate nastiness before walking straight past her dying husband with a look of relief on her face, taking full advantage of the Quarto playtext's singular stage direction '*Exit*' to create what Robert Smallwood described as 'one of the production's most chilling moments,

Illustration 17: Regan (Amanda Redman) in control as she looks down on Gloucester
(Timothy West), who is about to be blinded, in Richard Eyre's 1997 RNT
production of *King Lear*

her eyes burning for the power and sexual freedom that his death would give her'.[59]

What Eyre's production thus did in its negotiated reading of Shakespeare's *King Lears* was to strike a careful balance between the late-twentieth-century audience's expectation of mimetic realism and vindication of the sisters' viewpoint on the one hand and the playtexts' 'bemonstering' of them on the other hand. The staging showed an awareness of what Barbara Hodgdon terms the audience's 'expectational text' – the text that consists of the individual spectators' 'private notions about the play and about performed Shakespeare',[60] as well as, I would add, a more pervasive cultural perception of what *King Lear* 'is about'. This was combined with carefully edited playtexts and the production's own ideological subtext, which sought to reconcile compassion for the protagonist with at least some understanding of his antagonists. With the interval placed before rather than after the blinding, the play fell into two parts. While this interrupted the build-up that leads from the storm to the blinding (the natural structure of the play, according to Emrys Jones),[61] it also created a clear division between the first half of the play, where the sisters are given sufficient characterisation and lines to allow for a 'resisting' reading, and the second half with its exclusive focus on Lear's victimisation by his monstrous 'pelican daughters'.

All three daughters became types in the second part: Cordelia, who appeared in full armour and freshly cropped hair in the centre of a strong white spotlight to shout 'No blown ambition doth our arms incite, / But love, dear love, and our aged father's right' (F 4.3.27–8) as a battle-cry, had changed from a complex character into an emblem of love and justice no less than her sisters had turned into archetypes of sexualised female depravity. In the second half, Eyre's production, like Noble's, let Lear arrogate all the suffering, let him instrumentalise his subjects and turn them into objects, mirrors of his anguish. But it did so in a highly self-conscious manner, advertising the shift of representational modes so as to expose the gap between 'reality' and archetype. It is only in their deaths that the sisters once more became normal women, their bodies almost interchangeable in their lifelessness: Lear dumped the body of Cordelia onto the cart bearing the corpses of her sisters and that was shortly to be loaded with his own body. His statement 'this is a dull sight' (F 5.3.256) was prompted by his inspection of Goneril's face in a belated acknowledgement of their kinship and of his loss of all three daughters. In death, their bodies were neither

---

[59] Robert Smallwood, 'Shakespeare Performances in England', *Shakespeare Survey* 51 (1998), 251.

[60] Hodgdon, 'Two *King Lears*', 143.

[61] Emrys Jones, *Scenic Form in Shakespeare* (Oxford: Clarendon Press, 1971), p. 160.

sexualised nor instrumentalised, as they were in Noble's staging,[62] but more simply and distressingly irrevocably dead. In contrast to Othello's fantasy that killing Desdemona would allow him to project his own meanings onto her, Lear's desire to project speech and meaning onto the bodies of his daughters was here frustrated by the irrefutable unresponsiveness of their three corpses.

'THE WHEEL IS COME FULL CIRCLE': SIGHT, SPEECH AND THE
SEMIOTICS OF REVENGE FROM *TITUS ANDRONICUS*
TO *KING LEAR*

The contrast between Lear's (and, I daresay, the audience's) desperate desire to project life and speech onto Cordelia and the daughter's lack of response was emphasised in Eyre's staging when Ian Holm's Lear pointed somewhere off-stage for his injunction to 'Look on her'. Unable to cope with the reality of his daughter's death, Holm's Lear took refuge in a fantasy that was clearly distinguished from the bodies in front of him. He died, as he had lived, in a denial of reality. Lear's Folio-only dying lines are famously indeterminate about their object (body or vision) and meaning (does Lear attract attention to the fact that the lips *don't* move or to their imagined motion?), thus stressing once more the semiotic breakdown that marks the end of this play. At the same time, the lines unquestionably re-emphasise the importance of speech and sight at the very moment at which both fail:[63] Cordelia remains silent and the dying Lear's 'eyes are not o' th' best' (F 5.3.253). Speech and sight, thereafter, will not have their former power: the survivors of the tragedy 'must . . . / Speak what we feel, not what we ought to say. / . . . we . . . / Shall never see so much' (F 5.3.299–302).

The nexus of gender, speech and sight that is so prominent in the final moments of the tragedy also rules the opening scene of the main plot, where Lear fails to read his daughters' speeches correctly and to understand that appearance does not necessarily match reality. Used to the power of his own speech acts which allow him to divide the country, disclaim his fatherhood of Cordelia and banish Kent, Lear is unable to understand that saying 'I love you' bears no necessary relationship to the feeling 'professed' (to use Regan's suggestive term). He is faced with a daughter who bears resemblance to Desdemona in knowing how to distinguish appearance from

[62] Rutter, 'Eel Pie', pp. 212–14 and *Enter the Body*, pp. 1–27.
[63] James P. Lusardi and June Schlueter, *Reading Shakespeare in Performance:* King Lear (Rutherford: Fairleigh Dickinson University Press, 1991), p. 143.

reality ('I know you what you are' F 1.1.268) but who, unlike Desdemona, is not willing to maintain harmony at the price of being untruthful and therefore chooses to say 'Nothing'. Cordelia's 'Nothing' counters hyperbole with understatement and bases itself on a rhetoric of exchange: 'You have begot me, bred me, loved me. I / Return those duties back as are right fit' (F 1.1.95–6). From the start, Lear's belief in the absolute correspondence between words and deeds clashes with Cordelia's opposition between her sisters' (and Edmund's) Iago-like free-floating signifiers and her own wordless referent or action: 'what I well intend / I'll do't before I speak' (F 1.1.224–5). Significantly, the Quarto playtext does not read 'What shall Cordelia speak?' but 'What shall Cordelia do?' (Q 1.1.55), thus setting up an opposition between speaking (her sisters' choice) and doing.[64]

Lear's reliance on words alone prevents him from *seeing* Cordelia's true affection – his order 'Hence, and avoid my sight!' (F 1.1.122) is symptomatic of his refusal to look. Even when Kent explicitly urges 'See better, Lear, and let me still remain / The true blank of thine eye' (F 1.1.156–7), all Lear understands is that by questioning the relationship between speech and feeling, word and meaning, Kent is challenging *Lear's* power to pronounce irrevocable speech acts:

That thou hast sought to make us break our vows,
Which we durst never yet, and with strained pride
To come betwixt our sentences and our power
. . .
By Jupiter,
This shall not be revoked.   (F 1.1.166–77)

The consequence of Lear's absolute belief in the power and truthfulness of words is, paradoxically, his loss of linguistic and literal power. The last speech act in which his words become instant fact is 'I do invest you jointly with my power' (F 1.1.128). Thereafter, and well before his language disintegrates (first partly externalised in the figures of Fool and Edgar/Tom, later in his own madness), his words fail to translate into fact. Banished Kent never leaves the realm, and Lear will from now on have to wait for his dinner.

In a reversal that is familiar from *Titus Andronicus*, where Titus' words and deeds become ineffectual after the mutilation of Lavinia while his enemies usurp the power to speak, Lear loses his power to command speech and sight. In his full identity as the king, Lear could order his daughters

---

[64] See Pierre Alexandre Hecker's discussion of this textual difference, 'The Shakespearean Stage: Language and Silence', D.Phil, Oxford University (1999), pp. 216–17.

to 'speak' or 'avoid [his] sight'. But once he has yielded his rule to his daughters and thus created a topsy-turvy world in which his daughters have become his mothers, Goneril and Regan can arrogate the power to refuse to speak or appear when called for. Since Lear's identity as 'every inch a king' partly relies on the potency of his gaze ('When I do stare, see how the subject quakes' F 4.5.103–4), his loss of identity is signalled by his daughters' usurpation of this gaze and his own metaphorical loss of speech and eyes: 'Does any here know me? This is not Lear. / Does Lear walk thus? Speak thus? Where are his eyes?' (F 1.4.199–200). Such an aggressive gaze, Carol Rutter has observed, characterised the Goneril of Irene Worth in Brook's productions and film: what Goneril's eyes 'did not do was to turn away, nor allow the audience to turn away. Such sight was disturbingly aggressive: her illegible face, not registering reaction, closed off interpretation of Goneril while throwing back in Lear's face an exact, because unmediated, resounding of his own terrible imagery.'[65] Fool, who can be seen as an embodiment of Lear's conscience on the one hand and of his growing mental and linguistic disjunction on the other, becomes the first victim of Goneril's gaze that now has the power to disable speech: 'Yes, forsooth, I will hold my tongue; so your face bids me, though you say nothing' (F 1.4.168–9).

Not only Goneril's 'eyes are fierce' (F 2.4.161); her words are also violent, for the speech act through which she has deprived him of fifty knights is perceived by Lear as physically injurious:

She hath abated me of half my train,
Looked black upon me, struck me with her tongue
Most serpent-like upon the very heart.
                    (F 2.4.148–50)

The daughters' usurpation of Lear's power to pronounce speech acts, command speech and rob Lear of his sight is literalised in the blinding of Gloucester. In a grisly parody of the opening court scene, Regan has taken Lear's place in her command to Gloucester to 'speak'. Gloucester, both a figure of 'true' Cordelia (Quarto even has him echo her in his statement 'I am true' 3.7.31) and a displacement of Lear (Regan will pluck out his 'poor old eyes' instead of Lear's, F 3.7.54), goes through the same motions as Cordelia: he first refuses to speak before finally bursting out with an indictment of his interrogators that directly leads to his punishment. Word and deed are gruesomely united in Cornwall's 'Upon these eyes of thine I'll

---

[65] Rutter, 'Eel Pie', p. 190.

set my foot' and 'Out, vile jelly!' as well as in Regan's 'A peasant stand up thus!' (F 3.7.65, 80, 77).

Lear, meanwhile, disintegrates mentally and linguistically, his loss of identity signalled visually through increasing physical dispossession and corresponding down-scaling of his costume – in Ian Holm's case, all the way to nudity. The psychological violence inflicted on him by his daughters is made physical, 'objective' and legible on his demented, diminished body. When he hires the disguised Kent, Lear is still relying on words alone, significantly using Regan's term when asking Kent 'What dost thou *profess?*' (F 1.4.11; emphasis added). Kent's answer, however, is characteristically in Cordelia's style of truthful understatement: 'I do profess to be no less than I seem' (F 1.4.12). The Fool, too, insists on understatement in the speech he teaches Lear (F 1.4.111–16). It is a sign of Lear's progressive realisation of the value of understatement that, contrary to Goneril's command that Oswald should embellish her missive to Regan with 'such reasons of your own / As may compact it more' (F 1.4.307–8), he orders his own messenger to exercise linguistic restraint: 'Acquaint my daughter no further with anything you know than comes from her demand out of the letter' (F 1.5.2–3). However, Lear has to go through the humiliation of having his power of speech fail him completely (F 2.4.268–70) before he can see beyond appearance to the truth beneath and grasp that 'vile things' such as Cordelia's reticence or the hovel in the storm may be 'precious' (F 3.2.71). Faced with the disintegration of mind and language in the dislocated discourse of Edgar/Tom and his own madness, Lear understands that signifiers and referents may not be in a necessary relation to one another. Like Hamlet's newly found awareness of the commonness of humanity in death in the graveyard scene, Lear's confrontation with Edgar/Tom entails his realisation that 'Unaccommodated man is no more but such a poor, bare, forked animal as thou art' (F 3.4.99–100).

Paradoxically, at the very moment at which his madness makes him hallucinate, Lear no longer accepts appearances but seeks to know the reality beneath. His question to Edgar/Tom is not about what Tom professes to be now but rather 'What hast thou been?' (F 3.4.78), revealing his understanding that there may be a hidden depth beneath the surface of the mad beggar. His desire to 'anatomize Regan; see what breeds about her heart' (F 3.6.38–9) stems from the same awareness of hidden depths. In this, *King Lear* stands in striking contrast to *Othello's* insistence on the value of accepting the characters' self-presentation ('looking at') and of resisting the urge to look for hidden depths ('looking to'). Instead, *King Lear* follows *Hamlet's* lead in stressing the need to see beneath surface appearance. One of the elements of Cordelia's death that makes it particularly distressing, therefore, is that death ultimately renders her opaque, that it does not allow Lear to see beyond it to an ulterior truth or meaning.

Sanity and the ability to 'see' only return to Lear on his painful awakening from his death-like sleep. Restored to his identity as king by Cordelia's addresses, Lear no longer trusts words but finds that knowledge and meaning have to be grounded in physical pain ('corpo*reality*'). Pain becomes the proof that the signifier 'hand' has a direct relationship with the physical referent: 'I will not swear these are my hands. Let's see: / I feel this pin prick' (F 4.6.49–50). His recognition of Cordelia is tentative and relies on the knowledge of his own humanity that was established through his feeling of the pin: 'as I am a man, I think this lady / To be my child Cordelia' (F 4.6.68–9). His mistakes of the opening scene are unmade by his willingness to re-acknowledge her as his 'child' and to 'look upon' Cordelia (F 4.6.61). Unlike the protagonists of *Titus Andronicus*, whose achievement of linguistic restoration led to revenge and thus the restoration of the body politic, Lear treads a new path by relinquishing his early quest for revenge (F 2.4.268), replacing it with his simple demand 'Pray you now, forget and forgive' (F 4.6.77). If Cordelia is indeed not a rounded character but rather a plot device, then her and her soldiers' function here is to represent the revenge Lear rejects at this point in favour of forgiveness.

Critics have often been puzzled by the cursory nature of the war in *King Lear*. It is, indeed, noteworthy that whereas before Lear's return to Cordelia and sanity Cordelia's military attack on her sisters is important in its promise of revenge and political restoration, after the reunion of Lear and Cordelia the actual armed conflict becomes almost meaningless. A retributive war would jar with the keynote of harmony that is struck (even literally in the music of the Quarto playtext's stage direction) in the reunion of father and daughter. The audience is thus deprived of the opportunity to break out of the passivity of empathy with the victim of violence into the activity of vicarious enjoyment of an act of 'just' revenge. It is once more frustrated in its expectation of the 'thrill of moral rectitude' and, in accordance with Edgar's teachings, is offered a vision of the virtue of passive endurance instead. Although the plot dictates that Cordelia and Lear should be involved in warfare, the quality of their reunion demands that they be represented as sacrificial victims who with their newly restored linguistic power can rise above thoughts of revenge to create a world built entirely out of discourse in an abdication of responsibility for the body politic. Russian director Grigori Kozintsev glosses this moment as 'time is powerless before the fearlessness of father and daughter who have found each other. They can be killed but no one can take away from them that moment of happiness – like a blinding flash of light – not even the whole army has the strength to do that.'[66] Accordingly, in his 1969 film of the play, Yuri Yarvet's frail Lear and Valentina Shendrikova's ethereal Cordelia are oblivious of the bustling soldiers who try to hurry them along. Lear's words

We two alone will sing like birds i'th'cage.
When thou dost ask me blessing, I'll kneel down
And ask of thee forgiveness; so we'll live,
And pray, and sing, and tell old tales, and laugh
At gilded butterflies, and hear poor rogues
Talk of court news, and we'll talk with them too . . .
                                        (F 5.3.9–14)

are striking for the recurrence of verbs of utterance (ask, pray, tell, laugh, talk) and the chilling resemblance of the first line to Marcus' description of Lavinia's tongue in a premonition of Cordelia's imminent silencing ('that delightful engine of her thoughts . . . / Is torn from forth that pretty hollow cage / Where, like a sweet melodious bird, it sung' *Tit* 3.1.83–6). At the same time, Lear phrases these lines in terms of exchange that recall Cordelia's early statement of reciprocity in love. Edmund's statement 'The wheel is come full circle' (F 5.3.166) applies to Lear as well.

The distressing nature of the tragedy's final scene partly results from the juxtaposition of the active world of the subplot and the evil sisters with the indifference of Lear. Retributive aggression does take place outside the cocoon of love Lear and Cordelia shelter in. In a series of moves familiar from *Titus Andronicus* and *Hamlet*, the subplot attempts resolution: Edgar exacts revenge, the sisters are defeated in their rhetorical power and the 'gored state' is tentatively reorganised by Albany. It is into this 'conventional' tragedy that promises the satisfactions of retribution and order that the main plot intrudes. Lear's entrance with the dead Cordelia is so painful not only because it punishes the audience for its momentary forgetfulness and 'dissident reading', but also because it undoes all that has come before, including the efforts of the secondary plot to restore order and meaning. The escape into forgiveness and a revelling in the plenitude of speech with Cordelia has been revealed as a non-viable fantasy. In this tragedy, it is impossible to undo one's mistakes, it is derisory to say 'No cause, no cause'. If there is a return to the beginning, it is in Cordelia's initial 'Nothing'

---

[66] Grigori Kozintsev, *King Lear: The Space of Tragedy: The Diary of a Film Director*, trans. Mary Mackintosh (London: Heinemann, 1977), p. 224.

that is now literalised in the unresponsiveness of her body. Now that he *can* see, Lear has to test his new powers of distinction between appearance and reality on the body of his daughter: 'I know when one is dead and when one lives. / She's dead as earth' (F 5.3.234–5). Both Lear and the audience are straining to keep up the illusion that Cordelia might revive, that, like Desdemona, she might just 'stay a little' (F 5.3.245) to say one last sentence, but Cordelia is dead. No amount of looking for 'martyred signs' (*Tit* 5.3.36) will allow Lear to project meaning onto her silent lips. He who has learned painstakingly to look for hidden meanings is now confronted with the inscrutability of death. Language, which had been so precariously restored in Lear's 'prison' speech, breaks down under the strain of his terrible knowledge: 'Thou'lt come no more. / Never, never, never, never, never' (F 5.3.281–2). No restoration of state or language is possible after this. One last time, Lear's suffering upstages every experience around him: 'we that are young / Shall never see so much, nor live so long' (F 5.3.301–2). The gap Lear created by marginalising the other characters, the space he filled with his suffering, is, at the conclusion of the play, left wide open. What is left is a sense of the irrecuperable loss expressed by Edgar – or is it Albany? – which is shared by the male survivors and the theatre audience.[67] But while the tragedy's survivors mourn the loss of Lear, my outrage at the ending concentrates on the void left by the erasure of alternative viewpoints, alternative protagonists.

---

[67] The attribution of this speech to Albany in the Quarto and Edgar in the Folio constitutes one of the most important variants between the two texts, allowing for subtly different readings of the play's resolution.

Epilogue: Polly goes to Hollywood – a success story

Like Hamlet, I write from loss; like him, too, I write to remember.
— Barbara Hodgdon[1]

I started this book with a story of loss. I then attempted to fill the empty spaces left by the gravedigger's daughter; Cordelia thrown out of the picture by her father; her 'bemonstered' sisters; silenced Lavinia, Desdemona and Emilia; racialised Aaron and Othello; and the not-yet-quite-dead bodies of Old Hamlet, Polonius, Ophelia and Yorick, by telling their stories. By collecting the textual traces left by these violated bodies in performance and building a narrative out of fragments, I have sought to make them walk again like the walking dead in *Hamlet*, re-presenting their textual absence in the 'theatre of memory' of performance studies.[2] By filling the empty space with memories of performances, with alternative protagonists, with the narratives told by bodies that have no words to speak, by 'looking *at*' instead of 'looking *to*' these violated bodies, I have sought to turn the stories of loss into stories of re-membrance, resistance, hope and gain.

It is therefore perhaps particularly fitting that my initial story of loss, in which in a manner analogous to Virginia Woolf's musings about the material obliteration of 'Judith Shakespeare's' genius I had dreamed up a narrative of failure and oblivion,[3] should in the end have turned out to be a success story. For if the gravedigger's daughter never made it onto the stage of the Royal Shakespeare Theatre, she nonetheless appears to have survived my imagined confrontations with her director unscathed. In her answer to my worried question about the disappearance of the gravedigger's daughter, Claire van Kampen, speaking on behalf of the production team for the 1989 RSC *Hamlet*, reassured me that the woman actor's appropriation of the man's speaking part *did* take place, and that if the Stratford main house

[1] Hodgdon, 'Re-Incarnations', p. 191.   [2] Hodgdon, 'Re-Incarnations', p. 194.
[3] Virginia Woolf, *A Room of One's Own* (Harmondsworth: Penguin, 1945), pp. 48–50.

records did not mention her, this did not prevent her from appearing on provincial stages:

The gravedigger's daughter – well, she did make it to the stage, very much so! She was in fact the beautiful Polly Walker, now star of stage and screen (Enchanted April, Patriot Games, Sliver etc.) who was totally enchanting as a kind of peasant in National–Rubovian dress. However, when the production was revived for the Stratford season, after 100 performances or so on tour, . . . her role was taken over by one of the travelling players, William Oxborrow, while Polly went off . . . to Hollywood.[4]

Polly Walker might yet play the role of Horatio – if not on the stage of the Royal Shakespeare Theatre, then perhaps in the next Hollywood adaptation of *Hamlet*.

[4] Letter, 31 August 1999.

Appendix: Main productions cited

Title: *Titus Andronicus*
Director: Peter Brook
Cast: Titus   Laurence Olivier
       Lavinia   Vivien Leigh
       Tamora Maxine Audley
       Aaron   Anthony Quayle
Place: Shakespeare Memorial Theatre, Stratford-upon-Avon
Production company: Royal Shakespeare Company
Year: 1955
Archival materials consulted: Promptbook, production photographs, programme, reviews

Title: *Titus Andronicus*
Director: Jane Howell
Cast: Titus   Trevor Peacock
       Lavinia   Anna Calder-Marshall
       Tamora Eileen Atkins
       Aaron   Hugh Quarshie
Place: UK
Production company: BBC/Time-Life
Year: 1985
Archival materials consulted: Video, screenplay

Title: *Titus Andronicus*
Director: Deborah Warner
Cast: Titus   Brian Cox
       Lavinia   Sonia Ritter
       Tamora Estelle Kohler
       Aaron   Peter Polycarpou
Place: Swan Theatre, Stratford-upon-Avon; The Pit, London

Production company: Royal Shakespeare Company
Year: 1987, 1988
Archival materials consulted: Performance texts, promptbook, production photographs, programme, rehearsal notes, stage manager's reports, production correspondence, reviews

Title: *Titus Andronicus*
Director: Gregory Doran
Cast: Titus   Antony Sher
       Lavinia   Jennifer Woodburne
       Tamora   Dorothy Gould
       Aaron   Sello Maake ka Ncube
Place: Market Theatre, Johannesburg; National Theatre, London
Production company: Market Theatre and SABC
Year: 1995
Archival materials consulted: Video, reviews

Title: *Titus Andronicus*
Director: Silviu Pucarete
Cast: Titus   Stefan Iordache
       Lavinia   Ozana Oancea
       Tamora   Mirela Coiaba
       Aaron   Ilie Gheorghe
Place: Bucharest; world tour
Production company: National Theatre of Craiova
Year: 1992–7
Archival materials consulted: Performance (Cambridge Arts Theatre, 4 June 1997), programme

Title: *Titus Andronicus*
Director: Julie Taymor
Cast: Titus   Robert Stattel
       Lavinia   Miriam Healy-Louie
       Tamora   Melinda Mullins
       Aaron   Harry Lennix
Place: New York
Production company: Theatre for a New Audience
Year: 1994
Archival materials consulted: Reviews, interview with director

Title: *Titus*
Director: Julie Taymor

Cast: Titus   Anthony Hopkins
        Lavinia   Laura Fraser
        Tamora   Jessica Lange
        Aaron   Harry Lennix
Place: Italy / USA
Production company: Fox Searchlight Pictures, Clear Blue Sky Productions and Overseas Film Group
Year: 1999
Archival materials consulted: DVD (with commentary), screenplay, reviews, interview with director

Title: *Titus Andronicus*
Director: Xavier Leret
Cast: Titus   Lee Beagley
        Lavinia   Jane Hartley
        Tamora   Lisa Tramontin
        Aaron   Guy Burgess
Place: UK tour
Production company: Kaos Theatre Company
Year: 2001–2
Archival materials consulted: Performance (Riverside Studios, London, 23 February 2002); reviews; interview with director, actors and producer; video; production photographs

Title: *Hamlet*
Director: Laurence Olivier
Cast: Hamlet   Laurence Olivier
        Gertrude   Eileen Herlie
        Claudius   Basil Sydney
        Ophelia   Jean Simmons
        Polonius   Felix Aylmer
Place: UK
Production company: Two Cities Film
Year: 1948
Archival materials consulted: Video, screenplay

Title: *Hamlet*
Director: Buzz Goodbody
Cast: Hamlet   Ben Kingsley
        Gertrude   Mikel Lambert
        Claudius   George Baker

Ophelia   Yvonne Nicholson
Polonius   Andre Van Gyseghem
Laertes   Stuart Wilson

Place: The Other Place, Stratford-upon-Avon
Production company: Royal Shakespeare Company
Year: 1975
Archival materials consulted: Promptbook, production photographs, reviews

Title: *Hamlet*
Director: Ron Daniels
Cast: Hamlet   Roger Rees
Gertrude   Virginia McKenna
Claudius   Brian Blessed
Ophelia   Frances Barber
Polonius   Frank Middlemass

Place: Royal Shakespeare Theatre, Stratford-upon-Avon
Production company: Royal Shakespeare Company
Year: 1984
Archival materials consulted: Performance text, promptbook, production photographs, programme, rehearsal notes, stage manager's reports, reviews

Title: *Hamlet*
Director: Ron Daniels
Cast: Hamlet   Mark Rylance
Gertrude   Clare Higgins
Claudius   Peter Wight
Ophelia   Rebecca Saire
Polonius   Patrick Godfrey

Place: Royal Shakespeare Theatre, Stratford-upon-Avon
Production company: Royal Shakespeare Company
Year: 1989
Archival materials consulted: Performance text, promptbook, production photographs, programme, set photographs, set designs, rehearsal notes, stage manager's reports, production correspondence, reviews, interview with properties manager

Title: *In the Bleak Midwinter / A Midwinter's Tale*
Director: Kenneth Branagh

Cast: Michael Maloney
Richard Briers
Julia Sawalha
Mark Hadfield
Celia Inrie
Place: UK
Production company: Midwinter Films
Year: 1995
Archival materials consulted: Video

Title: *Hamlet*
Director: Kenneth Branagh
Fight directors: Simon Crane, Sean McCabe, Nicholas Powell
Cast: Hamlet   Kenneth Branagh
Gertrude   Julie Christie
Claudius   Derek Jacobi
Ophelia   Kate Winslet
Polonius   Richard Briers
Place: USA / UK
Production company: Castle Rock Entertainment
Year: 1996
Archival materials consulted: Video, screenplay

Title: *Hamlet*
Director: Matthew Warchus
Fight director: Terry King
Cast: Hamlet   Alex Jennings
Gertrude   Susannah York and Diana Quick
Claudius   Paul Freeman
Ophelia   Derbhle Crotty
Polonius   David Ryall
Place: Barbican Theatre, London
Production company: Royal Shakespeare Company
Year: 1997–8
Archival materials consulted: Performance, performance texts (24 June 1997 with Diana Quick, 7 August 1997 with Susannah York), promptbook, programme, rehearsal notes, stage manager's reports, reviews

Title: *Hamlet: First Cut*
Director: Jonathan Holloway

Cast: Hamlet   Peter Collins
     Gertred   Sally Mortemore
     King   Guy Oliver-Watts
     Ofelia   Rachel Nicholson
     Corambis   Tim Weekes
Place: UK tour
Production company: Red Shift
Year: 1999
Archival materials consulted: Performance (Mumford Theatre, Cambridge, 3 November 1999), programme, reviews, production photographs

Title: *Hamlet*
Director: Michael Almereyda
Cast: Hamlet   Ethan Hawke
     Gertrude   Diane Venora
     Claudius   Kyle MacLachlan
     Ophelia   Julia Stiles
     Polonius   Bill Murray
Place: USA
Production company: Double A Films Production, Miramax Films
Year: 2000
Archival materials consulted: Video, screenplay

Title: *Othello*
Director: Orson Welles
Cast: Othello   Orson Welles
     Desdemona   Suzanne Cloutier, Betsy Blair, Lea Padovani
     Iago   Micheál MacLiammóir
     Emilia   Fay Compton
Place: Italy / France / Morocco
Production company: Mercury (re-edited re-release: Castle Hill Productions)
Year: 1949–52 (re-release 1992)
Archival materials consulted: Video

Title: *Othello*
Director: Sergei Yutkevich
Translators: Boris Pasternak and Anna Radlova
Cast: Othello   Sergei Bondarchuk
     Desdemona   Irina Skobtseva

| Iago | Andrei Popov |
| Emilia | Antonina Maximova |

Place: USSR
Production company: Mosfilm
Year: 1955
Archival materials consulted: Video

Title: *Othello*
Director: John Dexter (stage production) / Stuart Burge (film)
Cast:
Othello	Laurence Olivier
Desdemona	Maggie Smith
Iago	Frank Finlay
Emilia	Joyce Redman

Place: National Theatre, London (stage) / UK (film)
Production company: National Theatre (stage) / British Home Entertainment (film)
Year: 1964 (stage) / 1965 (film)
Archival materials consulted: Video

Title: *Othello*
Director: Jonathan Miller
Cast:
Othello	Anthony Hopkins
Desdemona	Penelope Wilton
Iago	Bob Hoskins
Emilia	Rosemary Leach

Place: UK
Production company: BBC/Time-Life
Year: 1981
Archival materials consulted: Video

Title: *Othello*
Director: Janet Suzman
Cast:
Othello	John Kani
Desdemona	Joanna Weinberg
Iago	Richard Haddon Haines
Emilia	Dorothy Gould

Place: Johannesburg
Production company: Market Theatre Othello Productions, Focus Films and Portobello Productions
Year: 1988
Archival materials consulted: Video, correspondence with director

Title: *Othello*
Director: Trevor Nunn
Cast: Othello   Willard White
        Desdemona   Imogen Stubbs
        Iago   Ian McKellen
        Emilia   Zoë Wanamaker
Place: UK
Production company: Royal Shakespeare Company (stage production) /
    Primetime (video)
Year: 1989 (stage) / 1990 (video)
Archival materials consulted: Video, promptbook, reviews

Title: *Othello*
Director: Oliver Parker
Cast: Othello   Laurence Fishburne
        Desdemona   Irène Jacob
        Iago   Kenneth Branagh
        Emilia   Anna Patrick
Place: UK
Production company: Castle Rock Entertainment, Imminent Films
Year: 1995
Archival materials consulted: Video

Title: *King Lear*
Director: Peter Brook
Assistant director: Charles Marowitz
Cast: Lear   Paul Scofield
        Goneril   Irene Worth
        Regan   Patience Collier
        Cordelia   Diana Rigg
        Gloucester Alan Webb
Place: Royal Shakespeare Theatre, Stratford-upon-Avon
Production company: Royal Shakespeare Company (stage production) /
    Columbia Pictures in association with the Royal Shakespeare Company and Filmways Inc. (film)
Year: 1962–4 (stage) / 1971 (film)
Archival materials consulted: Promptbooks, reviews, production photographs, programme (1964 revival), video (film)

Title: *King Lear*
Director: Grigori Kozintsev

Cast: Lear   Yuri Yarvet
       Goneril   Elsa Radzin-Szolkonis
       Regan   Galina Volchek
       Cordelia   Valentina Shendrikova
       Gloucester Karl Sedris
Place: USSR
Production company: Lenfilm
Year: 1969
Archival materials consulted: Video

Title: *King Lear*
Director: Buzz Goodbody
Cast: Lear   Tony Church
       Goneril   Sheila Allen
       Regan   Lynette Davis
       Cordelia   Louise Jameson
       Gloucester Jeffery Dench
Place: The Other Place, Stratford-upon-Avon
Production company: Royal Shakespeare Company
Year: 1974
Archival materials consulted: Promptbook, reviews, production photographs

Title: *King Lear*
Director: Cicely Berry
Cast: Lear   Richard Haddon Haines
       Goneril   Joan Blackham
       Regan   Jill Spurrier
       Cordelia   Maureen Beattie
       Gloucester Desmond Barrit
Place: The Other Place, Stratford-upon-Avon
Production company: Royal Shakespeare Company
Year: 1988
Archival materials consulted: Promptbook, reviews, production photographs

Title: *King Lear*
Director: Deborah Warner
Cast: Lear   Brian Cox
       Goneril   Susan Engel
       Regan   Clare Higgins

Cordelia	Eve Matheson
Gloucester	Peter Jeffrey

Place: Royal National Theatre, London
Production company: Royal National Theatre
Year: 1990
Archival materials consulted: Promptbook, reviews, production photographs, rehearsal notes

Title: *King Lear*
Director: Nicholas Hytner
Cast:

Lear	John Wood
Goneril	Estelle Kohler
Regan	Sally Dexter
Cordelia	Alex Kingston
Gloucester	Norman Rodway

Place: Royal Shakespeare Theatre, Stratford-upon-Avon
Production company: Royal Shakespeare Company
Year: 1990
Archival materials consulted: Performance, performance text, promptbook, production photographs, programme, rehearsal notes, stage manager's reports, production correspondence, reviews, interview and correspondence with director

Title: *King Lear*
Director: Adrian Noble
Cast:

Lear	Robert Stephens
Goneril	Janet Dale
Regan	Jenny Quayle
Cordelia	Abigail McKern
Gloucester	David Bradley

Place: Royal Shakespeare Theatre, Stratford-upon-Avon
Production company: Royal Shakespeare Company
Year: 1993
Archival materials consulted: Performance text, promptbook, production photographs, programme, rehearsal notes, stage manager's reports, reviews

Title: *King Lear*
Director: Richard Eyre
Cast:

Lear	Ian Holm
Goneril	Barbara Flynn

Regan	Amanda Redman
Cordelia	Anne-Marie Duff (stage) / Victoria Hamilton (TV)
Gloucester	Timothy West

Place: Royal National Theatre, London
Production company: Royal National Theatre / BBC2
Year: 1997 (stage) / 1998 (TV)
Archival materials consulted: Performance, performance text, reviews, production photographs, video

Bibliography

Adelman, Janet, *Suffocating Mothers: Fantasies of Maternal Origin in Shakespeare's Plays:* Hamlet *to* The Tempest, London: Routledge, 1992.

Aebischer, Pascale, 'Black Rams Tupping White Ewes: Race and Gender in the Final Scene of Six *Othellos*', in Deborah Cartmell, I. Q. Hunter and Imelda Whelehan (eds.), *Retrovisions: Reinventing the Past in Film and Fiction*, London: Pluto, 2001, 59–73.

'Cutting/Framing Violence: The BBC/Howell *Titus Andronicus* (1985)', in José Ramón Díaz Fernández and Sofía Muñoz (eds.), *Shakespeare on Screen: The Centenary Essays*, forthcoming.

'*Hamlet*, mémoire, langue, action, et passion', in Olivier Pot (ed.), *Emergences et formes de la subjectivité littéraire aux XVIe et XVIIe siècles*, Geneva: Droz, forthcoming.

'Looking for Shakespeare: The Textuality of Performance', *SPELL* 13 (2000), 157–73.

'Women Filming Rape in Shakespeare's *Titus Andronicus*: Jane Howell and Julie Taymor', *Etudes Anglaises* 55:2 (2002), 136–47.

'"Yet I'll Speak": Silencing the Female Voice in *Titus Andronicus* and *Othello*', in Patricia Dorval (ed.), *Shakespeare et la voix*, Paris: Société Française Shakespeare, 1999, 27–46.

'Yorick's Skull: *Hamlet*'s Improper Property', *EnterText* 1:2 (2001), 206–25. http://www.brunel.ac.uk/faculty/arts/EnterText/hamlet/aebischer.pdf

Albanese, Denise, 'Black and White, and Dread All Over: The Shakespeare Theater's "Photonegative" *Othello* and the Body of Desdemona', in Dympna Callaghan (ed.), *A Feminist Companion to Shakespeare*, Oxford: Blackwell, 2000, 226–47.

Alexander, Nigel, *Poison, Play and Duel: A Study in* Hamlet, London: Routledge and Kegan Paul, 1971.

Allen, Jeanne, 'Looking through *Rear Window*: Hitchcock's Traps and Lures of Heterosexual Romance', in Deidre Pribram (ed.), *Female Spectators: Looking at Film and Television*, London: Verso, 1988, 31–44.

Allen, Shirley S., *Samuel Phelps and Sadler's Wells Theatre*, Middletown CT: Wesleyan University Press, 1977.

Almereyda, Michael, *William Shakespeare's* Hamlet: *A Screenplay Adaptation by Michael Almereyda*, London: Faber and Faber, 2000.

Anon., 'Music and the Drama', *Athenaeum*, 8 November 1845, 1084.

Anon., 'The Theatres', *Spectator*, 8 November 1845, 1065.

Anon., 'The Worrying of Willard! Conflict Mars Singer's TV Acting Debut', *Reading Post*, 22 June 1990.

Anon., 'Willard Rises to His Othello Challenge', *Evening Post*, 23 June 1990.

Ashcroft, Bill, Gareth Griffiths and Helen Tiffin, *Post-Colonial Studies: The Key Concepts*, London: Routledge: 2000.

Asp, Carolyn, '"Upon Her Wit Doth Earthly Honor Wait": Female Agency in *Titus Andronicus*', in Philip C. Kolin (ed.), Titus Andronicus: *Critical Essays*, New York: Garland, 1995, 333–46.

Bakhtin, Mikhail, *Rabelais and His World*, trans. Helene Iswolsky, Bloomington: Indiana University Press, 1984.

Bartels, Emily C., 'Making More of the Moor: Aaron, Othello, and Renaissance Refashionings of Race', *Shakespeare Quarterly* 41 (1990), 433–54.

Barthelemy, Anthony Gerard, *Black Face Maligned Race: The Representation of Blacks in English Drama from Shakespeare to Southerne*, Baton Rouge: Louisiana State University Press, 1987.

Bate, Jonathan (ed.), *Titus Andronicus*, by William Shakespeare, Arden 3, London: Routledge, 1995.

Beauman, Sally, *The Royal Shakespeare Company: A History of Ten Decades*, Oxford: Oxford University Press, 1982.

Belsey, Catherine, *The Subject of Tragedy: Identity and Difference in Renaissance Drama*, London: Methuen, 1985.

Berry, Philippa, *Shakespeare's Feminine Endings: Disfiguring Death in the Tragedies*, London and New York: Routledge, 1999.

Bertram, Paul and Bernice W. Kliman (eds.), *The Three-Text Hamlet: Parallel Texts of the First and Second Quartos and First Folio*, New York: AMS Press, 1991.

Billington, Michael, 'A Brutal Sort of Interrogation', *Guardian*, 14 July 1995.

'Get Shorter', *Guardian*, 10 May 1997.

'Horror and Humanity', *Guardian*, 14 May 1987.

Blumenthal, Eileen and Julie Taymor, *Julie Taymor: Playing with Fire*, New York: Harry N. Abrams, 1999.

Boaden, James, *Memoirs of Mrs. Siddons*, London: Gibbings and Company, 1893.

Boose, Lynda E., 'Grossly Gaping Viewers and Jonathan Miller's *Othello*', in Lynda E. Boose and Richard Burt (eds.), *Shakespeare, the Movie: Popularizing the Plays on Film, TV, and Video*, London and New York: Routledge, 1997, 186–97.

'Scolding Brides and Bridling Scolds: Taming the Woman's Unruly Member', *Shakespeare Quarterly* 42 (1991), 178–213.

Boose, Lynda E. and Richard Burt (eds.), 'Introduction', *Shakespeare, the Movie: Popularizing the Plays on Film, TV, and Video*, London and New York: Routledge, 1997, 1–7.

Bradley, A. C., *Shakespearean Tragedy: Lectures on* Hamlet, Othello, King Lear, Macbeth, London: Macmillan, 1983 [1905].

Branagh, Kenneth, Hamlet*: By William Shakespeare: Screenplay, Introduction and Film Diary*, New York and London: W. W. Norton and Company, 1996.

Brereton, Austin, *The Life of Henry Irving*, 2 vols., London: Longmans, Green and Co., 1908, vol. I.

Bronfen, Elisabeth, *Over Her Dead Body: Death, Femininity and the Aesthetic*, Manchester: Manchester University Press, 1992.

Brook, Peter, 'Come, Begin . . .', Programme for *The Tragedy of Hamlet* for The Young Vic Theatre Company in association with The Tara Ulemek Foundation, Young Vic, London, 2001.

  The Empty Space, London: MacGibbon & Kee, 1968.

Brownmiller, Susan, *Against Our Will: Men, Women, and Rape*, London: Secker and Warburg, 1975.

Burchill, Julie, 'Too Hot to Handle', *Guardian Weekend*, 6 July 2002.

Burt, Richard, 'Shakespeare and the Holocaust: Julie Taymor's *Titus* is Beautiful, or Shakesploi Meets (the) Camp', *Colby Quarterly* 37:1 (2001), 78–106.

Butler, Judith, *Gender Trouble: Feminism and the Subversion of Identity*, New York: Routledge, 1990.

Butler, Robert, 'Warchus Puts His *Art* into His *Hamlet*', *Independent on Sunday*, 11 May 1997.

Calderwood, James L., *Shakespearean Metadrama: The Argument of the Play in* Titus Andronicus, Love's Labour's Lost, Romeo and Juliet, A Midsummer Night's Dream *and* Richard II, Minneapolis: University of Minnesota Press, 1971.

Callaghan, Dympna, *Woman and Gender in Renaissance Tragedy: A Study of* King Lear, Othello, The Duchess of Malfi *and* The White Devil, London: Harvester Wheatsheaf, 1989.

Carlisle, Carol Jones, *Shakespeare from the Greenroom: Actors' Criticisms of Four Major Tragedies*, Chapel Hill: University of North Carolina Press, 1969.

Cartmell, Deborah, *Interpreting Shakespeare on Screen*, London: Macmillan, 2000.

Case, Sue-Ellen, *Feminism and Theatre*, Houndmills: Macmillan, 1988.

Catty, Jocelyn, *Writing Rape, Writing Women in Early Modern England*, Houndmills: Macmillan, 1999.

Cavell, Stanley, 'The Avoidance of Love: A Reading of *King Lear* (1987)', in Frank Kermode (ed.), *Shakespeare:* King Lear*: A Casebook*, London: Macmillan, 1992, 214–57.

Chakravarti, Paromita, 'Modernity, Post-Coloniality and *Othello*: The Case of *Saptapadi*', in Pascale Aebischer, Edward J. Esche and Nigel Wheale (eds.), *Remaking Shakespeare: Performance across Media, Genres and Cultures*, Houndmills: Palgrave Macmillan, 2003, 39–56.

Chambers, Colin, *Other Spaces: New Theatre and the RSC*, London: Eyre Methuen and TQ Publications, 1980.

Charney, Maurice, *Titus Andronicus*, London: Harvester Wheatsheaf, 1990.

Clover, Carol J., *Men, Women, and Chain Saws: Gender in the Modern Horror Film*, London: British Film Institute, 1992.

Cohen, Derek, *Shakespeare's Culture of Violence*, New York: St Martin's Press, 1993. *The Politics of Shakespeare*, New York: St Martin's Press, 1993.

Cottrell, John, *Laurence Olivier*, Sevenoaks: Hodder and Stoughton, 1977.

Cowhig, Ruth, 'Actors, Black and Tawny, in the Role of Othello, – and Their Critics', *Theatre Research International* 4:2 (1978), 133–46.

Cox, Brian, *The Lear Diaries: The Story of the Royal National Theatre's Productions of Shakespeare's* Richard III *and* King Lear, London: Methuen, 1995.

'*Titus Andronicus*', in Russell Jackson and Robert Smallwood (eds.), *Players of Shakespeare 3: Further Essays in Shakespearian Performance by Players with the Royal Shakespeare Company*, Cambridge: Cambridge University Press, 1993, 174–88.

Crowl, Samuel, '*Hamlet*', *Shakespeare Bulletin* 18 (2000), 39–40.

Danson, Lawrence, *Tragic Alphabet: Shakespeare's Drama of Language*, New Haven: Yale University Press, 1974.

de Lauretis, Teresa, *Technologies of Gender: Essays on Theory, Film, and Fiction*, Bloomington: Indiana University Press, 1987.

DeLuca, Maria and Mary Lindroth, 'Mayhem, Madness, Method: An Interview with Julie Taymor', *Cinéaste* 25:3 (2000), 28–31.

Dessen, Alan C., *Elizabethan Stage Conventions and Modern Interpretations*, Cambridge: Cambridge University Press, 1984.

Disch, Thomas M., 'Late-Winter Night of Tragicomedy', *Daily News* [New York], 14 March 1994.

Dolan, Jill, *The Feminist Spectator as Critic*, Ann Arbor: UMI Research Press, 1991.

Donaldson, Peter S., *Shakespearean Films / Shakespearean Directors*, Boston: Unwin Hyman, 1990.

Doran, Gregory and Antony Sher, *Woza Shakespeare!* Titus Andronicus *in South Africa*, London: Methuen, 1996.

Douce, Francis (ed.), *The Dance of Death: In a Series of Engravings on Wood from Designs Attributed to Hans Holbein*, London: G. Bell and Sons, 1902.

Duffy, Robert A., 'Gade, Olivier, Richardson: Visual Strategy in *Hamlet* Adaptation', *Literature/Film Quarterly* 4:2 (1976), 141–52.

Edmonds, Richard, 'Hamlet in the Shadows', *Birmingham Post*, 10 May 1997.

Eliot, T. S., *Elizabethan Dramatists: Essays by T. S. Eliot*, London: Faber, 1968.

Elsom, John, 'Family Crisis', *Listener*, 31 October 1974.

Enders, Jody, *The Medieval Theater of Cruelty: Rhetoric, Memory, Violence*, Ithaca and London: Cornell University Press, 1999.

Engler, Balz, 'Textualization', in Roger D. Sell (ed.), *Literary Pragmatics*, London: Routledge, 1991, 179–89.

Esche, Edward J. and Nigel Wheale, 'An Aaron for the Times', unpublished article.

Esslin, Martin, *The Field of Drama: How the Signs of Drama Create Meaning on Stage and Screen*, London: Methuen, 1987.

Everett, Barbara, '*Hamlet*: A Time to Die', *Shakespeare Survey* 30 (1977), 117–23.

Fawcett, Mary Laughlin, 'Arms/Words/Tears: Language and the Body in *Titus Andronicus*', *English Literary History* 50 (1983), 261–77.

[Fechter, Charles,] *Charles Fechter's Acting Edition: Othello*, London: W. J. Golbourn, 1861.

Fiedler, Leslie A., *The Stranger in Shakespeare*, St Albans: Paladin, 1974.

Fisher, James E., 'Olivier and the Realistic *Othello*', *Literature/Film Quarterly* 1 (1973), 321–31.

Foakes, R. A., *Shakespeare and Violence*, Cambridge: Cambridge University Press, 2003.

'The Texts of *King Lear*', in Jay L. Halio (ed.), *Critical Essays on Shakespeare's King Lear*, London: Prentice Hall International, 1996, 21–34.

Ford, John R., '"Words and Performances": Roderigo and the Mixed Dramaturgy of Race and Gender in *Othello*', in Philip C. Kolin (ed.), Othello: *New Critical Essays*, New York and London: Routledge, 2002, 147–67.

Frye, Roland Mushat, *The Renaissance* Hamlet: *Issues and Responses in 1600*, Princeton: Princeton University Press, 1984.

Furness, Horace Howard (ed.), *Othello*, by William Shakespeare, vol. VI of *A New Variorum Edition of Shakespeare*, 27 vols., Philadelphia: J. B. Lippincott, 1886.

Gadd, Ian, 'The Rat and Hamlet's Arras', *Notes and Queries* ns 44:1 (1997), 61–2.

Gaines, Jane, 'White Privilege and Looking Relations – Race and Gender in Feminist Film Theory', *Screen* 29:4 (1988), 12–27.

Gardner, Lyn, '*Hamlet: First Cut*', *Guardian*, 13 September 1999.

Gautier, Théophile, *Voyage en Russie*, ed. P. Laubriet, Paris and Geneva: Ressources, 1979.

Gay, Penny, *As She Likes It: Shakespeare's Unruly Women*, London and New York: Routledge, 1994.

Geertz, Clifford, 'Thick Description: Toward an Interpretive Theory of Culture', in his *The Interpretation of Cultures: Selected Essays*, London: Fontana Press, 1993 [1973], 3–30.

Genster, Julia, 'Lieutenancy, Standing in, and *Othello*', *English Literary History* 57 (1990), 785–809.

Girard, René, 'Hamlet's Dull Revenge', in Patricia Parker and David Quint (eds.), *Literary Theory / Renaissance Texts*, Baltimore: Johns Hopkins University Press, 1986, 280–302.

A Theater of Envy: William Shakespeare, Oxford: Oxford University Press, 1991.

Gledhill, Christine, 'Pleasurable Negotiations', in E. Deidre Pribram (ed.), *Female Spectators: Looking at Film and Television*, London: Verso, 1988, 64–89.

Godfrey-Faussett, Charles, '*Hamlet: First Cut*', *Time Out*, 26 January–2 February 1999.

Golding, Arthur, *Shakespeare's Ovid: Being Arthur Golding's Translation of the Metamorphoses*, ed. W. H. D. Rouse, London: Centaur, 1961.

Gordon, Giles, 'Mortality Explored', *London Daily News*, 13 May 1987.

Gowing, Laura, 'Language, Power and the Law: Women's Slander Litigation in Early Modern London', in Jenny Kermode and Garthine Walker (eds.), *Women, Crime and the Courts in Early Modern England*, Chapel Hill: University of North Carolina Press, 1994, 26–47.

Goy-Blanquet, Dominique, 'Titus Resartus: Deborah Warner, Peter Stein and Daniel Mesguich Have a Cut at *Titus Andronicus*', in Dennis Kennedy (ed.), *Foreign Shakespeare: Contemporary Performance*, Cambridge: Cambridge University Press, 1993, 36–55.

Green, André, *The Tragic Effect: The Oedipus Complex in Tragedy*, trans. Alan Sheridan, Cambridge: Cambridge University Press, 1979.

Greenblatt, Stephen, *Shakespearean Negotiations: The Circulation of Social Energy in Renaissance England*, Berkeley: University of California Press, 1988.

Gross, John, 'He Chips Away Here and There', *Sunday Telegraph*, 23 May 1993.

Guthke, Karl S., 'Renaissance und Barock: Der Tod und das Mädchen – und der Mann', *Ist der Tod eine Frau? Geschlecht und Tod in Kunst und Literatur*, München: Verlag C. H. Beck, 1997, 94–143.

Habib, Imtaz, *Shakespeare and Race: Postcolonial Praxis in the Early Modern Period*, Lanham MD: University Press of America, 2000.

Halio, Jay, 'Five Days, Three *King Lears*', *Shakespeare Bulletin* 9:1 (1991), 19–23.

Hamilton, A. C., '*Titus Andronicus*: The Form of Shakespearian Tragedy', *Shakespeare Quarterly* 14 (1963), 201–13.

Hankey, Julie (ed.), *Othello*, by William Shakespeare, Plays in Performance, Bristol: Bristol Classical Press, 1987.

Hawkes, Terence, *Meaning by Shakespeare*, London: Routledge, 1992.

Hawthorn, Jeremy, *A Glossary of Contemporary Literary Theory*, London: Edward Arnold, 1992.

Hecker, Pierre Alexandre, 'The Shakespearean Stage: Language and Silence', D.Phil., Oxford University, 1999.

Heilman, Robert B., 'Wit and Witchcraft: Thematic Form in *Othello*', in Susan Snyder (ed.), Othello: *Critical Essays*, London: Garland, 1988, 189–200.

Helms, Lorraine, '"The High Roman Fashion": Sacrifice, Suicide, and the Shakespearean Stage', *PMLA* 107 (1992), 554–65.

Higgins, Lynn A. and Brenda R. Silver, 'Introduction: Rereading Rape', in Lynn A. Higgins and Brenda R. Silver (eds.), *Rape and Representation*, New York: Columbia University Press, 1991, 1–11.

Hodgdon, Barbara, 'Kiss Me Deadly; or, The Des/Demonized Spectacle', in Virginia Mason Vaughan and Kent Cartwright (eds.), Othello: *New Perspectives*, London and Toronto: Associated University Presses, 1991, 214–55.

'Race-ing *Othello*, Re-Engendering White-Out', in Lynda E. Boose and Richard Burt (eds.), *Shakespeare, the Movie: Popularizing the Plays on Film, TV, and Video*, London and New York: Routledge, 1997, 23–44.

'Re-Incarnations', in Pascale Aebischer, Edward J. Esche and Nigel Wheale (eds.), *Remaking Shakespeare: Performance across Media, Genres and Cultures*, Houndmills: Palgrave Macmillan, 2003, 190–209.

The End Crowns All: Closure and Contradiction in Shakespeare's History, Princeton: Princeton University Press, 1991.

The Shakespeare Trade: Performances and Appropriations, Philadelphia: University of Pennsylvania Press, 1998.

'Two *King Lears*: Uncovering the Filmtext', *Literature/Film Quarterly* 11:3 (1983), 143–51.

Holden, Anthony, *Olivier*, London: Weidenfeld and Nicolson, 1988.

Holland, Peter, *English Shakespeares: Shakespeare on the English Stage in the 1990s*, Cambridge: Cambridge University Press, 1997.

Honigmann, E. A. J. (ed.), *Othello*, by William Shakespeare, Arden Shakespeare 3, London: Thomas Nelson, 1997.

Horsfield, Margaret, 'To the King, Nine Daughters', *Guardian*, 12 July 1990.

Howlett, Kathy M., *Framing Shakespeare on Film*, Athens: Ohio University Press, 2000.

Huet, Marie-Hélène, 'Monstrous Imagination: Progeny as Art in French Classicism', *Critical Inquiry* 17 (1991), 718–37.

Hughes, Alan (ed.), *Titus Andronicus*, by William Shakespeare, New Cambridge Shakespeare, Cambridge: Cambridge University Press, 1994.

Hunter, G. K., *Othello and Colour Prejudice*, London: Oxford University Press, 1967 (reprinted from *Proceedings of the British Academy* 53 (1967), 139–63).

Ioppolo, Grace, 'The Performance of Text in the Royal National Theatre's 1997 Production of *King Lear*', in Grace Ioppolo (ed.), *Shakespeare Performed: Essays in Honor of R. A. Foakes*, London: Associated University Presses, 2000, 180–97.

Iyengar, Sujata, 'White Faces, Blackface: The Production of "Race" in *Othello*', in Philip C. Kolin (ed.), Othello*: New Critical Essays*, New York and London: Routledge, 2002, 103–31.

Jackson, MacDonald P., 'Stage Directions and Speech Headings in Act 1 of *Titus Andronicus* Q (1594): Shakespeare or Peele?', *Studies in Bibliography* 49 (1996), 134–48.

Jackson, Russell, 'The Film Diary', in Kenneth Branagh, Hamlet*: By William Shakespeare: Screenplay, Introduction and Film Diary*, New York and London: W. W. Norton & Company, 1996, 175–208.

Jenkins, Harold (ed.), *Hamlet*, by William Shakespeare, Arden Shakespeare 2, London: Methuen, 1982.

Johnson, Robert, '*Titus Andronicus*: The First of the Roman Plays', in T. R. Sharma (ed.), *Essays on Shakespeare in Honour of A. A. Ansari*, Meerut: Shalabh, 1986, 80–7.

Jones, Eldred, 'Aaron', in Philip C. Kolin (ed.), Titus Andronicus*: Critical Essays*, London: Garland, 1995, 147–56.

Jones, Emrys, *Scenic Form in Shakespeare*, Oxford: Clarendon Press, 1971.

  The Origins of Shakespeare, Oxford: Clarendon Press, 1977.

Kaufman, David, 'Robobard', *Village Voice*, 22 March 1994.

Kaul, Mythili, 'Background: Black or Tawny? Stage Representations of Othello from 1604 to the Present', in Mythili Kaul (ed.), Othello*: New Essays by Black Writers*, Washington DC: Howard University Press, 1997, 1–19.

  'Preface', in Mythili Kaul (ed.), Othello*: New Essays by Black Writers*, Washington DC: Howard University Press, 1997, ix–xii.

Kendal, [Dame Madge], *Dramatic Opinions*, Boston: Little, Brown, and Company, 1890.

Kernan, Alvin, 'Barbarism and the City', in Susan Snyder (ed.), Othello*: Critical Essays*, London: Garland, 1988, 201–12.

Kerr, Darren, '"This Horrid Act": Blinding Gloucester on Screen', Conference paper, Shakespeare: Authenticity and Adaptation, DeMontfort University, Leicester, 9 September 2000.

Kerrigan, John, *Revenge Tragedy: Aeschylus to Armageddon*, Oxford: Clarendon Press, 1997.

Kingston, Jeremy, 'Curtains for Shakespeare's Worst', *The Times*, 22 May 1997.

Kiss, Attila, *The Semiotics of Revenge: Subjectivity and Abjection in English Renaissance Tragedy*, Szeged: *Acta Universitatis Szegediensis de Attila József Nominatae* Papers in English and American Studies 5, 1995.

Knight, G. Wilson, *The Wheel of Fire: Interpretations of Shakespearian Tragedy with Three New Essays*, London: Methuen, 1949.

Kolin, Philip C., 'Blackness Made Visible: A Survey of *Othello* in Criticism, on Stage, and on Screen', in Philip C. Kolin (ed.), Othello: *New Critical Essays*, New York and London: Routledge, 2002, 1–87.

Kott, Jan, 'Shakespeare – Cruel and True', in Philip C. Kolin (ed.), Titus Andronicus: *Critical Essays*, London: Garland, 1995, 393–8.

Kozintsev, Grigori, *King Lear: The Space of Tragedy: The Diary of a Film Director*, trans. Mary Mackintosh, London: Heinemann, 1977.

Lanier, Douglas, 'Drowning the Book: *Prospero's Books* and the Textual Shakespeare', in James C. Bulman (ed.), *Shakespeare, Theory, and Performance*, London: Routledge, 1996, 187–209.

Lapworth, Paul, 'Daniels' Hamlet a Degree Off Balance?', *Stratford Herald*, 5 May 1989.

'The Cubed Roots of Tragedy', *Stratford Herald*, 20 July 1990.

Larkin, Alile Sharon, 'Black Women Film-Makers Defining Ourselves: Feminism in Our Own Voice', in E. Deidre Pribram (ed.), *Female Spectators: Looking at Film and Television*, London: Verso, 1988, 157–73.

Lasky, Jesse, Jr with Pat Silver, *Love Scene: The Story of Laurence Olivier and Vivien Leigh*, Brighton: Angus & Robertson, 1978.

Levin, William R., *Images of Love and Death in Late Medieval and Renaissance Art*, Michigan: University Publications, 1975.

Lindfors, Bernth, '"Mislike Me Not for My Complexion . . .": Ira Aldridge in Whiteface', *African American Review* 33 (1999), 347–54.

Loomba, Ania, *Colonialism/Postcolonialism*, London: Routledge, 1998.

Lucking, David, 'Putting out the Light: Semantic Indeterminacy and the Deconstitution of Self in *Othello*', *English Studies* 75 (1994), 110–22.

Lusardi, James P. and June Schlueter, *Reading Shakespeare in Performance:* King Lear, Rutherford: Fairleigh Dickinson University Press, 1991.

MacDonald, Joyce Green, 'Black Ram, White Ewe: Shakespeare, Race, and Women', in Dympna Callaghan (ed.), *A Feminist Companion to Shakespeare*, Oxford: Blackwell, 2000, 188–207.

'Women and Theatrical Authority: Deborah Warner's *Titus Andronicus*', in Marianne Novy (ed.), *Cross-Cultural Performances: Differences in Women's Re-Visions of Shakespeare*, Urbana and Chicago: University of Illinois Press, 1993, 185–205.

MacLiammóir, Micheál, *Put Money in Thy Purse: The Making of* Othello, London: Virgin, 1994.

[Macready, William Charles], *The Journal of William Charles Macready, 1832–1851*, ed. J. C. Trewin, London: Longmans, 1976.

Maguire, Laurie, '"Actions That a Man Might Play": Mourning, Memory, Editing', *Performance Research* 7 (2002), 66–76.

Maher, Mary Z., 'Production Design in the BBC's *Titus Andronicus*', in J. C. Bulman and H. R. Coursen (eds.), *Shakespeare on Television: An Anthology of Essays and Reviews*, Hanover: University Press of New England, 1988, 144–50.

Marchitello, Howard, *Narrative and Meaning in Early Modern England*, Cambridge: Cambridge University Press, 1997.

Marshall, Cynthia, '"I Can Interpret All Her Martyr'd Signs": *Titus Andronicus*, Feminism, and the Limits of Interpretation', in Carole Levin and Karen Robertson (eds.), *Sexuality and Politics in Renaissance Drama*, Lewiston NY: Edwin Mellen Press, 1991, 193–213.

'Sight and Sound: Two Models of Shakespearean Subjectivity on the British Stage', *Shakespeare Quarterly* 51 (2000), 353–61.

Marshall, Herbert and Mildred Stock, *Ira Aldridge: The Negro Tragedian*, London: Camelot Press, 1958.

Märtin, Doris, *Shakespeares 'Fiend-Like Queens': Charakterisierung, Kontext und dramatische Funktion der destruktiven Frauenfiguren in* Henry IV, Richard III, King Lear *und* Macbeth, Heidelberg: Carl Winter Universitätsverlag, 1992.

Masten, Jeffrey, 'Playwrighting: Authorship and Collaboration', in John D. Cox and David Scott Kastan (eds.), *A New History of Early English Drama*, New York: Columbia University Press, 1997, 357–82.

Mayne, Judith, *Cinema and Spectatorship*, New York: Routledge, 1993.

McCabe, Eamonn, Interview with Henry Louis Gates Jr, 'Henry the First', *Guardian Review*, 6 July 2002, 20–3.

McGlone, Jackie, 'Fair Dos for Daddy's Girls', *Theatre Records* 166 (11 March–30 May 1993), 94.

McHale, Brian, *Postmodernist Fiction*, London: Methuen, 1987.

McKenzie, D. F., *Bibliography and the Sociology of Texts*, The Panizzi Lectures 1985, London: The British Library, 1986.

McLendon, Jacquelyn Y., '"A Round Unvarnished Tale": (Mis)Reading *Othello* or African American Strategies of Dissent', in Mythili Kaul (ed.), Othello: *New Essays by Black Writers*, Washington DC: Howard University Press, 1997, 121–37.

McLuskie, Kathleen, 'The Patriarchal Bard: Feminist Criticism and Shakespeare: *King Lear* and *Measure for Measure*', in Jonathan Dollimore and Alan Sinfield (eds.), *Political Shakespeare: Essays in Cultural Materialism*, Manchester: Manchester University Press, 1985, 88–108.

Miller, Jonathan, *Subsequent Performances*, London and Boston: Faber and Faber, 1986.

Mills, Sara, 'Reading as/like a Feminist', in Sara Mills (ed.), *Gendering the Reader*, London: Harvester Wheatsheaf, 1994, 25–46.

Miola, Robert S., '*Titus Andronicus* and the Mythos of Shakespeare's Rome', *Shakespeare Studies* 14 (1981), 85–98.

Mortimer, Owen, *Speak of Me as I Am: The Story of Ira Aldridge*, Wangaratta: Owen Mortimer, 1995.

Muir, Kenneth, 'Imagery and Symbolism in *Hamlet*', *Etudes Anglaises* 17 (1964), 352–63.

Mullin, Michael, 'Peter Brook's *King Lear*: Stage and Screen', *Literature/Film Quarterly* 11:3 (1983), 190–6.

Mulvey, Laura, 'Visual Pleasure and Narrative Cinema' (repr. from *Screen* 16:3 (1975), 6–18), *Visual and Other Pleasures*, Bloomington: Indiana University Press, 1989.

Munkelt, Margarete, *Bühnenanweisung und Dramaturgie: Hinweise zu Interpretation und Inszenierung in Shakespeares* First Folio *und den Quartoversionen*, Amsterdam: Verlag B. R. Grüner, 1981.

Murdin, Lynda, '*Titus Andronicus*', *Yorkshire Post*, 14 July 1995.

Nead, Lynda, *The Female Nude: Art, Obscenity and Sexuality*, London and New York: Routledge, 1992.

Neill, Michael, *Issues of Death: Mortality and Identity in English Renaissance Tragedy*, Oxford: Clarendon Press, 1997.

'"Mulattos", "Blacks", and "Indian Moors": Othello and Early Modern Constructions of Human Difference', *Shakespeare Quarterly* 49 (1998), 361–75.

'Unproper Beds: Race, Adultery, and the Hideous in *Othello*', *Shakespeare Quarterly* 40 (1989), 383–412.

Newman, Karen, '"And Wash the Ethiop White": Femininity and the Monstrous in *Othello*', in Jean E. Howard and Marion F. O'Connor (eds.), *Shakespeare Reproduced: The Text in History and Ideology*, London: Routledge, 1987, 143–62.

Nightingale, Benedict, 'The Raw Power of Emotion', *The Times*, 12 July 1990.

Norman, Marc and Tom Stoppard, *Shakespeare in Love*, London: Faber and Faber, 1999.

Novak, Peter, 'Shakespeare in the Fourth Dimension: *Twelfth Night* and American Sign Language', in Pascale Aebischer, Edward J. Esche and Nigel Wheale (eds.), *Remaking Shakespeare: Performance across Media, Genres and Cultures*, Houndmills: Palgrave Macmillan, 2003, 18–38.

Nuttall, A. D., *Why Does Tragedy Give Pleasure?*, Oxford: Clarendon Press, 1996.

O'Brien, Geoffrey, 'The Ghost at the Feast', *New York Review of Books* 44:2 (1997), 11–16.

Ogude, S. E., 'Literature and Racism: The Example of *Othello*', in Mythili Kaul (ed.), Othello: *New Essays by Black Writers*, Washington DC: Howard University Press, 1997, 151–66.

Olivier, Laurence, 'An Essay in Hamlet', in Brenda Cross (ed.), *The Film* Hamlet: *A Record of Its Production*, London: The Saturn Press, 1948, 11–15.

Confessions of an Actor: An Autobiography, New York: Simon and Schuster, 1982.

Orkin, Martin, 'Othello and the "Plain Face" of Racism', *Shakespeare Quarterly* 38 (1987), 166–88.

Owen, Michael, 'A Lear to Remember', *Evening Standard*, 6 July 1990.

Pavis, Patrice, 'From Text to Performance', in Michael Issacharoff and Robin F. Jones (eds.), *Performing Texts*, Philadelphia: University of Pennsylvania Press, 1988, 86–100.

Pechter, Edward, 'On the Blinding of Gloucester', *English Literary History* 45 (1978), 181–200.

Othello *and Interpretive Traditions*, Iowa City: University of Iowa Press, 1999.

Phelan, Peggy, *Unmarked: The Politics of Performance*, London: Routledge, 1993.

Pike, Luke Owen, *A History of Crime in England*, 2 vols., London: Smith Elder, 1876, vol. 1.

Pizzello, Stephen, 'From Stage to Screen', *American Cinematographer* 81:2 (2000), 64–73.

Pot, Olivier, 'Le Problème de l'obscénité à l'âge classique', *XVIIe siècle* 173 (1991), 403–36.

Powell, Kerry, *Women and Victorian Theatre*, Cambridge: Cambridge University Press, 1997.

Prosser, Eleanor, *Hamlet and Revenge*, Stanford: Stanford University Press, 1967.

Quarshie, Hugh, *Second Thoughts about* Othello, International Shakespeare Association Occasional Paper 7, Chipping Campden: Cloud Hill Printers, 1999.

Quince, Rohan, *Shakespeare in South Africa: Stage Productions during the Apartheid Era*, Studies in Shakespeare 9, New York: Peter Lang, 2000.

Radin, Victoria, 'Just the Man for the RSC', *Observer*, 27 June 1982.

Ray, Sid, '"Rape, I Fear, Was Root of Thy Annoy": The Politics of Consent in *Titus Andronicus*', *Shakespeare Quarterly* 49 (1998), 22–39.

Ricci, Digbi, 'Titus Topples into the "Relevant" Pit', *Mail & Guardian*, SA, 31 March 1995.

Richmond, Hugh Macrae, 'The Audience's Role in *Othello*', in Philip C. Kolin (ed.), Othello: *New Critical Essays*, New York and London: Routledge, 2002, 89–101.

Rosenberg, Marvin, *The Masks of Othello: The Search for the Identity of Othello, Iago, and Desdemona by Three Centuries of Actors and Critics*, Berkeley and Los Angeles: University of California Press, 1961.

Rouse, John, 'Textuality and Authority in Theater and Drama: Some Contemporary Possibilities', in Janelle G. Reinelt and Joseph R. Roach (eds.), *Critical Theory and Performance*, Ann Arbor: University of Michigan Press, 1992, 146–57.

Rovine, Harvey, *Silence in Shakespeare: Drama, Power and Gender*, Ann Arbor: UMI Research Press, 1987.

Royster, Francesca T., 'The "End of Race" and the Future of Early Modern Cultural Studies', *Shakespeare Studies* 26 (1998), 59–69.

'White-Limed Walls: Whiteness and Gothic Extremism in Shakespeare's *Titus Andronicus*', *Shakespeare Quarterly* 51 (2000), 433–55.

Rutter, Carol Chillington, 'Eel Pie and Ugly Sisters in *King Lear*', in James Ogden and Arthur H. Scouten (eds.), Lear *from Study to Stage: Essays in Criticism*, London: Associated University Presses, 1997, 172–225.

Enter the Body: Women and Representation on Shakespeare's Stage, London: Routledge, 2001.

Ryle, Gilbert, 'Thinking and Reflecting', in his *Collected Essays 1929–1968*, vol. II of his *Collected Papers*, 2 vols., Bristol: Thoemmes Antiquarian Books Ltd, 1990, 465–79.

Rymer, Thomas, 'From *A Short View of Tragedy* (1693)', in John Wain (ed.), *Shakespeare:* Othello*: A Casebook*, London: Macmillan, 1994, 39–49.

Sacks, Peter, 'Where Words Prevail Not: Grief, Revenge, and Language in Kyd and Shakespeare', *English Literary History* 49 (1982), 576–601.

Scarry, Elaine, *The Body in Pain: The Making and Unmaking of the World*, Oxford: Oxford University Press, 1985.

Schechner, Richard, *Performance Theory*, revised and expanded edition, London: Routledge, 1988.

'Race Free, Gender Free, Body-Type Free, Age Free Casting', *Drama Review* 33:1 (1989), 4–12.

Scuro, Daniel, '*Titus Andronicus:* A Crimson-Flushed Stage!', in Philip C. Kolin (ed.), Titus Andronicus*: Critical Essays*, New York: Garland, 1995, 399–410.

Seymour, Alan, 'A View from the Stalls', in Kenneth Tynan (ed.), Othello*: The National Theatre Production*, New York: Stein and Day, 1967, 13–19.

Shepherd, Anna, 'A Bloody Night with Titus', *Kenilworth Weekly News*, 8 February 2002.

Sher, Antony, *The Feast*, London: Little, Brown and Company, 1998.

Siemon, James R., '"Nay, That's Not Next": *Othello*, v.ii in Performance, 1760–1900', *Shakespeare Quarterly* 37 (1986), 38–51.

Simmons, James R., Jr, '"In the Rank Sweat of an Enseamed Bed": Sexual Aberration and the Paradigmatic Screen *Hamlet*s', *Literature/Film Quarterly* 25:2 (1997), 111–17.

Singh, Jyotsna, 'Othello's Identity, Postcolonial Theory, and Contemporary African Rewritings of *Othello*', in Margo Hendricks and Patricia Parker (eds.), *Women, 'Race', and Writing in the Early Modern Period*, London and New York: Routledge, 1994, 287–99.

Smallwood, Robert, 'Director's Shakespeare', in Jonathan Bate and Russell Jackson (eds.), *Shakespeare: An Illustrated Stage History*, Oxford: Oxford University Press, 1996, 176–96.

'Shakespeare Performances in England', *Shakespeare Survey* 51 (1998), 219–55.

Smith, Andrew, 'Lear's Blood Lust', *Chase Post*, 27 May 1993.

Smith, Peter J., '*Hamlet: First Cut*, directed by Jonathan Holloway for Red Shift, The Bull, Barnet, London, 4 December 1999, mid stalls', *Cahiers Elisabéthains* 57 (April 2000), 130–2.

Sofer, Andrew, 'The Skull on the Renaissance Stage: Imagination and the Erotic Life of Props', *English Literary Renaissance* 28 (1998), 47–74.

Spencer, Charles, 'Back from the Abyss to Invest Madness with a Human Face', *Daily Telegraph*, 22 May 1993.

'This Is So Bad, It Isn't Even Scary', *Daily Telegraph*, 14 July 1995.

Starks, Lisa S., 'The Displaced Body of Desire: Sexuality in Kenneth Branagh's *Hamlet*', in Christy Desmet and Robert Sawyer (eds.), *Shakespeare and Appropriation*, London and New York: Routledge, 1999, 160–78.

Stoppard, Tom, 'Pragmatic Theater', *New York Review*, 23 September 1999.

Suzman, Janet, 'South Africa in *Othello*', *Tanner Lectures on Human Values* 17 (1996), 273–94.

Tanner, Laura E., *Intimate Violence: Reading Rape and Torture in Twentieth-Century Fiction*, Bloomington: Indiana University Press, 1994.

Taylor, Gary and Michael Warren (eds.), *The Division of the Kingdoms: Shakespeare's Two Versions of* King Lear, Oxford: Clarendon Press, 1983.

Taylor, George, *Players and Performances in the Victorian Theatre*, Manchester: Manchester University Press, 1989.

Taylor, Paul, 'More Sinn'd Against', *Independent*, 24 May 1993.

Taymor, Julie, *Titus: The Illustrated Screenplay, Adapted from the Play by William Shakespeare*, New York: Newmarket, 2000.

Thaxter, John, 'Politics, Thrills and Revenge', *Stage*, 16 September 1999.

Tricomi, Albert, 'The Aesthetics of Mutilation in *Titus Andronicus*', *Shakespeare Survey* 27 (1974), 11–19.

Tynan, Kenneth, 'Olivier: The Actor and the Moor', in Kenneth Tynan (ed.), Othello*: The National Theatre Production*, New York: Stein and Day, 1967, 1–12.

'The Triumph of Stratford's Lear', *Observer*, 11 November 1962.

Ubersfeld, Anne, 'The Pleasure of the Spectator', trans. Pierre Bouillaguet and Charles Jose, *Modern Drama* 25 (1982), 127–39.

Vandenhoff, George, *Leaves from an Actor's Note-Book; with Reminiscences and Chit-Chat of the Green-Room and the Stage, in England and America*, New York: D. Appleton and Company, 1860.

Vanita, Ruth, '"Proper" Men and "Fallen" Women: The Unprotectedness of Wives in *Othello*', *Studies in English Literature 1500–1900* 34 (1994), 341–56.

Vaughan, Virginia Mason, Othello*: A Contextual History*, Cambridge: Cambridge University Press, 1994.

'Looking at the "Other" in Julie Taymor's *Titus*', *Shakespeare Bulletin* 21 (2003), 71–80.

'The Construction of Barbarism in *Titus Andronicus*', in Joyce Green MacDonald (ed.), *Race, Ethnicity and Power in the Renaissance*, London: Associated University Presses, 1997, 165–80.

Wagner, Valeria, 'Losing the Name of Action', in Mark Thornton Burnett and John Manning (eds.), *New Essays on* Hamlet, New York: AMS Press, 1994, 135–52.

Waith, Eugene M., *Patterns and Perspectives in English Renaissance Drama*, London: Associated University Presses, 1988.

'The Metamorphosis of Violence in *Titus Andronicus*', *Shakespeare Survey* 10 (1957), 39–49.

Walker, Alexander, *Vivien: The Life of Vivien Leigh*, London: Orion, 1994.

Walsh, Martin W., '"This Same Skull, Sir . . .": Layers of Meaning and Tradition in Shakespeare's Most Famous Prop', *Hamlet Studies* 9 (1987), 65–77.

Wardle, Irving, 'Barbarous but Unforgettable Assault', *The Times*, 28 April 1989.
 'Shakespearian Horrors Transformed into Farce', *The Times*, 14 May 1987.

Weis, René (ed.), King Lear*: A Parallel Text Edition*, by William Shakespeare, Harlow: Longman, 1993.

Weller, Philip, 'Freud's Footprints in Films of *Hamlet*', *Literature/Film Quarterly* 25:2 (2000), 117–25.

Wells, Stanley, 'Shakespeare Production in England in 1989', *Shakespeare Survey* 43 (1990), 183–203.

Werner, Sarah, 'Notes on Sharing the Cake', in Lizbeth Goodman with Jane de Gay (eds.), *The Routledge Reader in Gender and Performance*, London: Routledge, 1998, 108–12.
 Shakespeare and Feminist Performance: Ideology on Stage, London: Routledge, 2001.

West, Grace Starry, 'Going by the Book: Classical Allusions in Shakespeare's *Titus Andronicus*', *Studies in Philology* 79 (1982), 62–77.

Willbern, David, 'Rape and Revenge in *Titus Andronicus*', *English Literary Renaissance* 8 (1978), 159–82.

Williams, Carolyn D., '"Silence, like a Lucrece knife": Shakespeare and the Meanings of Rape', *Yearbook of English Studies* 23 (1993), 93–110.

Wirth, Jean, *La Jeune Fille et la mort: recherches sur les thèmes macabres dans l'art germanique de la Renaissance*, Geneva: Droz, 1979.

Women's Theatre Group and Elaine Feinstein, 'Lear's Daughters', in Daniel Fischlin and Mark Fortier (eds.), *Adaptations of Shakespeare: A Critical Anthology of Plays from the Seventeenth Century to the Present*, London: Routledge, 2000, 217–32.

Woolf, Virginia, *A Room of One's Own*, Harmondsworth: Penguin, 1945.

Worthen, W. B., *Shakespeare and the Authority of Performance*, Cambridge: Cambridge University Press, 1997.

Wymer, Rowland, *Suicide and Despair in the Jacobean Drama*, New York: St Martin's Press, 1986.

Index